ALMANACH

OTHER BOOKS BY SHARON KIVLAND INCLUDE

Abécédaire, Moist, 2022

Unable to achieve broad recognition in my lifetime, I laboured in obscurity until my death last year, Ma Bibliothèque, 2019

Reading Nana. An experimental novel, Ma Bibliothèque, 2017

A Lover's Discourse, Ma Bibliothèque, 2017

Freud on Holiday. Volume IV. Part 1. A Cavernous Defile, Cube Art Editions, 2013, and three earlier volumes

A Case of Hysteria, Book Works, 1999

ALMANACH

A YEAR IN THE FRENCH REVOLUTIONARY CALENDAR

SHARON KIVLAND

grand
IOTA

Published by
grand**IOTA**

2 Shoreline, St Margaret's Rd, St Leonards TN37 6FB
&
37 Downsway, North Woodingdean, Brighton BN2 6BD

www.grandiota.co.uk

First edition 2025
The illustrations are from:
Sharon Kivland, *The Bloody Radicals*, 2023-2024,
a series of 120 drawings in watercolour
on Arches Grain Fin paper, each 23 cm by 31 cm

Extracts from earlier versions were published as follows:
'Nivôse', a recording for *Pamenar* online magazine, 2022.
'Messidor', in *Prototype* 5, ed. Jess Chandler et. al., 2023.
'Floréal', in *Firmament*, ed. Jessica Sequiera, Seattle, 2024.
'Nivôse', in *The LARB Quarterly* 37, Spring 2023.

Typesetting & book design by Reality Street

A catalogue record for this book is available from the British Library

ISBN: 978-1-874400-93-6

ACKNOWLEDGEMENT
Lines from *A Revolutionary Calendar* (2020) by Zoë
Skoulding are included by kind permission of the author
and Shearsman Books.

TO THE HONEST PEOPLE
AUX HONNÊTES GENS
&
FOR MY 'FELLOW-BRETHREN AND COMPEERS'
POUR MES 'CONFRÈRES ET COMPAIGNONS'

NI VÔSE

It is the last day of the month of *nivôse* in the French revolutionary calendar, day thirty, *décadi*. The year is CCXXX, and it is two hundred and thirty years after the revolution that is so dear to my heart, or at least, since the counting began. *Nivôse* is the month of snow, though it is not snowy here and now. Mist and frost have passed, while rain and wind have yet to come and then seed will be sown and after there will be blossom, meadows, harvest, heat and fruit and fine vintage (if we are lucky). Today is a day of rest in this old new short-lived republican calendar formed of four sets of three: months of three weeks of ten days, days with ten hours, hours with a hundred minutes, minutes with a hundred seconds. It is a calendar of natural and attractive names, plants, animals, tools. It is the calendar of Jacobin history. There is rain, yes of course, for this is Brittany, in whose capital, Rennes, the revolution, my beloved history, started. This thirtieth day is the day of the *crible*, a sieve, from the Latin, *criblum*, a tool with calibrated openings that is used to separate solid fragments according to their size, the smaller from the large, the latter remaining while the former passes, a tool that this evening I will use to wash and steam the grains of couscous to accompany the modest stew of sweet potato in a sauce of tomato, onion, garlic, lime, cumin and cardamon. It is also a weighty metaphor for this book, as I will separate solid fragments; I will sift and riddle.

It is the day of Saint Germanicus in another calendar, the one delivered by the postman, who, after Alain, followed by Jean-Luc, is now a very pleasant young woman whose name I do not know; it was delivered before Christmas and I paid ten euros for mine, after carefully selecting from those she offered, this time, kittens in various appealing and playful poses. The calendar is particular to each department in France, printed in its modern form by the company of François-Charles Oberthur; in 1810 it was the *Almanach des Postes*, in 1880, the *Almanach des Postes et des Télé-*

graphes, in 1945 the *Almanach des P.T.T.* and in 1989 the *Almanach du Facteur*. Now I buy this *almanach du facteur* myself, paying the lavish tip of ten euros, but my neighbour Marcelle, for whom I had both the pleasure and bore the burden of being her 'second daughter', used to give it to me as a Christmas present on Christmas Eve. She kept all her almanachs over many years, each marked with the weather, the sowing and planting or the gathering. She marked the deaths of all the dogs and cats buried in our gardens: Belle, Nora, Fifi, Samy, and now, in mine, there lies Jean-Balthazar (named after the son of Père Fouettard, who takes Marie Noël, the daughter of Père Noël, in his arms after he has spent the night whipping the bad people while she has been giving presents to the good children. This is a song by Jacques Dutronc). There is Zéphir (named after the monkey in the stories of Babar the elephant-king), and Limpet (because she stuck like one to the shelf where the cats climb up to eat and because one of her legs had been damaged when she was a kitten at the decrepit farm next door). Others will in due course appear, including those who survived Marcelle. There are some whom I never knew (but I suppose I could ask Monique, her daughter, her true daughter, her first daughter), including the partially mummified body of a cat in the barn, whom Marcelle thought may have been the vanished Mélanie. Every living beast was a word, yes, and every kind being a sentence, and all of them together, my fellow-commoners, a large history, continuing if not for ever yet to the world's end. Saint Germanicus was a martyr, a disciple of Polycarpe of Smyrna, now Izmir, condemned by his faith and a Roman judge to end his life in the jaws of a beast, the ferocious wolf who devoured him.

What else is this day? Or rather, what is this day to me, writing as I look out of the window of my study onto the garden, where the geese and ducks and chickens have been released from their enclosure for the winter months, so they may have the pleasure and nourishment of scratching at compost heaps, of scattering leaves and straw and uneaten peelings over the gravel paths, while the geese try to break into the winter vegetable garden, nibbling at spinach and chicories and winter salads, avoiding the over-abundant kale entirely. Or rather, I stop writing to track their zig-zag wanderings, to listen to the geese cry out, to observe the ducks, Indian runners, the drake fawn and white, foul-flanked, the female black and beetle-green sheeny, follow the geese, whether in admiration or with faint menace. They call out constantly to each other. I marvel at the terrestrial creatures that live with us, and, like Montaigne, believe them to have as many rights or more than we, in our near resemblance.

This is first day of writing. There is always a first day but there is never entirely a last day, as what is written continues to be rewritten, even when done and dusted, when its metaphorical ink (the ink of a letter) is blotted or sprinkled with pounce, the fine powder made from dried cuttlefish, or with sand, the paper vibrated gently so the excess powder or sand falls off, is shaken off to be scooped up, rebottled for re-use, the paper folded, the letter despatched. It is also the last day of the job I have held for over thirty years, which has not made me who I am but has brought in the small income that sustained my life and that of others around and with me, human and animal. It is the first day of the physiotherapy that I hope will restore the mobility I have lost since an accident in the autumn last year that confined me to hospital and then to bed. It is to be my *vita nova* or my *vita nuova*, even if 'on the one hand, I have no time left to try out several different lives', as Roland Barthes writes. This is my last life, this new life, and I will plant, when I can walk again, I will plant my feet once again firmly on the ground, and I will understand something about how I must live the life that is left to me, as it is measured out to me and by me.

What was this writing to be? I knew what it would be very clearly until I started it, when the form, which had been so clear in my mind and rehearsed there for several months as though I were reading it aloud, became vague, as misty as the month of *brumaire* or as full of holes as a sieve. This much I knew: it was an almanach, and I would recount my days, my own calendar, including the five days of the *sans-culottides*, should they occur, the days of virtue, talent, labour, opinions (of which I hold many), reward, and revolution, though the last occurs only in a leap year, and this year is not one unless I were to use the Jewish calendar, in which case 2022 is a *shanah meuberet*, a pregnant year with an extra month, two months of Adar, the twelfth month of the religious year, when moon and sun are aligned. There would be, no, there are already, animals, saints and martyrs, radicals, gardens, plants of all nature, including seeds and leaves and flowers, household tips, meals, and there are useful objects, including tools, books and small items of furniture; there are embroideries and woven cloths and some children's shoes and jackets, a little coat of faded and scuffed black velvet with a cream and black striped lining, a cap or hat or a pair of red kid gloves (ten pairs, in fact); there is a pair of small cream and maroon patent leather boots. I should have time, all the time in my world, seconds into minutes into hours into days into weeks into a year.

This is a book of little times.

It begins in Year I. It ends in Year II.
My years.

PLUVIÔSE

The second month of the winter quarter and the fifth month of the Jacobin year, the month of rain, starts with spurge laurel and ends with a sleigh. It passes through plants and objects, and contains a bull, a cow, and a hare. Last year there was an unprecedented number of hares in the field behind the house and in the lanes, long limbs leaping, stretched out behind them, haring away in fact, or sitting still, bolt upright and alert. Hare statues. The peasant who used to farm the field behind Jean-François's garden hidden in the forest declined to plough it once he discovered a hare had her litter there, hidden above ground in the grass, the leverets born with eyes open, fully furred, and able to hop within a few hours, but lying low in a depression in the earth, visited once or twice a day by their mother. The hare was thought to be a messenger between the worlds of the living and the dead, and had its own saint, Melangell, beneath whose skirts the hunted beast took refuge from the dogs that pursued it. When we still ate meat, which we have not done for a long time, I used to make a civet, a stew of hare with red wine, bacon, onion, shallots and carrots, thyme and garlic, perhaps juniper berries, some cognac, sometimes truffles if by good fortune they came my way (and sometimes they did), the blood of the creature added towards the end of cooking to thicken the sauce, and the stew eaten with the liver, fried separately. Yet now that is a terrible thought, unimaginable to me even as I remember its unctuous flow and I can almost taste the incredible savage richness, to be eaten with a good red burgundy accompanying it. Any would do, but a Pommard in preference, if the budget allowed, depending on further good fortune, such as from Hospices de Beaune, a bottle of Dame de la Charité, a wine that requires a long sleep of twenty years to reach its – *her* – excellence, or more modestly, Chateau de Meursault, Les Petits Noizons. Some cooks add mushrooms, but I never did, nor did I add croutons of bread fried in oil. Some cooks said the hare for the civet should be a male.

Nature converged with revolution in the calendar, for Gilbert Romme, its main architect. Time started again, anew, according to reason and nature and the intentions of history. It was Year I of a new order, one in which there was collective time, human time, no gods or masters, tyrants abolished, kings, both their bodies, done away with and their queens too. There was no longer a divine order of the universe. Our time, our space, it was a difference between *temps voulu* and *temps veçu*, the measured time of the clock and the unmeasured time of existence, between *chronos* and *kairos*. Nothing but the changes of nature marked the changing of the hours, the days, the years. The king was deposed, and the sovereign body, no longer sovereign, a body now in pieces, ceased to serve as any kind of measure. That sovereign body always was two bodies, a natural one that lives and dies, and an enduring symbolic body assumed by the successor to the throne. The real and symbolic body of the ruler expired; the head, the responsible part of the body politic, quite literally rolled in 1793, 'forcibly undressed, his voice drowned out by the drums, trussed to a plank, still struggling, and receiving the heavy blade so badly that the cut does not go through his neck, but through the back of his head and his jaw, horribly'. And by then, the King was Citizen Capet, and then, the principal personage was *caput*. The baker, the baker's wife, and the baker's son, all gone. Some said there should have been a Year Zero.

For a long time, oh years and years, I forget how long (*tempus*!), I posted the day's date on Facebook, the date as it appeared in the revolutionary calendar, accompanied by an image – an engraving or drawing, a photograph or postcard – of the plant or tool or animal of the day. Days that ended in zero were assigned to an agricultural implement. Days ending in 5 were assigned to an animal. All other days were assigned to a plant, or a mineral. I collected my images and then I stopped doing this in the late autumn after my accident, not because of that, but rather because I knew this book would take the place of my activity. Today it would have been moss, and I would have found a lovely image: dense green, clumped or massed, shady locations, damp places, soaking up the rain of *pluviôse*.

The weather in 1788 alternated between heavy rains and extreme droughts, and when the winter came that year, the winter seeds froze and the fruit trees and grape vines died. It was very cold today, and on returning from the small market in Pleurtuit, we were chilled to the bone. In my wheelchair, despite the rug over me, the cold seemed to pierce my damaged leg. In the market the man who sells cheese from the mountains looked half-frozen, clapping his hands together, his face red and chapped, but was quite cheery, nonetheless. His cheese is excellent, good comtés and tommes, a Beaufort and an Abondance. He says *septante*, *huitante,* and *nonante* instead of *soixante-dix, et cetera* because he is from the Savoie, but they say this in Switzerland, and the Congo as well, no doubt by way of Belgium as the language of the colonisers echoes, occupies, and hardens, one word unleashing another. It rolls nicely enough off the tongue as one parts with one's *sous*, however. Next to him a woman sells fruit and vegetables, sometimes helped by her fragile daughter, to whom she speaks gently but firmly. The fish van was there after a few weeks of absence, and Bertrand gave the handsome tabby cat with a red collar, sitting up in front of the van, a small piece of fish. The cat belongs to the woman who was the florist, but now is retired, her shop at the corner of the square has closed and she has moved up the road. The cat continues to return to the market on Friday mornings. Today he disdained the fish, moving to stand in front of the *galette* van in a most pleading way, but he did not want the morsel of ham thrown to him either. It is simply his habit to return to the market square. We bought *merlan*, whiting fillets, to fry in clarified butter and to be accompanied by a sauce of white wine, butter, egg yolk, bitter orange zest and juice from the bergamot lemon Arnaud gave me on Sunday. The lemon is orange rather than yellow, sweet and sour at the same time, the lemons of Marrakech. We bought an extra fish fillet for Monique, my neighbour, the daughter, the real daughter, of Marcelle; it was left hanging in its plastic bag from her doorknob as she was confined with the corona virus, which so far, we have escaped (or it has escaped us).

There are six saints of these days, two of them for a weekend that was not one yet under the regime of the calendar (one of the reasons it failed to hold, too many days of work without repose): Fabien and Sébastien, Agnès of Rome, Vincent, Ildefonsus of Toledo, Francis de Sales, Titus and Timothy, and yesterday, the conversion of Saint Paul. What I know about some of them (and it is only a little, from memory, and some details may be inaccurate):

> Fabien and Sébastien were martyrs, and their tombs are on the via Appia, their names are coupled in the litany of saints; first they were apart, two separate cults, and then they were together; Agnès is the patron saint of young girls and chastity and women who have survived rape. Christ was, she said, her only spouse, rejecting all suitors, offending the governor's son she refused so that he had her first chained, then sent to a brothel, then beheaded, though in some accounts I have read that he had her dragged naked through the streets and her hair grew to cover her whole body and men who looked at her were struck blind;
> Francis became a mystic after meeting a woman he had already met in a dream, and he wrote a popular book of letters about leading a devout life, which had jokes and an encouragement of dancing, and his last word on his deathbed was 'humility', and that he is the saint of Catholic writers, journalists, and the deaf;
> Ildefonsus wrote a book on the perpetual virginity of Mary, who once appeared to him, descending from heaven to offer him a chasuble as a sign of her gratitude for his devotion, his love and fidelity. He is the subject of paintings by El Greco

and Velázquez; in the former, he is writing, seated at a table covered in a velvet red and gold-embroidered cloth, and he pauses, lifting his silver pen, to look at a statue of the Blessed Virgin; in the latter, the Virgin holds a red chasuble over the saint, who is not yet sainted.

For many, I suppose, it would be possible to become bored with saints quite quickly, though I have always enjoyed reading about their martyrdoms, the many ways in which their bodies are torn or burnt, how their blessed limbs and breasts are severed or their beautiful eyes are removed. And I have enjoyed visiting and admiring their many polychrome wooden statues in the small chapels of Brittany, in the villages and towns where they have settled to take on local appearance as patron saints and on occasion to play roles in local narratives. Saint Agnes, virgin and martyr (I remind you that no man could touch her without losing his eyesight, though the story changed later), appears in Tréfumel, next to Saint Armel, wolf-prince, who defeated a dragon in the forest and who cures the lame and whom some think was King Arthur. There is no story about Agnes here, and indeed, her appearance is considered unusual, unlike that of Saint Anne, the mother of Mary, who everyone knows *for a fact* was Breton.

The saints and martyrs, the dead, those who died for their devotion, their beliefs, the *croyant/es*, measured time in the Christian calendar with its distinction between sacred and profane days, indicating the way time should be spent according to the dictates of the church. Such a parade of saints and martyrs, but sometimes, on certain days, they were replaced with 'great men', sun-kings, for example (after Apollinaire: *soleil cou coupé*, sun corpseless, sun cutthroat, the sun a severed neck, solar throat slashed, and let the sun beheaded be, and so on) or other illustrious figures – even with Voltaire, imagine!

Sylvain Maréchal's *Almanach des honnêtes gens* of 1788 is a calendar of lived experience. He undid the authoritarian measure of time, calling for a *reestablishment of things for once and for all on their original footing, their original state, which is to say on the most perfect and most legitimate equality*. It was all a story, he said, at the time he wrote it, but he was telling the truth, he said, and it would become history one day. *Histoire* and history and fable: once upon a time and there was and there was not. We all tell stories in our village, about our village of six houses, with four outliers (considered not as part of the village for reasons I do not always understand, even when the families that inhabit or inhabited the houses are interlinked, enlaced by name and marriage, Bonnier, for instance, or Béréchel or Lemoine, identified as *la mère*, *le père*, and so on, in endless family ties, intermarriages, multiple *cousinages*) though my stories come late to the telling of its history and in the end, they may play little part in what remains to be told when I am gone, and I will not figure at all, *l'anglaise*, as they call me still, to my vexation.

In the *potager*, which I can only see from the window of my study as since my accident I cannot climb the stone steps into the garden, there is now chard, parsley, kale, wretchedly small Brussel sprouts... I cannot see beyond the towering and toppling kale, where there might be various Italian chicories, Palla Rossa, Castelfranco, Treviso (how irritated Stephen was when I called these chicory, and he gave me quite a long lecture about witloof). The Florentine fennel has gone to seed, but its ferny fronds remain. I cannot see if there is still Puntarella or Catalogna. The poultry have been confined to quarters today. They have scattered earth over the gravel paths, that much I can see, and nibbled (the geese did this) the tips of emerging bulbs and scratched up (the chickens did this) some new planting from November before my accident. They have disturbed the compost heaps to such an extent that the half-rotted debris lies in front of the containers in a little mountain. The slow worms who were living in the warmth of the compost have departed or the cats have eaten them. Annick once cried out to me to come quickly, quickly, for Smudgelina was eating a snake, but it was a slow worm she was swallowing, like a python.

Outside the house in the courtyard tips of the tulips planted before my accident are visible in some pots but not in others, the consequence, no doubt, of buying cheap bulbs from an indifferent supplier – I am always too tempted by what appears to be a bargain. I planted 'Queen of the Night' (dramatic), 'Foxtrot' (like a peony), 'Foxy Foxtrot' (such a delightful name), 'Black Parrot' (whimsical), 'Purissima' (elegant), 'Gavota' (a Czechoslovakian hybrid), 'Sun Lover' (colour-changing), 'Princess Irene' (sweetly scented), 'Apricot Beauty' (exquisite). I planted a hundred new bulbs and replanted the bulbs of last year in the garden beds. I can see that the dahlias, a new passion, have gone, declined completely now, and I hope they will return in the spring. I ordered new plants, unable to resist their names and their descriptions: 'Verrone's Obsidian', almost black and like stars, 'Coffee at Midnight', as homage to the great Peggy Lee in my mind, 'Fancy Pants', and 'Clair Obscur'. I regretted that I did not order 'Great Silence' – perhaps there is still time for the great silence. I fear that I will never be able to garden again, and what then?

Mysteriously, two fine black hens appeared a week ago, R. said. They are handsome and curiously tame. They started to lay this week, large brown eggs with a curiously narrow point. They bob back and forth by the gate, he says, and sometimes hop up to balance precariously on its narrow top bar. The others have accepted them, unlike the brown hen who appeared last summer, who took months to become part of the flock. She at last goes into the henhouse at night, but for weeks every evening at dusk I had to climb a ladder in the hanger to grab her as she roosted, succeeding only occasionally as she flapped off, squawking indignantly and so I would shout furiously OK then stupid creature the fox will eat you, he will snap you up, the fox will crunch your bones and you will be nothing but a pile of feathers. I was looking for the fable to tell this differently, but the story usually ends in the same way, I suppose. Snapped up. Swallowed. Dead. Dust to dust. A pile of feathers. A pair of shoes.

Our land measures... what does it measure in hectares or any other form of measurement? I could not find the deeds of the house. I am often asked this measure, but I cannot ever remember. Once I described the size in relation to the restaurant in Le Mans in which I was dining with friends, and was completely wrong, shrinking it in my measure, making it no larger than the bourgeois dining-room where we were seated. I suppose some would consider that with its gravel paths and small clipped box hedges around the beds, it is a bourgeois garden, because of the box, Vincent Victor once said, but I think it is too untidy, too optimistic in its exuberance for that to be fully justified; *trop de végétation*, remarked Geoffroy, in a critical way; Adrian looked around once at lunch and said he could not decide if he wanted a garden like mine or if he preferred one with a few carefully placed shrubs like Jacques'. Later that night in Le Mans, lodged in a convent in the city, I was violently sick several times, the result, I think, of ordering fish too far from the sea. I had to teach the next day. In the class I taught that morning I climbed on a table and walked around the room, following the path of the tables neatly arranged in a block. I was trying to explain to the students how one must take possession of the space in which one works, as a duty, as obligation, as an ethics. I was also trying not to throw up. The body always returns, in whatever form, whole or in pieces, healthy or diseased, and for a few months, I have been shattered, confined by the limits of my form, by my broken bones, held together by metal plates and bolts, inhuman and all too human.

In medieval times, bodies and souls existed in duality: one was flesh, mortal, and corrupt, while the other was perpetual, without matter and connected to God. But the women mystics, some of them anyway, did not accept the separation of one from the other, for the body was both an instrument and a battleground for the condition of the soul; sin and corruption were not solely associated with the body, no, not at all. Parts of the body were enshrined; as sacred relics, more esteemed and valued than gold or precious stones, they were housed in lovely reliquaries, of gold or ivory or silver, displayed in the churches whose form echoed bodies, the cruciform architecture reflecting the crucified body of Christ, their interiors described as the womb of the Blessed Virgin. The reliquaries most commonly were caskets, but others were made in the form of the parts they contained, or they were fashioned as complete bodies or as busts. Later the reliquaries were made with windows or as vials of rock crystal so the bone or tooth or Virgin's milk were no longer hidden. The relics had the power to heal. They performed miracles. They were not impure idols, receiving the worship of an oracle or of sacrifice; they were pious memorials, before which the faithful heart felt strongly touched by solemnity, imploring more fervently the powerful intercession for its sins.

Yesterday I made marmalade, my annual production. The oranges from Arnaud in the village market were slowly simmered for hours the day before, filling the house with a lovely fragrance. This is not the best way to make marmalade, but it is the easiest. The soft skin is sliced finely, the pulp squeezed out, the pips tied in muslin, then boiled with an equal quantity of sugar for thirty minutes. It must rest to cool a little, then is ladled into the warm sterilised glass jars. This morning I wrote AVE MARIA on the labels, the blue-edged stickers for school exercise books. Hail Mary is either the name of the producer or the variety. I poured melted wax over the marmalade to keep it sealed against corruption. Patrice called by to collect a jar, leaving a bottle of Château Chasse-Spleen in return. He also took away medlar jelly from fruit set to blet from the end of October. Medlars are called dog's arse, *cul de chien*, in French; they are most particular in flavour – like an apple butter mixed with dates. He also took away a jar of apple and lavender jelly from the summer, which Bruno once said (ungratefully, in my view) tasted like soap.

In Siena in 2018 my son and I were most excited by the head of Saint Catherine. I found the postcard of this splendid and unbelievable relic this morning as I rifled through a pile of cards for a less disturbing image to include in a small package to an elderly friend, forgetting for a moment that I too am elderly. Catherine's marvellous and incorrupt head is preserved in the Basilico of San Domenico, but her body is in Rome, in Santa Maria sopra Minerva. There is a story that her head was smuggled out of Rome in a bag, but the people from Siena who had taken it were stopped by the guards; when they opened the bag, it appeared to be filled with rose petals rather than the head of a dead saint and that is miraculous. A miracle! She dictated to her secretaries her treatise on divine providence while in ecstasy, it was reported, but she is believed to have edited it subsequently; therein she said that God was the sea in which we were the fish. That she was illiterate did not prevent her political activity and influence, her constant writing of letters to cardinals and princes, exhorting them to defend the vessel of the Church, her work to return the papacy from Avignon to Rome after the Great Schism. The cardinals and princes were in awe of her. She was their scourge. Her right thumb is preserved, too, as it should be. Her foot and three fingers are in Venice. Catherine could levitate during prayer, she ate nothing but the Sacrament, she received the stigmata, pierced by five red rays from a crucifix. A miracle! She bore on her finger the ring that was placed there by Christ in a vision, a ring from his own foreskin. A miracle! Once the Blessed Sacrament, the body of Christ, flew directly from the hand of the priest into her mouth. A miracle!

During the revolution the measure of bodies, a thumb (*pouce*), a foot (*pied*), of human bodies was made standard, for the size of individuals is not. A foot in Paris was not the same as a foot in Normandy. The first *mètre* is conserved in the Archives de France, a ruler a little longer than a metre in an X-shaped cross-section that minimises the risk of deformation, for two lines engraved in the groove of the X establish the distance. The international prototype is a copy, cast in a platinum-iridium alloy, made in 1889, kept in the Bureau international des poids et mesures in the Pavilion de Breteuil, Saint-Cloud, a building inaugurated by Louis XIV and later, acquired by Marie-Antoinette. I had to stop writing, leaving my writing table to wash some very muddy and unimpressive spinach from the garden. Anything like this takes me time, negotiating from crutch to walking frame to wheelchair. I descend the stairs on my arse, slowly.

Sunday was the saint day of my neighbour Marcelle. While she was living, I would bring her mimosa from the tree that is no longer in my garden. I had it cut down for it was only lovely in flowering and that was not quite enough for me. Mimosa is given as a gesture of mourning or of sensitivity. I wanted it for the funeral of my grandmother, but my mother felt it to be improper, inappropriate, and I was not old enough to insist. My mother used to put the candied flowers, hard little mimosa nubbins, on a lemon cream that as a child I felt to be the height of sophistication, served in deep-blue glass bowls from Sweden at dinner parties where the main course was beef Stroganoff, at which some people now sneer, but it was delicious with its sour cream mushroom gravy livened by Dijon mustard, paprika, and Worcestershire sauce, served with broad noodles.

Some more saints: Martine, Angèle, Ella, Véronique, Agathe, Eugénie, Jacqueleine, Apolline. All are virgins and martyrs. One is a little warrior, another an *abbesse*. Or a princess arousing profane passions (oh no, that's another Ella entirely, who was far from saintly). Or disguised themselves as men. They miraculously restore sight, they bring succour to those grieving the loss of parents, to the sick and the disabled, they are called upon by bell-founders, wet nurses, the victims of rape, sufferers from breast cancer, dentists, and those with toothache. They intercede for the victims of fire, for photographers and laundry workers, for donkeys and bad pupils. They give marzipan cakes to the poor and die piously and in good spirits. They collect the fallen baby teeth from children as they sleep, leaving a gift in return. They appear with shears and tongs and breasts on a plate, or holding a cloth impressed with the face of Christ, or grasping pincers in which a tooth is held. I read a poem by Rosmarie Waldrop: 'Even books spot with secret menstrual blood and propagate their species. My hand forms letters of unambiguous design. Or are you preparing me for new ways of behavior?' Oh, indeed.

Some more plants: butcher's broom, snow drops, laurel, lungwort, hellebore, pennycress; and some trees: hazel and yew and poplar and box. And shrubs, two varieties of daphne. My daphne is dead. No longer may I take its fragrant and delicate branches into the house in winter or enjoy its scent as I pass from the courtyard to the garden. Broccoli for the twelfth day. Cyclamens are yet to come in the calendar, but are already in the garden, though fewer than I had hoped, a discreet scattering. Fabre d'Églantine gave images to Gilbert Romme's mathematics of a new time, to the time when the labourer would be held in higher esteem than all the kings of the world together and agriculture would be considered as the highest of the arts of a civil society. Time would be natural, as nature itself, most energetic, in all its fecundity in the month of July when the sun is at its zenith, and when the French people also reach their full height and force to harvest the precious seeds of reason and independence, when red is the colour of the blood of kings and their henchmen, more livid, darker than the blood of other men. Like droplets of blood, the seeds fall or are scattered: a scrap here, a scrap there. Little bits. *Pluviôse*, however, was slow and foggy and rainy, gloomy-cold, wrote Baudelaire, dark chills, musty odours, and his cat sought a bed, its thin and mangy body shaking restlessly.

One of the cats, young Orphée, brought in a female Mallard duck through the cat flap in the door to the road this morning. We thought she was dead, but under her wings her heart gave faint flutters. Taken outside she raised her head and suddenly flapped her wings with vigour. She was taken up to the other poultry, where she drank and ate some wheat and looked rather shocked. The two Indian Runners ducks stared at her. She showed no signs of imminent departure. It is uncertain what she – or we – will do when night falls. R. kept going to check on her, delightedly reporting from each visit that she was very bright, very smart, very clever. Orphée seemed indifferent to the fate of his duck once he had deposited her, though he appeared to have a somewhat pleased expression – of course, it is difficult to discern a cat's emotions from its face.

The tip of the month in my postman's calendar advised me how to make taps shine: I should cut a lemon in half and rub the pulpy side on my fittings, making sure they are well covered in the juice. Then all I must do is rub off the juice and the limescale deposits with the clean tea towel with which I have already furnished myself, *et voilà*, my taps will be sparkling. But my half lemons were going in a Kilner jar in the refrigerator, rubbed with a little *gros sel* and when the jar is full, I will add more salt and cover them with good olive oil to preserve them, and they will be a fine thing.

The local paper comes out weekly. Once it was called the *Le Petit Bleu des Côtes-du-Nord*, under the editorship and direction of René Pleven, France's last foreign minister under the Fourth Republic, whose father accompanied Captain Dreyfus to his appeal. It is now *Le Petit Bleu des Côtes d'Armor*, as the northern coast became the coast of the land of the sea in 1990 after many years of negotiation. The newspaper is published in Dinan every Thursday and covers news across the department. In this week's edition, there was reportage of the arrival of a mysterious wreck, a little sailing boat abandoned in the river in the village of Le Chatelier. The story took a more mysterious turn: the boat, which the gardener who found it had initially tied to a tree, was moved to a mooring at the private pontoon of the property he maintains. Who could have attached this boat to the pontoon, the article speculated. Last Friday, on watch at the roundabout of the *Pigeon Vert* in Lanvallay, over the afternoon, the gendarmes noted seven offences: two drink-driving offences, one under the influence of drugs (a motorcyclist), one failure to observe a stop sign, one failure to present a vehicle registration document and two vehicles that were overdue for a technical inspection. Is there to be a blues-rock festival in Broons, another article enquired. Is life with wind turbines a living hell? – are the readers for or against them? I was mildly surprised to see a photograph of Hervé, co-founder of an ecological association that firmly supports them, as his interview makes clear. And in the same edition, there are reports of three tribunals, each concerning a woman who had suffered violence from a man. One was found in her pyjamas by the police on the pavement, her face bleeding. Her neighbour, who saw the event from her window and called the police, described the man as methodical and calm as he hit his wife's head against the cement path. The man's lawyer said his client was already broken by his life in the army and his trauma, that prison would not repair him. The second woman was hit by her husband who escaped from his psychiatric hospital. It was as if he could not hear her cries, she told the police, and then he suddenly stopped hitting her, dashed a bottle of water in her face, then started to cry. At the tribunal, he said he did not know what he was doing for he was so full of medication from the hospital and that he wanted peace, in fact, to be left to continue his life tranquilly. The third woman, four-months pregnant, refused to make a complaint against her boyfriend who punched her repeatedly after dragging her by her hair, and this was for the second time, for in October he had punched her in the stomach and hit her face, and her neighbours heard her cries. The man laid the blame on the excessive amount of alcohol he had consumed. The woman said she did not want to make a complaint as he helped her with her rent, even if he did not live with her. It was his twelfth conviction for conjugal violence.

Saint Valentin, Saint Valentine's Day, of course, patron saint of epilepsy, of beekeepers, interceding for lovers and marriages as well as for the plague, fainting, and travelling. There were three saints, all Valentines, all martyred, and one Valentine replaced Faunus, the Roman god of agriculture, and the day became a parliament of fools, a day of tokens and flowers and propositions, none of which I have kept. I wanted only to write in the past, though a future tense might be acceptable, in the hope of a future, as troops gather on the border of Russia and Ukraine and Israeli settlers attack Palestinian farmers in the West Bank and teachers in American schools cannot teach that any crimes were committed towards race or gender (though one said it will be clear enough what kind of Texans he means when he talks to his students about slavery). The present is hard enough: tense, immediate. It gives the impression that it is written in the present moment, in real time as events occur, unfold, without filter or absorption, before one's very eyes or through one's very eyes without later reporting of the continuous present. It is supposed to be intimate, to be dramatic and dynamic and vivid. It is supposed to reveal what I am thinking or reading or doing, and what I am doing before *your very eyes* if only you could see me, is applying a *cataplasme*, a poultice of green clay, to my shiny red ankle through which stabs of pain are shooting, in the hope of calming the inflammation and relieving the soreness, and particularly, to avoid taking some of the morphine I have kept for precisely this purpose: to no longer feel pain in the present but to relegate it to the past. But I want, I wanted, to move around in time, and I would use the future tense, when I will walk, when I will travel, or when I will go out into the garden to prune roses and plant potatoes, covering them with straw, and shallots and onions and broad beans and peas. That was the past, and perhaps it will be the future, but it is not the present.

28 *pluviôse*, and yes, of course, *c'est la Bretagne*, as everyone here always says when anyone complains, it is raining, grey, and for a long time I watched the little white and grey cat Luna sitting under an arch in the garden next to the stout black and white cat who has been visiting to the great annoyance of our own rotund black and white cat Aristide – there have been savage and angry mewlings and hissings in the night and everyone, cats and dogs, rushed to the doors, back and front. The two cats sat together in a companionable manner for some time until something alerted the visitor to a matter demanding his attention elsewhere and he shot off.

Treacherous Luna, *infidèle*. She lives her own life, in inward and secret motion, hah! With a flick of her tail and a whiskery twitch. It was pleasant to watch them unobserved.

I would like a 1930s chaise longue in the window, one made of rattan woven in two colours, in two parts: a seat and a stool, the latter slipping in neatly under the chair when no extension of the legs is required, with supports for the elbows and a reclining back that may be adjusted to three or even four positions. I would put down the book I was reading and look from the window at the rain and the wind and the cats, and in the distant garden, the geese and chickens and ducks moving this way and that, the mallard was still with us, until the next day when she was to be taken to the river in a cat's basket to lead a more mallard-like life in water with her kin.

I was reading the historian Mona Ozouf's book about her childhood in Brittany. She lived in the cramped and closed territory formed between the school, the church, and the house, where her maternal grandmother still wore her *coiffe*. At home Mona, then Mona Annig Sohier, had to profess her allegiance to Brittany while at the school she had to show her indifference to local identities. Ozouf's father Yann, who died when his daughter was four, was a militant activist for an independent Brittany. From the library in Lamballe, the one he left behind after his early death, housed in a glass-fronted cupboard decorated with carvings inspired by celtic illuminations, made by Joseph Savina, an artisan from Tréguier, she read books that she felt to be incomparable with others. There were more books scattered about the house, of course, children's books for her, the countess of Ségur (*Les Malheurs de Sophie, Les Petites Filles modèles...*), Perrault (*La Belle au bois dormant, Le Petit Chaperon rouge...*), and books from her schoolteacher mother's childhood and youth and from the canon deemed suitable for teachers, Estaunie, Pérochon, Colette. But it was to her father's library she turned: grammars and dictionaries, histories of Brittany, folktales, legends, proverbs, chronicles, songs, prayers... and journals, literary *revues*, political tracts. From her reading, she retained images more than ideas.

For her grandmother, Marie-Scholastique, there had never been any question of school; she was ten-years old when the Ferry Laws established mandatory education while undoing religious authority in the public system; she did not learn to read or write until much later when, driven by the feeling of dignity that never left her, so she would not be obliged to hand over her love letters to her husband who was aboard the *Furieux* or the *Isly* to the public scribe, the scrivener of the illiterate. In the childhood house of her grandmother in Kervenez, there was one book, *Buhez ar Sent*, the lives of the saints. Her grandmother read slowly, pushing at each letter one by one with her index finger. Her granddaughter was always astonished by this. It was as though material were matter, stuff to be rubbed. Writing was performed like a ceremony, laborious, and invariably beginning with the same formula, that she was taking up her pen (*la plume*) and that the winter had been cold. Her granddaughter saw the capital letters rise in the text like air balloons, *montgolfières*. Letters left Paris during the siege of 1870 in hot air balloons without pilots, the *ballons non-montés*, postbags in their cradles, their calico canopies sewn by volunteer dressmakers in the abandoned railway stations. Letters rose into the air, envelopes endorsed with the name of the balloon, franked for despatch to be forwarded on landing.

Later Ozouf wrote about the feast days, the festivals and holidays, of the Revolution, as history in the making, as new festivals were declared with each shift in the regime to celebrate each alteration and efface reminders of the past.

There was, she wrote, a transfer of sacrality from the *ancien régime* to the new. Individuals were rebaptised as citizens. Social bonds that had come undone were remade and good events ripened like good fruit. She wrote about the thousands of festivals celebrated everywhere under a single name: Youth, Old Age, Spouses, Agriculture, the Sovereignty of the People. These festivals were failures in the imagination of causal connections, bearing only the signs of the time but not its meaning. Time was divided by new festivals, finding new objects or events worthy of celebration, to guarantee against unforeseeable change, and to make the Revolution eternal, against time. Festivals began, divided, commemorated, and closed, placed new time beyond argument, showed history derived from a founding act.

For over ten years Vincent Victor took photographs and made films of the *comices agricole*, the agricultural shows, in the villages and town around where he lived (still lives). The work was titled under the name of his own village; there were scenes of the preparation of farm animals, cattle and sheep competitions, banquets, festive and convivial, demonstrating the *savoir faire* of producers, that they know their animals. The fairs still take place but are declining. They are advertised, often magnificently and absurdly, by elaborate constructions of enormous straw bales turned into the life-size models of tractors or appearing as huge amusing figures or faces. Densely packed round bales have largely replaced the small square or rectangular bales now hard to find and can only be moved by tractors. He was concerned, he said, with the conservation of popular traditions, with the memory of gestures, the future of our society's relations with the agricultural world, and with how collective gathering might take place at a time of globalisation. At the centre was his house, his childhood home (perhaps), from which extended in concentric enlacements, hamlet, village, town, region, his natal territory, and back to his house, around which watercress grows and where he has both a winter kitchen and a summer kitchen. His house is designed as a body – each room representing a part or organ: the head, the stomach and guts, the heart, the rectum. I have not seen him for more than a year, when he appeared agitated, and I could not understand what he was saying. Another time at an opening I told him that I had written about him, about the work and he was completely uninterested, asking not even a single question. I was a little surprised, I must admit, but I did not pursue the matter.

I remembered that there is a *comice agricole* in *Madame Bovary*, and that Flaubert had written to Louise Colet he had returned from a *comice*, dying from exhaustion and boredom, but he needed to see one of these inept rustic ceremonies for his Bovary, for his account of provincial seduction and hypocrisy. He wrote that he feared his *comice* scene might be too long, that he had all the characters of his book in action and in dialogue, intermingled with each other, and over this a great landscape enveloping them; that there, voices would interlace, producing a polyphony from the bellowing of bulls, sighs of love (Rodolphe chooses to declare his love to Emma at the fair, but she responds to his advances as she thinks a respectable woman should), and the phrases of administrators and councillors from the *prefecture*.

A contemporary of Saint-Just, an anonymous companion, described Saint-Just as yearning for the Revolution to be over so he could return to the contemplation of nature and the enjoyment of a restful life in a country haven with a young woman intended by heaven as his companion. It was a pastoral dream, one depicted in so many toiles de Jouy in pastoral scenes where peasants labour joyfully, planting, harvesting, making wine, and are joined by aristocrats in utopian scenes where work becomes recreation. Richard Mique designed Marie-Antoinette's *hameau* – her own hamlet –

and her English garden. Her little village had a mill, which was only decorative, a *boudoir* where with her entourage she received guests. On the other side of the river there was a working farm, established as a business concern, with sheep, chickens, pigs. There was a barn, a model dairy, a working dairy, a fisherman's cottage, stables. They said the Queen played at being a farmer, a shepherdess dressing up her sheep in ribbons, but it was not true. Instead, she educated her children about farming, *la vie agricole*.

Claude, Julienne, Alexis, cyclamen, celandine, and sleigh... The body of the saint did not decay, was marvellously preserved, incorruptible, until it was burnt during the iconoclasm of the Revolution; the left forearm was the only part to escape destruction: numerous miracles. The saint was plunged into a bath of molten lead but to her it seemed no more than a warm bath, and then she was beheaded: numerous miracles. The saint was a prodigal son or he was a beggar or he was a blind soldier, but in any case, lived unrecognised under the stairs of his father's house and in a seventeenth-century opera by Stefano Landi, his role was sung by a *castrato*: numerous miracles. I have written too much about cyclamens elsewhere, yet now I was delighted that the bulbs I planted in the autumn have surfaced. Celandine is used to cure diseases of the eye, for treating ulcers and eczema, to cure jaundice and colic, and for cleansing the throat. If a tincture of celandine is taken with the heart of a mole, all enemies are overcome; it removes warts and expels roundworm; with celandine, swallows restore the sight of their blind nestlings. I have nothing to write about a sleigh, *traineau*, not now, not today at least, though once I wrote about Walter Benjamin's ride in one through the streets of Moscow in the snow, when he believed himself to be in love.

The last day of this month, 30 *pluviôse*, and it rained, as properly it should, though later it stopped and there was that strange winter sunlight against grey. The wind rose, was rising as *ventôse* enters; a red weather warning was issued in Britain and trains and boats were cancelled. According to the memoirs of Madame Campan, in the severe winters of 1775 and 1776 Marie-Antoinette reintroduced sleighing parties to France, recalling the pleasures of her childhood. Sleighs belonging to the Dauphin, the King's father, were found in the stables and she had more modern ones made, as did the princes and noblemen of the Court. It was quite the fashion. The snow lay on the ground for six weeks and provided great enjoyment for the Court. The harnesses of the horses were decorated with bells and pompoms, their bridles embellished with white plumes, the sleighs were trimmed with gold, what delightful parties, what innocent amusement! The sleigh journeys sometimes extended from Versailles as far as the Champs Élysées, even crossing the boulevards. The women wore masks on their nocturnal sleigh-rides and the enemies of the Queen claimed she had travelled *incognito* through the streets of Paris in her sleigh. The public did not like the habits of the Northern Courts, not at all, and although one or two subsequent winters lent themselves to this amusement, Marie-Antoinette herself did not resume it. She wrote in January 1776: 'We were driving yesterday, and today there is a great "course" in Paris; but as they have never yet seen a queen take part in one, they would invent stories, and I would rather give up the pleasure than be bothered by more stories.' Poor little queen. She became acquainted during the sleighing-parties with the Princess of Lamballe, encountered wrapped in fur, her face peering out from sable and ermine. Oh, she was so like a little flower.

VENTÔSE

Storm Eunice passed lightly on Friday and Saturday, and Storm Franklin rose at four this morning, with lashing rain and howling wind, such clichés of weather. Three of the cats rushed in, their fur crackling wet, and fought sturdily for the best positions on the bed. One left a carefully dissected mouse in the upstairs bathroom: head, spleen, liver or bile duct to three sides of the partially eaten body, the back legs and tail neatly stretched out from the centre of the once living *nature morte* on the blue and white chequered rug, now in the washing machine – the rug, that is, not the mouse, which was cremated in the woodstove, sizzling a little. I could not sleep again after three o'clock, and read two books until seven, finishing Andrew's excellent novel about Rousseau in England, where he was remembered as being kind to the poor, and starting and finishing Lauren's book of notes made on an iPhone on the 91 and 92 buses from Montparnasse, neither which I used to take when coming back to Paris from Brittany.

I would take the 96, Montparnasse to Piscine des Tourelles, when I lived off the rue de Rivoli for a little time at Saint Paul and my son went to the little infant school, in French a *maternelle,* next to the delicatessen called Izraël, run by monsieur and madame Izraël, who said if something is good, it has its place with them, though sometimes, it must be said, they were really quite rude to customers. It has 'exotic products', oils and spices and dried fruits and pickles and loukoums, oh, everything you could want, from the Magreb, Israel, China, Turkey. So many kinds of peppercorns: from Sichuan, from Maniguette in Guinée, from Cameroun, from Tellichery, from Muntock, from Jamaica... and in an emergency, there is Marmite and Golden Syrup ('from the strong came forth sweetness' printed on the gold and green tin, part of Samson's riddle to the Philistines in Judges 14:14, 'for what is sweeter than honey, what is stronger than a lion', omitting 'out of the eater, something to eat'; the wager's prize was thirty *sedin* and *chalipha* and it got complicated after that, for the Philistines made his wife betray the answer and thirty men had to die in the end to provide the soft undershirt and the robes of the bet). The school is no longer there, though the shop is, and a few years ago my son and I made our first nostalgic visit to both shop and absent site, to which a little later he took his then girlfriend, and I suppose other women since, and then we took to visiting there when I came to Paris, to buy a little loukoum, some pistachios, a yellow and red packet of ras-el-hanout, the mix of star anise, white ginger, fennel, clove, cinnamon, nutmeg, cumin, cayenne, and black pepper.

The postman's almanach offered a recipe for *verrines de betteraves*, but I had the last of the pumpkins, a huge marina di chioggi, with warty grey-green skin and sweet firm orange flesh, to use up in every conceivable fashion – it has been roasted with cinnamon and butter, with sage and black garlic, with sumac and white beans; it has been soup and tonight more will be roasted, mashed, and added to a risotto. Arnaud had vanilla oranges in the market, which was lively, full of Parisians with their children on half-term holiday, buying Erwan and Cathy's expensive artichoke purée and fish soup. I bought another case of bitter oranges from Italy for marmalade, and pears from Holland, lemons from Sicily, wrinkled apples from Arnaud's orchard, delicious tiny dried figs, and avocados, as well as the famous vanilla oranges, which had to be 'transformed', he said, so they will become a salad with watercress and black olives. Arnaud gave me a Maltaise orange, the queen of oranges, which are also sometimes called vaniglia oranges, but come from Tunisia, from Cap Bon, once the Cape of Mercury, and not from Malta, and as he always does, wished me *pleines bonne choses* for the week to come, the week now entered. Sunday was the day of Sainte-Aimée, noted for her austerity when she entered the convent of the Clares in Assisi, though she had been very worldly until then, it was said.

On one nostalgic tour my son and I visited also the metre cut in marble (Garamond, I was told, or perhaps a version of Bodoni, but surely, I think, it must be Didot, the font of the Enlightenment, 'modern-style', cut by Firmin Didot and cast as type to be used in print by his brother Pierre), a lovely graven line with a brass stop at each end, rue Vaugirard, in the arcade near the Jardin de Luxembourg in the sixth *arrondissement* of Paris. Others were installed in sixteen accessible locations, the busiest places, to which the public could bring its lengths of string, taking a measure home, but only another remains *in situ*, in the Place Vendôme on the facade of the Ministry of Justice. Each year, for six years and then much later, the year he entered the École normale supérieure in rue Ulm, a seventh image, I photographed my son against the latter. His arms are outstretched; he is measuring himself against the measure of logic and reason. His mother obliges him to take measure.

There was a child, my beloved son, photographed every year between the ages of seven and thirteen, from the entry into the age of reason, when the Oedipus goes on hold, so to speak, in favour of producing a good citizen, to the return of the Oedipus at puberty. The Oedipus complex finds its resolution in prohibition (for the son, anyway), when the child renounces his desire for his mother. Hah! The *école maternelle*! The way in which each subject navigates the passage through the Oedipal relation will determine both the assumption of a sexual position and the choice of sexual object. For Jacques Lacan, it is a passage to the symbolic, one that passes through a complex sexual dialectic. The child, a boy, holds out his arms against the *mètre étalon*. He returns there, *majeur,* at twenty-one, our last visit to pose and photograph. He is a citizen. On one of his ribs this boy, *my* boy, has the word *mère* tattooed in Didot typeface – out of the eater, the eaten, out of the strong, sweetness.

As a measure, the age of majority changed: under the *ancien régime* it was thirty years for a *garçon*, twenty-five for a *fille*. In 1792 it was determined as twenty-one for both. Now it is eighteen (we were late), when, according to the Code Civil, article 414, 'à cet âge, chacun est capable d'exercer les droits dont il a la jouissance' ('at this age, each is capable of exercising the rights to which they are entitled'), and yes, without parental control or responsibility, to *jouir*, to enjoy, and to be subject to ordinary criminal law. In *mètre*, one may hear *m'être*, to be myself. In *mètre*, one may also hear *maître*, master. To master oneself – but one is never master in one's own house and the master's tools will never dismantle the master's house.

For a long time or what seemed so, I was unable to decide as whom I could write: as myself or as another, and as well as the matter, the question, of tenses, it was a matter of subject position, of which person. I imagined what it would be to write as she and her (and never for a moment as they and them, perhaps oddly under the current manner of identities and identification). I imagined looking at myself, who would be herself, of course, commenting on this woman who was largely confined to her house for several months, perhaps for longer, who would then start, step by step, quite literally, going out into the garden and then, I would see her taking trains to cities here and there. I would see her learning to walk again. I would see her and I would write her. I would watch her go once again into her studio and lay out her paper, her inks, her paints, and draw wolves holding women's underwear, and bleeding seed pods or roots, and observe her dyeing kid gloves with madder so when dry they shrivelled up like claws, and painting the arms of rather kitsch Dresden figurines of dancers wearing real lace tutus or gowns, the lace covered or transformed or merged with a fine thin layer of porcelain, with the quite expensive red paint specially made for porcelain and other china products. I would comment on this, considering her actions. I would wonder what she was doing and when, if she was writing or embroidering or if she was disinfecting the small wound on a black and white cat's back with Betadine, when a tick had lodged and was removed too rapidly leaving part of its detestable being in the cat's vulnerable body, or if she was wiping the eyes of the oldest cat with a solution to cleanse them, then holding him tightly so to squeeze in a line of eye ointment expertly and quickly. I would see her bidding at auction online for a taxidermised wild boar (*sus scrofa*), no information on its sex given, and a male roe deer (*capreolus capreolus*) with six points to his horns, in preparation for an exhibition she had not been offered but was forming in her mind already, assembling its parts slowly and in great anticipation but without any real expectation. I would watch her as the good weather, *les beaux jours*, came, and this morning, 5 *ventôse*, the day of the billy goat, the *bouc*, and of Lazarus, who rose again on the fourth day after his death, I would have seen that she was able to hobble up two steps into the garden where she picked a bunch of daffodils, ten to be exact, taking them into the house to put them in a white glazed vase with a gold trim in the form of an Empire-style dress made by her friend Jeannie, and where she noted with surprise and delight the tiny freckled iris or irises (whose plural form she had to look up in the dictionary, where she found either would do). Then later I would see that she lay down on the 1930s burgundy-and-cream-patterned velvet-upholstered divan in her study to read Mona Ozouf again, the chapter on time and festivals, keeping her right leg elevated on several cushions because of the constriction in circulation, and that she noted Joseph Le Maistre's observation that d'Églantine and Romme's calendar was a 'conjuration', a talisman with irrational hold, and that Saint-Just, the magnificent, the admirable, the beautiful, tried to have bonds between people renewed every year during *ventôse*.

I could have continued like this, of course, writing about myself as another, but suddenly it seemed disagreeable to me. I thought that I might return to it at some point, despite thinking it to be no more than an affectation. Too much was taking place in the world. Russia invaded Ukraine last night, as it was evident would happen. The news was intolerable. I looked at the atlas, registering the territories, the lie of the lands, closed it again after tracing the borders with my finger, where countries touched, like Freud's porcupine dilemma, elaborating Schopenhauer's parable of proximity and separation. (Note to self: 'Animals have the vegetable kingdom for their nourishment, and within the animal kingdom again every animal is the prey and food of some other. This means that the matter in which an animal's Idea manifests itself must stand aside for the manifestation of another Idea, since every animal can maintain its own existence only by the incessant elimination of another's. Thus the will-to-live generally feasts on itself, and is in different forms its own nourishment, till finally the human race, because it subdues all the others, regards nature as manufactured for its own use'.) The porcupines are brought together for warmth but driven apart by their quills, back and forth, and the human porcupine's neighbour is not only a potential helper or sexual object, 'but also someone who tempts them to satisfy their aggressiveness on him, to exploit his capacity for work without compensation, to use him sexually without his consent, to seize his possessions, to humiliate him, to cause him pain, to torture and to kill him'. Back and forth. *Fort* and *da*. Repetition and compulsion.

Freud had a bronze model of a porcupine on his desk among the other figures, the little statues of gods and goddesses so dear to him at the end of a day when it was impossible to look at human faces any longer. I won the deer at auction, but not the boar. I could not get out of the car to collect it.

When R. brought it back to the car, he tapped on the window with its nose, and a young man passing by laughed aloud, as did we. I saw a living roe deer at the edge of the forest this morning, where the trees touch the field. In the building where we store works there are ten deer heads, trophies mounted on wooden plaques of varying size, each deer with a red velvet ribbon around her (or even his) neck, and perhaps I would write about them later. Today was the day of wild ginger.

I read this, from Jacques Lacan, that anxiety is not doubt, but that anxiety is the cause of doubt; that doubt arises to fight anxiety, to avoid what is in anxiety and to hold on to certainty.

Against the *mètre étalon*, in a work I entitled *Mes semblances*, I placed other bodies in conjunction, bodies cut in stone or modelled, always the same body, the body of a woman, and manly artists, pipes in mouth, working from life, the same body of a woman. Look, I said to my audience in a lecture I gave in Berlin four years ago – no, now five years ago or is it six, even seven? – shortly after I took the final photograph of my son against the metre, here are artists, pointing to the men with pipes in their mouths. Look, here, out of view, is a model, a woman who is produced by the men, these manly artists, in various sizes. And look, here is another studio, one more decorous, more domestic, a ladies' salon of artistic production, where another woman is modelled without mess, pipe-smoking, beer bottles, or indeed, a body. (I may have been making too much of the pipes.) A pair of callipers, a *compas* in French, chrome-plated, was also on display, the tool for taking precise measurements and transferring them to the work of the serious sculptor, from subject to object or perhaps object to subject. The distinction between public and domestic space was evident in the two artists' studios. There were two regimes of production divided by a radical standard raised at a moment when subjectivity changed forever.

And I was walking then, carefully placing one foot in front of the other. I was walking, steadily and with trust in myself, making sure that I placed weight first on my right heel, then pressed my foot down to my toes, so I could feel them spreading in my unattractive shoes, the only shoe that would fit over my still-swollen foot. I was very conscious of my body, alert to where the stress fell. No, I was not sport-ive, I admitted to the physiotherapist. But I could feel a sen-sation run through the muscles of my right calf, and I could hold my position, which I could call a pose, and I thought about how as a student, earning a little money working as a life model, I found the extended holding of a pose, some-times for up to thirty minutes, quite soothing. And then there were the quick poses, held long enough only to be rapidly registered in a sketch. However, one had to stay still and silent, at least in the life room. The pose had to be main-tained. Strict rules were followed in institutional settings, applied to admission to the life room, visibility, disrobing, touch, periods of rest, and conversation. In some institu-tions, only the teacher could speak to the model. Once a man was caught masturbating in the hall outside the studio where I maintained a pose, and was chased away by the life-drawing instructor, a woman who later had an affair with the man with whom I was living at the time, a violent and abusive philanderer. A few years ago, he sent me a friend request on Facebook, such breathtaking impudence at best. I wondered if he remembered trying to kick my head as I crouched under a table. I wondered what he thought about that now. Most art schools no longer have a 'life room', but nonetheless, it seems to exist in some collective memory, with particular furniture: the model's 'throne', a raised stand or dais that in sculpture studios has a 360-degree rotation so that each artist may have a complete view of the figure, and those peculiar benches combining a seat and an easel, called, in English, donkeys. For clay and plaster modelling there were three- or four-legged stands, sometimes folding up for easy storage, with square tops that revolved, called, in French, *selles* or *sellettes*, and as well as a turntable, a *selle* is also a breed of horse and a saddle.

Emails came from friends in Russia. The letter from Ekaterina was titled 'letter from hell'. Katya wrote that it came from the lowest part of hell, deathly cold. She wrote of her shame and anger. She ended by saying she did not know if this might be the last letter she could send, and please, she begged, please know that she and many others were against the terrible regime. I wrote back to her with all my heart. There was nothing else to offer and it was not enough. She did not reply. There was silence again. I listened to the wireless; I heard Yelena speaking, with her son Arkady. A translator could not hold back her tears. I listen to other women in Ukraine, or fleeing Ukraine, stuck at borders or crossing borders, or in other countries, hoping families and friends are safe or on their way, that visas will be offered freely. No one could hold back their tears.

Mahmoud Darwish wrote in 1982 from Beirut that he would pay no attention to what was happening outside the window, to the shells, rockets, artillery... blowing his way like a raging wind... that human will can't do anything against these; they're a fate that can't be turned back. He wrote that he hoarded his treasure of water, using each drop with extreme care, each drop with its role: five hundred for washing the hair and two thousand for washing the body. Yet no-one was washing the dead. The dead cannot repay that good act, the last duties, the offices, *officium*, in any case: service, duty, business. Antigone poured water over her brother. The dead must be washed if they are to rest. (She scattered a thin layer of earth over him, Hades and the dead were witnesses, and her choice was to die. So it goes.) Family, friends, neighbours, any might undertake the duty. Often, too often perhaps, it is left to strangers. One should be present at a death.

A report came on the radio: a hump-backed whale had been observed in the sea near Perros-Guirec on the coast of pink granite. It was photographed from the customs path of Plouman'ach. The amateur photographer could not believe his eyes and would have thought he had gone crazy if the sight was not confirmed by his companion. The whale re-emerged from the sea and its breath condensed into a cloud. Incredible, the photographer said, just incredible, and it was. The whale stayed by the semaphore of Perros for half an hour before swimming out into the ocean. It was thought to have made the detour into the bay to follow a shoal of sardines or mackerel.

A sparrow was tapping on the windowpane of my study all morning. It hopped from the gutter that runs across the top pane to the frame, intent on the corner of the glass. One of the cats, Luna, the little white and grey one, waited patiently in the dog basket by the window for hours after the sparrow disappeared. Then suddenly the sparrow returned, and Luna shot up, startled, rigid and intent, and the sparrow flew off again. Distracted, I looked up *Walter Presents* for a Nordic noir to watch that evening, and I was amused, as always, that as I tapped 'Walter' on the keyboard, that *Walter Benjamin Archives*, an exhibition, was the first to come up on the search engine. If I followed that, rather than crime drama, I was led to an *abécédaire*: archive, atlas, aura, auto-portrait, each entry an apposite quotation from a work by Benjamin. *Barbarie*, barbarism, had an image (a building) accompanying a quotation from 'Experience and Poverty', an essay in which he advised his reader to remember the paintings of James Ensor, in which the streets of cities are filled with ghosts and philistines disguised with cardboard crowns and masks roll endlessly down those streets. He wrote that the economic crisis was at the door, and behind it lay the shadow of approaching war; he wrote that holding on to things had become the monopoly of a few powerful people, no more human than the many, and for the most part more barbaric, but not in the good way. Everyone else had to adapt, he wrote, beginning anew and with few resources. In the same essay he wrote that Paul Klee's figures obey the laws of their interior; he placed stress on their *interior*, rather than their inwardness, that this is what made them barbaric. We know one such figure too well, too obviously, and that is the angel of history, with chicken feet and spindly legs, slack-mouthed face turned to the past, seeing a single catastrophe rather than a chain of events, a storm blowing its wings with such violence that it cannot close them. I tried to remember and counted angels: Gabriel, Raphael, Uriel, Michael, Phanuel, Raguel, Sariel, Jeremiel, and two named only as the Fallen. There is a hierarchy among angels and their orders. They have a roster of duties, of watchfulness. They keep watch – we all knew this as children – along with the apostles. They bless the bed that we lie on.

I pruned some of the roses – I was still unable to stand for very long. I wished I had maintained their labels from their planting, remembering only a few: 'Cuisse de nymphe' (the colour of flesh), 'Reine Victoria', 'Reine des Violettes', 'Louise Odier', 'Félicité Parmentier'... two 'Ena Harkness'. Such delicious names. Women and roses. The peonies were beginning to emerge and following the calendar, violets, narcissi, also in the garden, but I did not have buckthorn or goat willow or elm for the days to date. The Madonna lilies planted in the autumn seemed to have disappeared, as had their markers, but the new fritillary was there, though it was not the variety I thought it was. I missed *mardi gras* and today was *cendres*, Ash Wednesday, when we are reminded that we are sinners and that our time in this world is no more than a passage, that we are from dust and to dust we will return, when we are marked with the ash from the burning of the holy palm of last year, when Lent begins, and some will fast. My *almanach* gave me a recipe for a *matelote* of fish and shellfish with saffron: take hake, monkfish, four small squid, some eel if you can get it, mussels and langoustines cooked apart, the latter for two minutes in a *court-bouillon*; in a frying pan sauté three onions in olive oil, then add the eel and squid, add three soup-spoons of tomato purée slackened with white wine, then the water in which the mussels have been opened and transfer to a casserole; gently brown the fish in the frying pan then add to the casserole, cover and cook gently for fifteen minutes, adding more wine if needed; chop some garlic, some parsley, slacken with oil and mussel water, add to the casserole, very gently, do not break up the fish with your wooden spoon, then add saffron, a pinch of threads; lastly, add the mussels and langoustines and serve at once. Some people add shrimps or scallops. Some people add potatoes to the stew – I am not one who does, instead thinking a few plain boiled potatoes should be served alongside, with good crusty bread and then a green salad, perhaps some cheese to follow, for as Jean-Pierre often says, a meal is not a proper meal without cheese. Among the saints I neglected to mention is Honorine, the hope of prisoners, who, liberated and joyful, brought their chains as *ex-votos*, and boatmen, especially the tugmen of the rivers and canals of the north who venerated her.

Marcelle's husband, Monique's father, was in the merchant navy. He died in mysterious circumstances in Le Havre, leaving his small family in reduced circumstances, living with his mother. Monique told me how her grandmother would hold a piece of bread in one hand and with the other hand, she smeared the bread with butter for her *goûter* when she returned from school. The dirty marks of her fingers imprinted the butter, grimy letters. Monique was disgusted. Her grandmother lived on the ground floor, the earth floor, she and her mother in the rooms above. Sometimes they were so poor that all they had for supper was a bowl of *lait ribot,* buttermilk, with a potato mashed into it, or a *galette*, the Breton buckwheat pancake, folded into the milk in the coffee bowl. When she was a child there was a well at the end of the village and clothes were washed in a stream in another corner of land, now divided from the village by the road and where a walnut tree grows. Monique is my age, and when I was a child, my grandmother lived with us in north London and did the laundry every Monday in a Hotpoint twin tub in the corner of the kitchen, a machine I inherited. Gaël's grandmother used to hold the loaf in the crook of her elbow and with the knife, draw a cross on it before slicing – this I saw in her house in the interior of Brittany, in a tiny village on a hill next to the pig farm with those poor little squealing porkers.

Tridi of the second *decade*, and the plant is *fumeterre*, common fumitory, sometimes called earth smoke as from a distance it looks like smoke rising, sometimes called jaundice herb for its use as a liver remedy. It is a plant of disturbed and bare soil and cultivated land and meadows and fields, spreading by dispersal of its small, warty seeds. It has sprays of purple or pink or white flowers. Boiled in milk, it was used as a cosmetic, clearing the skin. In the *almanach du facteur,* the day is Casimir's, the patron saint of Lithuania and Poland, a prince who rejected wealth. A million people fled Ukraine in the last two days, crossing to Poland, Slovakia, Hungary, and Moldova. Others went to Russia and Belarus; some have headed further west to other European countries. Many waited for sixty hours or longer to cross into Poland. It was reported that it was quicker to cross by foot than by car and that many people were unable to board trains. Most of those arriving at the borders were women and children. Some walked for days to reach the borders. The weather was freezing. At the Hungarian border points, refugees were given flowers and little charms to mark the start of spring as well as food and hot drinks.

I thought that I remembered Marcelle giving each house, each woman (for we were a village of women then), a tiny clutch of snowdrops from her garden in March, but I confused this with her gift of a spray of three strands of lily of the valley on 1 May. Sometimes the lily of the valley, *muguet*, is called Mary's tears or Our Lady's tears. It chases away the maledictions of winter. Anyone can sell flowers on May Day without a license. Once workers wore a red triangle on May Day, the three sides representing eight hours of work, eight hours of sleep, eight hours of their own time, or they wore a red wild rose, *églantine*, the sweet briar, the dog rose; later, under Pétain, the rose was replaced by the lily of the valley. I also confused the days of the saints for *tridi* was not the day of Casimir but of Guénolé, the Benedictine abbot of Landévennec. He parted the sea to cross the estuary to found his abbey on the other bank; he gave the eye of a goose to his little sister to restore her eyesight; he calmed a violent tempest at sea by the sign of the cross. Obviously, he is the patron saint of ophthalmologists and also of the wives of fishermen, the fishwives. He is one of the phallic saints, coming to the aide of sterile women. In Brest, by the river Penfold, the site of a ruined chapel named for him was once the place of a cult of fertility. There are other chapels with his name and to these the women used to come to light a candle to his statue, telling their rosaries, rubbing their infertile bellies against the statues. There was so much the invocation of this thaumaturge could cure: warts and headaches and sick children who could not walk, and giving protection against rain during the harvest, accomplishing miraculous healing and as well as that miraculous fertilisation. Saint-Guénolé is the name also of a port to the north of the point of Penmarc'h in the Finisterre, a fishing port confronting the winds of the south-west, from which the sardine boats, of the *sardiniers* or *bolincheurs* go to sea at night, returning for the market at 6.30 in the morning. I thought about fishwives, those who had license to sell, noted for their strong character and language, or I thought that a fishwife is a shrew, or I thought that Jamie told me fishwife is a slang name for the wife of a gay man, but I was mistaken, for the wife in his work was called a false one, without any piscine reference. I thought about the resemblance of a skate's reproductive organs to its human counterpart, the supposed arousal of the fishermen when landing an attractive skate, that skate is not kosher and should not be eaten because it menstruates (some say). Mermaid's purses.

The sparrow continued to tap against my window, hopping from the gutter then flying to the electricity cable when startled by one of the two cats who have set up what appears to be a rota of surveillance, leaping at the pane, claws outstretched. The bird went away at night, to sleep, I supposed, but during the day she was always there, tapping or simply looking at me, trying to find a place to perch from which she could observe, then swoop and tap. There was something desperate about her activity at times, though she would rest for short periods, then fly off, return, perch, tap, stare, launching herself against the glass, wings fluttering quite furiously, as though she simply had to find a way to enter. It was discomforting. I felt that I should open the window to allow her entry but knew this would lead only to her death. Once I tried to save a wren from the claws of Alexandre, the young cat who returned with me from Rome, a magnificent cat. Once in the courtyard, Cosima took down a swallow from flight. It was wonderful and terrible.

The magazine of the department, the *Côtes d'Armor*, arrived in the letterbox, an issue on the rights of women. The editorial was written in French, Breton, and Gallo, the *dialect continuum* of this part of Brittany, extending to the Pays de Retz and into lower Normandy, a link in the chain of language. It was one of the languages almost eradicated under the later stage of Revolution when regional languages were no longer tolerated, though in the early heady liberal days they were seen as no more than a little obstacle to the rapid diffusion of revolutionary ideas and the new laws and decrees were translated. Later the local languages or dialects became the sign of superstition or the hand of the priest or connivance with the enemy of the new regime, or a barrier in the communication between the representatives of the state and those of the territories, hostile or indifferent. Gallo means 'foreigner', or rather, 'not-Breton' or French. Marie used to say that her mother was Breton, but her father (she would pause), he was French. Marcel's family spoke Breton at home in the Finisterre, and he was punished when he went to school for the first time, punished for not speaking French, for replying instead to the teacher in the language he knew, his maternal language, the words of home. He said that he felt as if thereafter he never spoke properly with his parents again. He does not remember telling me this.

When Marie was cremated, there was silence; no flowers, Marcel said, but only when we arrived and I was ashamed, embarrassed really, that I had brought a bunch of roses from my garden as I always brought flowers to her when she was alive. Inside the building I tried to take my son's hand, but he pushed me away, roughly, without looking at me. Later I told him it was for me as much as it was for him, and he nodded. He has a cold heart. His cold, cold heart once beat warmly against mine: *I tried so hard, the more I learnt to care for him*, but that is a sentimental song, one of the heart. There was music, but only Yvette and Jean-Marc spoke a eulogy. Later they told me that they had insisted they did so, that they would speak for and to Marie, Marie who was no longer with us, Marie who had slowly faded away and never until the end told her mother that she was dying. Her children were lost at her death, even before it, only Thomas with his nun-like girlfriend (who keeps her mobile phone on when she is at home, connected throughout the day to her parent's house so she can hear about their domestic business and they can hear her likewise, and it drives Thomas crazy, this shared habitation from which he is excluded or to which he is other, unnecessary) mustered the force to host the aftermath of the service, making coffee and laying out dry biscuits that no one had the heart to eat.

Of course, as I should have known, the sparrow was not a female, but a male, intent on battling what he perceived to be another male in his territory. He was young so I misread his plumage, did not see the dark down around his neck. I hung a pair of linen cloths at the window so he could no longer see the self whom he took to be another – *je suis un autre, je est un autre*, and the other was no other. No longer would he exhaust himself against the glass when he should be finding a mate instead. No more tapping. No longer would he be captured by an image. Unlike the child of the mirror stage whose identification with an image gives mastery of its body, until I suspended the cloth the sparrow was trapped in his aggressive tension, in the death drive, the Hegelian fight to the death, without the human yield of jubilation wrought by identification. A day later: he had not returned, and I was overwhelmed with relief for his continuing seemingly anxious and angry presence had been upsetting and I could not make him stop save by replacing the linen hangings at the window, which blocked my light on these still dark days. The youngest cat stayed sitting on a wooden chair near the window, just in case the bird came back, but now he too had relinquished his obsession. My cats are not greatly interested in mirrors. There is nothing for them in a reflection. However, I have on occasion caught sight of at least one of them glancing at itself with moment- ary interest or patting awkwardly at the glass with a soft paw.

Carême, Sunday, 15 *ventôse*, was the first Sunday of Lent, and once there would have been the veiling of images, and fasting, praying, the giving of alms. In the wilderness Christ resisted the temptation of Satan, fallen angel. It was a time of spiritual combat for many, for some it was the time of the preparation for the resurrection. We bought oysters in the village market. I bought stupidly expensive fish soup in a glass jar, a bag of croutons and a pot of rouille, the red pep- per mayonnaise for the soup, from Erwann and Cathy, because for weeks I had felt guilty about passing their stall, where they stood expectantly but a little hopelessly until the weekend the Parisians came to their second homes. Actu- ally (and sadly), Erwann was rather without charm. The soup was fine, as it should be at the price. In my version, when I can be bothered to make it, it is made from a bouil- lon of various fish heads, whatever I can get from Bertrand, olive oil, white wine, some carrot, onion, celery, and fennel. I add orange peel, saffron, thyme, rosemary, bay, red chili, garlic, crushed tomato to the stock and simmer it for a few hours, then pass it through a sieve. The chickens get what is left in the sieve, enjoying what remains of the fish heads, the stripped and shiny bones, the blind white eyes.

Carême, *quintidi* of the second decade, is the day of the goat in the postman's calendar. Gilles and Annie-France kept miniature goats. The little goats could be seen from the main road to the supermarket, climbing the wood pile and the tree stumps in their garden. Once we went over for supper and when I asked where all the little goats were, there was a silence, an uneasy pause in the conversation. Quietly, eyes lowered, Annie-France said they were in the freezer, and we passed on to other subjects quite quickly. I hobbled up to the garden to advise on the position of a new arch at the top of the steps, the one inexpertly woven from hazel branches having at last collapsed. It was a task that Esteban had been going to do, but then he had a serious car accident, and was dead for a few minutes until his friend pressed on his heart, breathed into his mouth. He was in a coma for weeks. He is angry and sad now on returning to a life of sorts. I pruned more roses but was unable to reach the rambler over another arch, the rampant *moschata* 'Rambling Rector' or 'Shakespeare's Musk'. It appears in *A Midsummer Night's Dream*, part of the canopy of Titania's bower, with eglantine, and woodbine, and on the ground, wild thyme and violets and oxlips, and Titania was lulled in these flowers with dances and delight. In the late summer I cut it back severely after its flowering in July. Two clematis grow through it; I do not know their variety. The tamarisk was not dead, as I feared, nor the quince tree. In the beds, there was far too much *arum maculatum*, also called Cuckoo Pint, Lords and Ladies, Jack-in-the-pulpit, Snakeshead, Naked Boys, Adam and Eve. I staggered as I tried to dig up all the root, the bulb, for even a tiny fragment, the smallest bulblet, left in the soil will grow and spread. Its orange berries are poisonous; if they are eaten, they will cause mouth and throat to swell, breathing will be difficult, the belly will ache, and then it is curtains. But birds can eat the berries and the birds propagate the seeds freely without harm to themselves.

In Ukraine, bodies lined the streets, it was reported. Humanitarian corridors were opened to let people leave, but these were not respected by the invading army. Some people drove eighteen hundred miles across Europe to bring their families to England, but there was no visa centre at Calais and people were told they had to go to Paris or Brussels to apply, or wait until a centre was established in Lille, over seventy miles away. Even those who succeeded in getting visas were held by immigration officials. The Home Secretary denied that anyone had been turned back at the border, but this, like much of what she said, now and in the past, was a lie, as was her statement that there would be a support team at Calais. She appeared to lack any sense of moral urgency. I recalled a paragraph in Daisy Hilyard's book *The Second Body*, in which she wrote that when life is examined on a global scale, one loses sight of oneself. The global scale, she wrote, is the intellectual experience of a body functioning beyond its personal boundary, and it becomes a matter of accounting, scales, categories (she also wrote 'explaining'), rather than living inside something or feeling inside something. She was writing about an essay by Timothy Clark, in which he described a world of destabilised borders, of inundated boundaries: everything opening on everything else, dissolving. Individuals are lost.

Today, *octidi*, was the day of the pimpernel, also called poorman's weatherglass, mirror of time, adder's eyes, and of Saint Françoise. Luna, the white and grey cat, hid behind the grey linen curtain drawn back at my study door. I never close the curtains; they are the remainder or reminder of when my son lived here, markers of his desire for privacy, to separate himself from the rest of the house, from his parents, to keep us out. He used to call us *les étrangers*, the foreigners, and said we were always creeping about. Luna often hides there, waiting for another cat to pass, usually for Céleste, the one with whom she feuds jealously. A work by Katharina hangs from the curtain rail, a long red glove from which very long streamers emerge; where the glove would slip onto the arm, the opening is a mouth with puffy lips and teeth made from pearls, china beads, and jewels. The cat likes to play with the strands. Katharina wrote of the mystics, the wound-lickers; she wrote of transformations and dissolving states; she was writing about holes and wounds, and the importance of keeping them open. Saint Françoise, patron saint of widows and motorists (the latter because of the story that an angel lit the road before the saint when she travelled), founded a community of oblates, women who shared their lives without taking religious vows. Before this, she lived on vegetables, though some said instead it was bread, and pure water; she helped the poor and undertook the meanest of tasks, the severest penances. She wore a dress of coarse green cloth, and under it a hair shirt. An angel appeared to her and commanded her to stop: the body, servant to her soul, should not be despoiled, the spirit should not be allowed to ruin her flesh. The pimpernel may be applied to the skin to ease painful joints, irritation, wounds that do not heal, or it may be taken internally against depression, herpes, disorders of the liver and kidneys.

I went into the garden to plant sets of onions and shallots, or rather to oversee their planting, for bending still was painful and my balance uncertain. My foot was swollen again. I could not stand upright easily or for long. Proofs of my book *Abécédaire* were sent out by its publisher yesterday and I felt embarrassed to have written it, as I will no doubt feel embarrassed about this one, should it ever appear in the world of readers. I was not rewriting it here. No. A friend in Paris, Ricardo, wrote to me, asking to read some extracts of *Abécédaire*, and in an excess of response, I sent him the whole thing. He replied in a characteristically thoughtful manner, explaining why he could not read it, finding it too dense and not at all like the embroidery sampler he had envisaged from the book's description; he included an image of a sampler as his example to demonstrate to me what it was that he had supposed of my book (what he had hoped for, I suppose). Or he had imagined the book sharing a relation with Michel Butor's *La Modification*, which he had been reading, a book in which time and space are condensed and where the narrator is a second person: *vous*. He thought there would be a similar approach to description, to the precise detail of each action or observation. Instead, my book was about subjects he had never considered, like Freud or sisterhood, but then, he wrote, the latter was perhaps no different from Jewishness – the same kind of instinctual correspondence, fellowship, solidarity, and pride (he excluded the occupied territories), victimhood, and hubris. I had forgotten that he appears in my book, albeit briefly. I wondered if he would get to that part eventually. There is another R. there, too, one less favourably mentioned, but not the R. here, my companion. I wondered if that other R. would encounter himself here one day, read himself: *vous*. I knew he would not, too caught up in his own image to recognise himself in the unfavourable light.

I listened to a woman interviewed on the wireless. She was speaking about the foundation she and her husband had set up to support children with cancer, to help with specialised treatment. The foundation was called after their daughter who died at eight months from leukaemia. The woman's voice was charged with emotion and provoked in me not sympathy, I regret to note, but a strong sentiment of resistance or embarrassment, the way one feels when cornered or collared by an obsessive in a public space from which it is difficult to escape (this happens to me far too frequently, as my friends and family observe, as though it were my fault, and indeed, perhaps it is). The child, a baby, was described variously: as a little lion, as an angel looking down on her parents from above with love and pride in their fundraising activities; the mother said her child lit up the world, that she inspired and gave hope. I (mis)heard the child's name as that of a shrub, a subgenus of the rhododendron species, and coldly wondered why they had named her after a woody plant. I was relieved when the feature ended but I was a little ashamed of myself, of my callousness, at the same time. It had been a few weeks of hearing women being interviewed, but this had been usually at borders, in stations, on trains, women in transit: holding their children or a cat or a dog, women crying, or two women, a mother and daughter, beautifully dressed in unusual matching brown coats from the high fashion shop they left behind them. The mother said, tartly, that she felt that there was no reason they should not be well-dressed, even when fleeing their country. I remembered Holly telling me about her now-elderly friend in Paris who always wore high heels to the barricades in 1968, holding out her arm for a gallant man to help her over the cars, the railings, the trees, the street signs, the pavement gratings, maintaining her sophisticated step. Perhaps I imagined this; however, it should be a true story.

Saint Rosine and Saint Justine and Saint Mathilde. Mandrake and parsley and daisies. Once when I was planting daisies, pushing them between the granite stones of the wall, *paquerettes*, *bellis* from *bellus* which might mean elegant and pretty or might mean war, for they did often grow on the fields of battle or can be used to treat deep wounds, Aline was very critical, asking me why I was planting weeds. Another time she came out into her courtyard in a state of great vexation to tell me I could not plant a tree in my garden, even though it was not *at all* near her fence, and once she stopped me planting a lilac, which I admit *was* very close to her fence, and another time, she and her daughter Annick said I could not weave a clematis into the ugly grille that tops an even uglier breeze-block wall separating their courtyard from ours, though now I have sneaked in some hydrangeas and an oleander, and *euphorbia melliferia*, honey spurge, has self-seeded with abandon. When Aline died, we were invited into the house to see her body laid out. She had been there for several days and there was a faint odour of decay (it seemed). Her skin was pale, flushed faintly with a delicate pink, like Turkish Delight, loukoum-flesh. Their dog Charlie was released into our courtyard every day to pee on my lavender bushes. We have no right of passage through their courtyard, but they have one through ours – the width of a wheelbarrow. Annick used to wash Charlie in bleach to get rid of his fleas. When he died, she asked me to bury him, and fortunately Philippe was in his mother's house in the village to help. The dog was buried under the walnut tree across the road from their house and while we dug away in the rain, Philippe told me that he thought Annick was too sad to come out with us to lay her dachshund to rest. He was surprised when I explained that Annick was inside eating the meal her mother cooked for her every day when she returned home for her lunchbreak. This was a long time ago, but when Philippe visits we still laugh about it.

Saints and martyrs: virgins of Padua and Sardinia and Arezzo, a Benedictine nun, a Saxon queen, but also a scent by Poiret, a novel by Dumas, and Rosine was the real name of Sarah Bernhardt. The parsley restored itself in the garden and would serve us yet for a month or two. The onions and shallots were in, not without dispute. A space was left for garlic. Coriander and dill began to come up in the polytunnel and the winter lettuces eaten by the wily little Araucana hen were returning, although still raggedly pecked-looking. There was Turkish cress, and some frisée remained, enough for a little salad with toasted walnuts, walnut oil, and croutons, though some bacon pieces with their fat would have been better, *hélas*.

Explosions continued in Ukraine and some cities were without power or heat. Those who had not fled received text messages from the local authorities advising them if someone died, they should just put the body outside, tie up the hands and legs, cover it, and leave it. There were bodies lying in the streets. People were collecting snow, melting it, boiling it. An aerial bomb hit a maternity hospital and women and children were caught in the blast or buried in the rubble. A woman and her two children dashed across an exposed bridge, a man came to help them, running to take the suitcase from the woman, and a mortar struck them. A photograph showed their luggage scattered near their bodies, a grey suitcase, some rucksacks, a blue case with wheels, a green carrying case for the small dog still barking furiously inside it. The husband, the father, recognised the luggage from the news. That was how he knew, he said. He said he had nothing left to lose.

The mandrake has thick roots; forked, they look like the legs of a human body. Its rootlets are like hair, like a little beard or moustaches. Once it was called *antropomorphos*, a human figure. Or in Persian, *mardum-giyah*, a plant-man. It did not come from seeds like other plants but grew from the sperm of hanged men or those crushed on the wheel. Or it grew from the blood or sperm of a god or a giant. It eased pain and tremors, sedated, anaesthetised, brought luck and fertility, but it also caused hallucinations, seizures, and death. It screamed when it was pulled from the ground and those who heard it died, so a dog was used to uproot it. The poor old dog was tied to the plant's stem and reaching out for food that was beyond its hungry reach, it would pull the mandrake from the earth and the mandrake would scream and scream and the dog would die at once as the mandrake continued to scream. The mandrake also could moan and speak and sing, it could cry, sobbing. At her trial, Jeanne d'Arc was accused of carrying a mandrake, as though it were her unholy magical child. In Michel Tournier's novel *Friday*, the earth appeared as living flesh to Robinson stranded on his island and he heard the voice of nature in the accents of the mandrake. Robinson woke one morning to find that his beard had taken root in the soil. There are other novels about the plant-man, plant monster, fossil plant. In one, the mandrake sang, and its song perfumed the air.

Ghost Party, in the first exhibition that was possible for me to visit since my accident, was a film by Manon de Boer and Latifa Laâbissi, who had been speaking and reading with and to each other for seven years, a correspondence of collage and conversations and gardening. Each took over the territory of the other; it was slow, over time that dilated. Before the space of the film was a video on a monitor with headphones with short clips of women directors talking about what it entailed to be a woman artist. Chantal Akerman was nervous, Delphine Seyrig was animated. It was, the two women said, a question of how their identities were revealed or exposed in their work. In the film there were bodies, but the bodies were not human, the human was replaced by character-vases whose role was to embody those admired by the artists. These were diverse, among them: Sophie Taeuber-Arp, Pasolini, Beyoncé, Lygia Clark, and the glass vases moved or were pushed across the floor of the modernist Van Wassenhove Villa in Belgium. The house is a concrete shell; the structure follows a topography without divisions, but particular functions are delimited geometrically: a square office, a cylindrical bedroom, a triangular kitchen. The character-vases had their own geometry and their movements were a ballet. There were flashes of other bodies, but the voice or voices were in the foreground, those of Marguerite Duras and Serge Dany, Valeska Gert, Casey, others who were of importance to the two artists. Look, one would say, here comes Oum Kalthoum (a rotund turquoise-blue vase with tiny handles on its / her short neck); or one would say I am Black and feminist, or her mother would ask Where is Franz Fanon, where? and then he came along as well. One woman stacked transparent glass vases, cups, jugs, carefully, making towers. There was constant reflection in the glass of the villa, and the garden entered the house or there was no separation between exterior and interior, subject and object, human and non-human.

The day of tuna, *thon*, the day of Saint Louise, and today, Louise wrote to me. In a part of her letter, she described writing as a ghost-writer for a woman friend, a politician. She wrote her speeches, her responses to the media, her social media. She learnt to become her – it was not a mimicking, she was clear – but rather an inhabiting, speaking in the woman's voice, or rather in both of their voices, collectively. She described it as inhabiting different identities in order to understand the structures of power. All these things, I thought, are as fragile as glass vases, as fragile as bodies. Vases and bodies tumble, smash, shatter, they are smithereens. They explode. They always explode.

An apartment building was bombarded with shells. A woman called her daughter who lived there or perhaps it was the daughter who called the mother. The daughter told her mother that the building had been hit. The mother could not make out very well what her daughter was saying as the daughter was crying hysterically. There was a second call: the daughter told her mother that at least the piano was safe (the mother said her daughter loved music). Perhaps there was a third call: the daughter said she was buried, but she may have said this in the second call. Perhaps there was a fourth call, or it may have been the third, and this time, definitely, it was the mother calling the daughter. There was no reply. There was only silence.

Sometimes I seek fewer words.

Sometimes I wish to draw a line under.

Sometimes time expresses the intentions of history.

A wind came from the Sahara on *sextidi*, the last decade of *ventôse*. There was a strange light in the sky yesterday, an unearthly yellow glow though some reports described it as orange or ochre. The colour deepened, darkened, during the day. The rain magnified it, held the light in liquid. The sky was veiled. It was not beautiful. The wind, the Sirocco, or some said the Calima, carried sand, yes, it was a sandstorm or a rain of sand, passing over the southwest and reaching Brittany in the afternoon, then progressing northwards. It passed over Strasbourg, Lyon, Paris, Rennes. It swallowed some cities, they said. It would continue traversing France until Friday. Carried by the wind the sand from an African desert covered the cities and mountains and countryside of France. The next day, the cars, the roads, the pavings, all had a fine veneer. The sand had mingled with the rain, making a gritty paste that dried to a skin. It was not dangerous, but still might provoke respiratory problems in those people who are sensitive to dust. The weather report described it as caused by a particularly virulent depression. Its only useful aspect was for agriculture, to nourish the fields. I was told the particles lay over the snow of the Alps. David wrote from Portugal that he could taste the sand, that it was gritty in his mouth.

The cunning tip of the week in the *almanach de facteur* was how to make a fertiliser from eggshells, which are rich in minerals, especially calcium. So that one's plants should benefit, the empty eggshells must be dried, then crushed as finely as possible with a rolling-pin (for example). All that remains then is to incorporate the resulting powder in the earth. I crush my eggshells in my hand, not at all finely, and give them back to my chickens. There is a pleasant crackling as the hollow shell shatters in the palm or between the fingers. Sometimes the dogs take the shells from the bowl where I have left them with peelings and leftovers for the poultry, crunching them lightly, then wilfully they scatter them over the kitchen tiles.

A woman was released at last from her detention in Iran. She arrived in England early this morning. When I turned on the wireless this morning, I heard her crying as she met her daughter. In fact, I heard only the crying, raw and unmediated. It was unbearable. How does one describe this cry between joy and sorrow and silence? The British government paid a historic debt to Iran, a matter of some two thousand or so undelivered Chieftain army tanks and other vehicles to the former ruler, the Shah, undelivered because the US-backed Shah was toppled from power. The two governments denied there was any connection between the payment of the debt and the release of the woman and of a man. They said it was done from a humanitarian viewpoint. The woman's husband, who had staged hunger strikes in front of the Iranian Embassy, said they were looking forward to a new life. He said that the time that was gone could not be retrieved, that was a fact, but they lived in the future not the past. The man's wife had said goodbye to her husband at Gatwick airport, expecting to see him in three weeks not nearly five years later. How would presence include and reconcile the past and future?

In Brittany there were three earthquakes, in the Morbihan near Vannes, then Ploëmel, and a little later, in Pacé, during the early morning yesterday. They were weak and caused no damage. The préfecture reassured inhabitants that no specific intervention by the emergency or security services was required at this stage. Some people said they felt them, were woken by them. Accounts differed: one reported the third was in the centre of Ploëmel and did not mention Pacé; another said the third was near St-Meen-le-Grand. But yes, *la terre a tremblé*, the earth definitely moved for some. A Parisian newspaper reported six little quakes, and that they started in the evening and some people thought it was an explosion. The earth trembles often in Brittany, and scientists are divided about the recurrence of earthquakes. It remains an enigma why the Armorican earth trembles regularly. Some scientists lean towards a deformation linked to the thrust of the African plate while others consider it is due to the presence of an ancient ice cap. In the same Parisian paper, there was an article about Karine Branger's two sculptures of giant clitorises in the entrance hall of the *mairie* of the *18e arrondissement*. One visitor, a pharmacy student, asked if they represented the Eiffel Tower. Her companion, a medical student, smiled, a little mockingly. The reporter, perhaps quoting the artist (I was not able to read more without subscribing to the newspaper), reflected that it was a way of raising awareness of this still enigmatic sexual organ and of calling attention to the female condition. The works are entitled WHAT and WHY, in capitals, reports the newspaper, omitting part of each title, the word *Trophy*. Another article, elsewhere, describes the works or work as relating to a 'source of pleasure, a source of suffering, a symbol of femininity and of a woman's control over her own body, as well as of her subjugation by men who, since the dawn of time, have shaped our societies by placing themselves at their head. It refers to the self, it refers to others. It reflects joys and sorrows, intense ecstatic sensations, and intolerable mutilations'. It is an extra organ (or two), one whose anatomy has not been stable, erectile in the heart of administration. The clitoris was rarely depicted with any degree of accuracy or considered to be an organ. Vesalius argued that it did not exist in healthy women; others thought it to be the devil's teat, which if found on a woman would identify her as a witch. Later, if and when it was found, it was sometimes cut off, to prevent or cure hysteria, to curb masturbation, or to ensure a clear distinction between what is male and what is female. As well as to remove malignancy, it is still removed for non-medical reasons; *khatna, khafd, khitaan,* the cutting has many names. The girl-child is restrained: her external genitalia are removed or damaged using a knife, scalpel, or other sharp instrument. The maidenhair fern is assigned for *octidi,* the third decade. It is sometimes called Venus's Hair, and its leaves can turn brown when touched, as if in protest.

Saint Joseph and the ash tree, and it was nearly a new month. We returned to Rennes for a performance by the two women whose film we saw a week ago. The performance echoed or repeated or reflected the film though often it had the air of improvisation. There were corrections to my memory and to my description of the film. The vases were not all transparent, and some were not even glass but pottery. Those that were transparent glass had no name, and one fell, crashed, shattered, as it was placed on another. Donald Winnicott was a tall green glass vase, Chantal Akerman a tiny yellow one. One artist and her mother were small round brown and beige striped pots. The women defined a border between themselves and their audience, drawing it with sand scattered through one little bag and with golden dust from another, which later was placed on the face and the eyelids of one woman as the other held her face between her hands, and then this one sprinkled it on the hands of the other. Both wore white dresses over black leotards. They asked again, who speaks, thinks, and moves when we speak, think, and move. They welcomed their co-habitation: hosts and ghosts, the same thing. The voice, their voices, were objects, and their objects had voices. The work ended with the two women standing together, held apart and held together by the large vase wedged between their bodies. Cleave: severed and bound. Their hands were by their sides. They looked into each other's faces, despite the difference in their height. That night I read a story in *Master of the*

Eclipse by Etel Adnan, who died last year. Listening to Um or Oum Kulthum or Kalthoum, she writes that we shall listen, drown in her voice, fade into it, *and she will die, and we will feel terribly lonely.*

A dibble, sometimes called a dibber, as Mark reminded me, or even a dibbler, on the last day of *ventôse*, for making holes in the ground. The tool is pressed down in the earth with the hand. Seeds, bulbs, plants, cuttings. Sunrise is earlier each morning and soon the time will change, go forward, such a mutable measure. A hole.

GERMINAL

rimèvere and Saint Clémence: a cold wind though the sun shone quite brightly, warmly even, in the courtyard. The house, my study, was cold but I had to work. I was sick and anxious, trying to come to terms with the French tax system and our rackety life and our lack of planning, our stupidity, our ignorance. For each step forward in the whole sorry business, there were two steps back of misunderstanding, naïve optimism, and a base fear of being found out when ignorance was no excuse. My teeth were ground down and I had not slept for many nights now, not more than a few hours before the nagging, no, *wrenching* anguish ate at me. My mouth was dry. My stomach was disturbed. There was no respite from this. I did not know what steps to take, as every avenue was an impasse. If only, I thought, if only things could be simple. Benoît and Marion said they would help when they stay with us at the weekend, coming from Paris to oversee the work on their country house. They have builders there, a Polish man and a Portuguese man. They make a fire outside in the evening and grill meat. The dogs scavenge the bones, crunch and swallow them, then throw up on the sofas and in the car. We took the builders some eggs. The Polish man was very worried about the war; though he has been in Paris for forty years he still has family in Poland, near to the border. We have found out that Ida, the little dog, goes into the kitchen at the Metairie, where he gives her little slices of sausage as she sits patiently by him while he cooks.

Germinal is the month of fertility, new growth. The potato tubers lay nestled for chitting in old egg cartons in the polytunnel, only two varieties this year: Linzer Delikatess, as usual, a second early, pale skinned, smooth, yellow, a fingerling, and Belle de Fontenay, which is similar, an old French variety. I regretted their closeness in type. I was given a little net of another variety but lost its name tag. As soon as the soil warmed up more, they would be planted, and the ridges earthed up over, covered with straw from the poultry houses. Once I grew them on the earth, not in it, with a thick blanket of straw over them. It was successful and I do not know why I have never repeated this. The hydrangeas at the back of the house were cut back, but never as severely as I intended. All but one lavender survived the winter. Verbena *bonariensis* has self-seeded over the gravel, and again I was not as ruthless as I might be, for it is too lovely. The plants come up in neat clumps, but I have found that if I try to plant these in other parts of the garden, they seldom take. I give them away, however, and hope the gifts settle in the gardens of my friends, producing their filmy towering heads of delicate purple flowers.

If my son had been a daughter, her name would have been Clémence, Clémence Madeleine. Oh, *clementia* and *clemens*, sweet and indulgent, good and kind and fair. Or associated with justice, profoundly. Or vivacious, rapid, spontaneous, and blue, yes, the colour of her sapphire, her precious stone of wisdom. Clémence held out her hand, stretching it in forgiveness. Four hundred people were confined in a school as shells exploded. A convoy of cars left the besieged city, but later, for the third time a convoy of aid was not allowed to enter. Those defending the city refused to surrender, and it was a city dying a most painful death. It took me a few hours to write very little, for the trivial things I would write about my daily life, as the sun shines although the wind is chill, were too small to encompass the enormity of grief and anger. I stopped writing or trying to write, and instead peeled potatoes for a gratin with sage from the garden, a bundle of it, garlic, olive oil, cream, and then parmesan would be added towards the end of the cooking in the oven, and there would be fresh spinach, slick with butter and a scrape of nutmeg, the salad leaves and Erica's cheese. I was conscious of the sad ironic juxtaposition in this paragraph and I do not need anyone to point it out to me, then or now.

The tulips started to perform in great showy bursts, opened wide in the sunlight, especially 'Purissima' in the beds, and 'Foxy' and 'Foxy Fox Trot' together snugly in a pot are exquisite. The garden should have calmed me, but I could do so little still, and I was too anxious. I was reading the letters of Rosa Luxemburg. She loved plants, collecting flowers and leaves for her herbarium. She could be a flower or an animal, she thought. From Breslau, a hundred and four years ago, she wrote to her friend Sophie Liebknecht that spring had come again and the days were growing long and so light. She wished she could stroll about the countryside, talking with her friend about anything that came into their heads. She asked Sophie to go out for her, and especially, please to go the Botanical Gardens so Sophie can tell her all about it. The birds were earlier that year: Rosa heard the nightingale on 10 March, the wryneck on 15 March, the golden oriole was already singing the week before, a bird that did not usually appear until May. She watched the birds from the window of her prison cell. She hoped that the following year they could all enjoy the spring together. A call went out on a Facebook page, a message that came from an address in Poland, asking that seeds should be sent, which would be given to the elderly people who have remained in their Ukrainian villages, unable or reluctant to leave. Seed companies have withdrawn from the country. No seeds are left. We are asked to send tomatoes, carrots, beets, cabbages, beans. But not artichokes, definitely no artichokes, please, because the elderly people of the Ukrainian countryside do not know artichokes. It was a matter of survival, the message said; time was running out, the time to sow.

Quintidi germinal, the day of the Annunciation and the day of the hen (I could hear one calling loudly that she has laid an egg, there are six or seven a day now, including a duck egg, which is often deposited on the ground in the most casual manner). I planted three Madonna lilies in the autumn – the bulbs were cheap and only one appeared to be coming up. The little black cat, Nana, rescued from a hole in a wall in Saint-Denis by Florentine, came into my study. Very carefully she sniffed the wall by the window, then made a tour of the room. Last year I was concerned about her vomiting one day and feared it was a reaction to the lilies in the pot in which she liked to lie. I rushed her to the vet, explaining my anxiety about lily poisoning, a plant toxic to cats, but Alberto dismissed it. I did not know what to think. Perhaps I should not have planted the Madonna lilies. Or I should fence them off, make an enclosure for them, like the secluded garden of Mary, where the angel made his surprising announcement to her. In many paintings of this event or scene there are two spaces, the garden, the *hortus conclusus*, and the portico or loggia that opens onto the garden. The angel crosses the threshold. Sometimes the angel holds a lily or there is a lily in a lovely vase in the scene. Sometimes a ray of light enters through a window, piercing its solid form with imperceptible subtlety, as St Bernard of Clairvaux remarks. Mary is disquieted by the angel or, she reflects, the mouth of the angel. The angelic words are painted on the canvas, speech impregnating Mary, word by word: word-sperm.

There was a handwritten note on the door of the eccentric bookshop in Dol de Bretagne, indicating its (unusual) closure due to a death. My son called me on his way to the station from the Café de l'Univers, usually called Bistrot Boris after the *patron*, where he had spent a few hours between our departure after lunch and his train to Paris, asking me if I had seen it, fearing the owner had died. I replied that had been my first thought, but then I felt it was more likely that he was attending a funeral. The bookshop is tiny and every surface, the floor, is piled high with towers of books;

each shelf has two or even three rows. Some books have their prices in old francs and the owner must make a rapid conversion to euros. The bookshop is called L'Herbe Rouge. Today I found that I was wrong about the reason for its closure, for in fact, the owner, Philip Marvier, died in September last year. I read his obituary in *Ouest France* online. He said that the apparent disorder of his stock gave a chance for readers to discover books they would not have dreamt of reading. He was always welcoming, kind, generous, erudite, modest. Perhaps L'Herbe Rouge will cease to exist now.

The hour changed, went forwards, and time shrank again, lost time or not enough time or too much time that had to be taken up by the many things I did not want to do. I wished for time well-spent, not time wasted, though I knew the tasks were necessary. Nervous and anxious and panicky, I brought all the geraniums out from their winter quarters, trimmed them of dead stems and leaves, potted them in new soil, and placed them on the exterior windowsills where they looked a little floppy, thin and sad and wan. I listened to a woman in Ukraine speaking on the wireless; she was crying, we have no water, she said, we melt snow, we have no food. I could not stop crying for a long time. I had not been able to eat for some days now. I could not sleep again. My mouth was very dry, my fists clenched by my sides at night. The week went from the daffodil, the alder, and to the hatchery, and the first goose egg was laid in the house where the three young Araucanas still go to sleep at nightfall. The Sentinel narcissi were starting to come out, the tight buds yellow and they will change to ivory as the flower opens. They have a green eye and ruffles that range in colour from salmon-pink to apricot. They are charming.

Not only did months and days change in the revolutionary calendar. For seventeen months the hours and minutes and seconds also were calculated differently. There were ten hours in a day and a hundred minutes in an hour and a hundred seconds in a minute. How beautiful and strange the ten-hour clocks are, but it was very expensive to replace all the clocks and watches, and finally it seemed only to be to the advantage of the mathematicians. I used to measure time by the programmes on the wireless, but for some time now I have found it was too distracting when I was writing, although when I am drawing or making something, say, embroidering or stitching white feathers to antique communion stockings, I can listen; I can do two things simultaneously, and especially when working in the garden, I must have the wind-up solar radio nearby, even if I pay it little attention. It had stopped working, after twenty years, but Marion touched it and miraculously, it played again, the winding clockwork lever making its cranky rustling sound as it turned, wound down. A miracle! It has stopped again since, but that may be due to the lack of sunlight. The sound of the news or the theme music of various programmes tells me the time. Often in the distance I hear the bells of the church clock in the village.

A story about two paintings was told by Marion over dinner. It was a family affair. It concerned two seventeenth-century Dutch still life tableaux in the Louvre. These were stolen from her family in the war and are now subject to restitution to the descendants, even though they belong to a national collection. Later, Florian remarked that disputes over ownership, where works of art belong, to whom, is a tricky question, suggesting I might not wish to take a stance on this. There are forty-five members of the family, dispersed through France, Luxemburg, Switzerland, *via* America back to France. Of course, some were killed, taken to the camps in the *rafales*, the great-aunts, and some were saved, the mother, for instance, of the daughter who claimed she was an illegitimate daughter of her father and saved herself.

The paintings cannot be divided; they must be sold. Through the tracking of the family, the meetings with lawyers, Marion discovered cousins, second-cousins, other removes of *cousinage*, one especially who lived really not very far away at all, but they had never met before, did not even know of each other, who is an art collector with a work by Jeff Wall on her walls and beautifully constructed vitrines to house her objects – many painted wooden or *papier maché* heads of which I was deeply envious, with expressions not unlike those of the impassive faces of the polychrome figures of the saints in the chapels of the countryside, elaborate fans, and other lovely barely-glimpsed things in excess but lined up nonetheless and arranged with irritating delicacy and taste. It was hard to see the photographs of the two paintings on Marion's mobile phone screen in our dark kitchen lit by candlelight. She had photographed them in the Louvre where they remain until the legal decision is established. One seemed particularly enchanting, a table scene of bread and bacon and cheese, abundant yet also precise and somewhat anatomical, perhaps the effect of so much carefully exposed meat and bread and cheese revealing their flesh and crumb and wax.

Adrian posted a picture of a painting entitled *L'Énigme du citron* on his Instagram. A lemon lies on a pewter plate, two slices cut from it, partly peeled, the long twist of peel with the cap hanging over the table edge, the rim of the plate overlapping the edge too. There is a pip and a hazelnut on the plate. To the left, there is a roll of bread, hazelnuts, a walnut broken in half. There are olives in a bowl, green ones, a wine glass with an elaborate stem, a tankard lying on its side, what appears to be a glass of beer behind it. It is one of the paintings Jean-Louis Schefer writes about in *La Lumière et la table*, a book about the arrangements or composition in Dutch painting, a book in which he allows himself to write about paintings that attract him, other than a fifteen-century anonymous Rhenish painting of a Virgin in a garden in *Questions du style*. Adrian wrote: 'time to attend, to reflect and stay quiet? Foucault insists, indeed it is a structure of his thinking, that the *souci de soi et des autres* entails learning how to stand back and not speak as well as to speak, something typically elided by professional commentators and *philosophes et autres grande.e.nds personnes*'. He continued: 'right now we are all shouting in yellow and blue and it is turning to an unseemly green'. He wrote that Schefer's study of this 'enigma of the lemon' is the perfect overlapping of speech and silence in the attention paid to the all there is, the surface, and that falling into this surface is to re-equilibrate, perhaps. How elegantly he writes. How ugly my writing is, I thought, after reading his, and went out to plant more potatoes. I wondered about the flow of time in a painting. I thought about the curl of lemon peel as a shard of skin and the scatter of nuts. I thought about the little *cerveau*, the walnut hemisphere that resembles a brain, or perhaps it is our brain that looks like a nut. I thought: nutjob.

The first day of the second decade of *germinal*: periwinkle. A lovely thing. But it is invasive. It was once called the flower of death; its trailing vines were woven into the wreaths for dead children or those worn by criminals on their way to execution. The path that winds through the forest from the top of the road was called the *chemin des pendus*, leading to a crossroads where the execution took place. Buried, profane burial, at a crossroads the soul of the dead would be confused by which path to take, buried at a liminal point for outcasts between worlds. From the war a journalist reported that civilian bodies lay by the roadside; some were burnt by the Russian soldiers, to hide them, he supposed. The periwinkle was associated with marriage, perhaps it was the 'something blue', and with sex, for its supposed aphrodisiac qualities. It is a poison, just a little toxic, but a variety from Madagascar is used in cancer treatment. It is a colour, and it is also a kind of snail. I pull out great clumps of periwinkle every year. There was three-cornered leek everywhere in the garden – it yields bulbs a little like spring onions, but rather slimy, and every part can be eaten, though I would prefer not. I do not know from where it came and I wish it would go away.

The rain and cold returned and snow threatened from the east. Julie wrote from England, from the Midlands, that it was snowing, *for heaven's sake*. I covered the earthed-up furrows of potato tubers with straw. The Indian Runner ducks were now in the garden as their aggression towards the geese had become intolerable, absolutely odious. The male duck is a sex fiend. They snout up (do they snout or do they beak instead?) the straw but do little damage otherwise. I hoped they will eat the slugs and snails. I must keep them out of the strawberry bed. At night, bedtime, they wait at the gate, restless, anxious to be allowed to return to the company of the others, but I told them it was their fault they had been separated. They came down into the courtyard while we were out yesterday, Régine told me; they are inquisitive, vociferous. I remembered reading that Sylvain Maréchal wrote poems in his notebook for Lucille Duplessis, who became the wife of Camille Desmoulins, but he never wrote about her. Quack quack, *coin coin*, this has nothing to do with ducks, unless it is simply to follow a pastoral train of thought, and thus to follow other forms of life or living. Hah! New beginnings in a rustic idyll. The kitchen drains were blocked. R. said it was because I rinse the basin in which I have made the sourdough bread dough in the sink, but I do not believe this is true.

The periwinkle is a sea snail, a winkle. They are easy to forage. If bought uncooked, they should smell sweet, of the sea, and move very slightly. They should be soaked first in fresh water, then salted water, then simmered in salted water for a few minutes only. Some people roll them in oil then to make their little shells shiny. The curl of flesh, their spiral of a body, is extracted with a pin. There is a little black disc, a tiny flat shutter that closes the neck of the shell – it must be removed and laid aside to get to the event of the winkle. They can be eaten with melted butter or garlic mayonnaise, but I feel these are unnecessary accompaniments.

Sigmund Freud recounted a dream: there was the Devil dressed in black, in an upright posture. He was pointing with his outstretched finger at a gigantic snail. This Devil was the Demon in a love scene with a girl in a very popular picture. Freud said he would never engage in the work of scientific research while involved in the clinical act of listening. He said that he must instead make himself vulnerable and receptive. He said that he must lay himself open to another person. He said he must allow himself to be taken by surprise. He said there must be floating attention, an evenly hovering attention. The inner ear, the bony cochlea, is shaped like a snail shell, with two and a half turns, housing the membranous labyrinth surrounded by perilymph fluid. Freud's ear, yes, the most famous ear of our epoch. To be heard, yes, even when one is saying nothing, even when one is silent, still, but attentive on both sides, listened/ listener. Listen to syntactical displacements: ellipsis and pleonasm, hyperbaton or syllepsis, regression, repetition, apposition. Listen to semantical condensations: metaphor, catachresis, antonomasia, allegory, metonymy, and synecdoche. From Freud's diary, an entry on 19 July 1938, a single word: 'Deafness'.

Emmanuel Swedenborg's ear-bones are in the Swedenborg Collection in London. They were collected from his tomb in 1790 when the vault in the Swedish Church in Princes Square in East London was opened. The bones passed to the possession of Doctor Spurgin, a friend of John Keats and president of the Swedenborg Society, then were donated to the Society in 1881 by a Mrs Bateman of Islington. They rest in a little round green leather case, nestling on discoloured velvet. The bones, *incus* and *malleus*, anvil and hammer, are the smallest bones in the human body, making up the inner ear. They work by picking up small vibrations. Swedenborg wrote an essay entitled 'On Tremulation', in which he proposed the possibility of telepathy by means of thought vibrations. Swedenborg used to walk in his garden, alone or with others. There is a little metal tin that contains bark from a poplar tree in his garden, a square garden ornamented with animal and other figures cut in box. The scrap of bark is like a piece of withered skin, a reliquary; *écorce*, peel, not *écorché*, peeled. He liked to walk in pleasant groves, composing his thoughts on the vicissitudes of time. He went to his summerhouse to write, such a grand idea (so did the poet Anna Mendelssohn, who was not at all grand, I think, but splendidly unruly and raging). He wrote of his conversations with angels and declared, with full confidence based on his experience, that angels were completely human, that they have faces, eyes, ears, chests, arms, hands, and feet, that they see each other, hear each other, and talk to each other. They lack only a material body. Some are so beautiful (those closest to God) that not even the most skilled painters could render a fraction of their light with their pigments or rival a thousandth of a part of the light and life in their faces. Sometimes the angels came forth from the mirror hung on the green walls of his garden house and his mind delighted in these things.

Last week my son and his father ate snails with garlic butter. They were bought in a shop; they were not gathered and then purged by me, perish the thought, though Guy, the son of Marie, used to collect them when he visited, and in the past, I have collected them, leaving them for a week with light sprinkle of flour or bran, or with grape leaves, or with apple peelings and lettuce leaves. They must be sprinkled with water daily to keep them moist. Then after they have had another period of a day or two without any food, starved and hung up in the sunlight in a mesh bag, they are placed in cold water with vinegar, and the water is replaced several times as it becomes foamy. At last, they are simmered in boiling water, and any that float to the top must be discarded, and all the slime, the mucus, skimmed from the surface. They can be taken from their shells, sautéed with butter, garlic, and parsley. I no longer eat snails, after the time in a small restaurant near Rome many years ago where I was enjoying a plate of small snails braised in red wine and olive oil, with tomatoes and garlic and herbs, and as I lifted one towards my mouth with my tiny fork I saw its little upper tentacles, on the tips of which are the eyes, and then the lower set with which the snail smells, oh goodness, where it raises its head to see the light and to sniff the air... and it was as though a shutter slid closed at the back of my mouth, sealing my throat against any further swallowing. Bryan described the photograph of the snail *hors d'œuvre* as resembling a Caravaggio in a Chardin. It was a matter of light, of darkness, the move or contrast or tension between states. It is nice, very pleasant indeed, when people think of what they see in terms of painting. Walking with John by the farm here over thirty years ago, he commented on every view, every scene, as though it were a painting, and his framing, his reference, was always correct, always charming. One of his paintings hangs on the stairwell to the library, a painted blue and green frame surrounding a blue and green ground on which there is a small grey-blue rock upon which lies a little hand, the fingers partly curled towards the palm. I wonder what has become of him.

Today: the day of *charme*, hornbeam, the day of the April

fish or the April fool, the day of Saint Hugues, whose piety was so great that he knew only one woman, and that was by sight. The calico cat lay curled like a snail beside me as I wrote. She is tortoiseshell and white, and these calico cats are always female. They bring good luck. Sometimes they are called 'money cats'. Good luck and economy, *miaow*, *miau*. Despite the cold wind from the north-east, I decided to brave the weather to paint the new wooden arch leading up to the garden so I could plant the 'Pierre de Ronsard' climbing rose I bought this morning before physiotherapy. Sandrine thought my sessions could go down to once weekly now; she worked on my balance with me, for I still stumbled. She made me rise repeatedly on my toes, then stand on one foot, raising my arms above my head, bringing them down to my sides, repeating the movements with the weight then on the other foot. The 'Pierre de Ronsard' rose is also called the Eden rose. It is a modern tea hybrid from 'Haendel', 'Kalinka', and 'Danses des Sylphes', bred by Marie-Louise Meilland in 1985. It is repeat flowering, and arguably it lacks a little in fragrance, but compensates for this in its vigour and resistance to disease and its heavy pink blooms, fading to white. It would grow fast, I hoped, and I might plant a clematis to grow through it, a winter clematis to replace the 'Winter Beauty' that died. I loved its bell-shaped flowers, so elegant against its glossy green foliage, flowering from December to the end of February if not longer, and I was saddened by its loss. Around the rose, I thought I would plant bulbs of Abyssinian gladioli and purple *liatris spicata*, and sow seeds of *nigella damascena*, 'Miss Jekyll', sky-blue 'love-in-the-mist', and already everywhere the columbines were growing crazily, despite the sudden chill. Lisa, Sonja, and I feared for our wisterias, for our peonies, all starting to come into blossom in the Poitou-Charentes and Brittany. Should they be covered, protected by pillowcases or blankets or fleece, asked Sonja.

Rameaux. Palm Sunday. We used to be given little branches of bay when we entered the church or as we left it, and these were blessed by the village priest on the steps. In other places the bay is replaced by olive branches or box or palm leaves. *Hosanna*, one should reply as one received the little branch or sprig, blessed are those who come to the name of the Lord. The branches are taken home and decorate the crucifix. On the wireless I heard a woman keening as she was interviewed about the death of her son. His body was held by her, or he was next to her or in the same room – it was not clear at all – but although there was a translator giving her words, as though putting them in her mouth, it seemed there were no words, no language, only sounds, raw and brutal and heart-wrenching. In some countries women put stones in their mouth to make their voice ugly, so men will not be seduced. A stone in the mouth of a corpse will prevent its return. I planted three claret-coloured *astrantia*, masterwort, sometimes called 'Hattie's Pincushion', neat, self-seeding, modest, to join the white- and pink-flowered varieties in the same bed. I scraped the ground around some of the vegetable beds, making them free of weeds and grass, until my hands bled. Suddenly R. shouted from the poultry run: our last remaining full hive of bees was swarming. He and Yves threw on their bee suits and raced after the swarm, but it had lodged in an inaccessible tree and then it moved on through an impassable hedge. An hour later the two men returned, trudging despondently. Of his three hives, Yves has only one still active, we have half a hive now from our four, and Rosie has none. Last year was a catastrophe for beekeepers. R. did not think he can continue. Next Saturday would be the day of the hive. Clusters of old wax linger in the frames I used to block the gap where one of the hens, the elder Aracauna, hops up and jumps through, clever girl, pretty girl, my own girl raised from an egg.

In the market in Pleudihen we bought splendidly fresh mackerel. *Madame est en service!*, Bertrand remarked. The fish were filleted, silver and pink, their bones and guts were given to the chickens. I made a delicate pink rhubarb sauce with red chili to accompany the pan-fried fillets. There were Udon noodles on a stall with sushi and gyoza; I bought the noodles for next day's soup, ginger, spring onion, tofu, carrot, shiitake mushrooms, spinach, some flakes of nori perhaps, a broth of vegetable stock, miso, soy, sesame oil. *Germinal* lurched along in fragments. Days compressed and days expanded. Sadness. Few words. A hundred words. Two hundred words. How many words are enough? I listened again to the recordings of Emmanuelle and Florence reading from their books, reading together and with others, with Ed and Iris. Their voices ebbed and flowed, playful or dirge-like, overlapping at times. I longed for more structure.

I wanted to read about the medieval saints: someone (my son, I thought, but later I found it in my library in London) had taken from my library Caroline Walker Bynum's *Holy Feast and Holy Fast*, though I found *Fragmentation and Redemption*, which later disappeared and Francis denied having it. I wanted to read about the relation of the part to the whole, about living matter and divine embodiment, and perhaps also about bloody wounds, sweating blood, and medieval views about Christ's conception from the menstrual fluid of his mother. I wanted to read about the image of paradise. I wanted to read about women's voices, cloistered or screened from view. I wanted to read about overclothing and how werewolves rolled back their skin to reveal a human body beneath their fur and how some bodies are not one and other bodies are of no consequence. The saints rolled by, yes, the saints marched in, go marching, otherwise to a catchy tune, travelling in the footsteps of those who have gone before, a tempo that is slowed for a funeral and when the moon turns red with blood, bad moon rising: Stanislas and Jules and Ida, and tomorrow, Maxime, and then Good Friday, *vendredi saint*. In the studio I took out packets of madder, consulting dying instructions and rearranging the pairs of kid gloves, gloves from the skin of little goats, some with a row of impossibly small buttons along the wrist, with tiny finger sheaves so narrow that a wooden stretcher, like a pair of pliers, was required to put them on, easing them over the fingers; its pointed end must be inserted into the finger, then the handle is compressed on its metal spring hinge so its two end splay out, stretching the kidskin. I thought about some new drawings of women I had been holding vaguely, too loosely, in my mind, women with hooves in the place of hands, holding gloves in their hooves, extended like the forelimbs of sleepwalkers. But hooves, as I knew from my drawings last year of women with hoofed feet like buskins, are very difficult to draw, and this was why the drawings were still only in my mind with no place to go as I could not bear the thought of more failure. The glove stretcher was also used to restore the gloves after washing, which stiffens and wrinkles the soft leather, the kidskin, the second skin or fitting like a second skin: overclothing, in the manner werewolves wear wolves, and elderly women wear werewolves, until their skins are peeled back so they can be given the Eucharist.

Sextidi, lettuce, *septidi*, larch, *octidi*, hemlock, ah yes, hemlock, which I drew with bleeding roots and seedpods, a light sprinkling of blood on the foliage and the flower-heads, for the cover of Zoë's book, her exquisite cycle of three hundred and sixty-five-line poems in twelve sections of thirty poems each, responding to an element, a single element, of the phenomenal world, another fashion of the temporal intersection between recursive, cyclical time and progressive, linear time. For hemlock, *ciguë*; 'a drowsy numbness / (clustered umbels hollow / stem streaked red) / laces the spring's inaudible nightingales.' Zoë wrote about looking for Rosa Luxemburg in all the cities, the towns, the streets, the bridges, the *u-Bahn* station, the electric lamp factory, the public gardens, oh all the places that bore her name, but no, she was not there and we would not find her, she would not be there, it was a rose for Rosa, but although we might find roses we would not find Rosa. In prison Rosa sang the Countess's aria from *The Marriage of Figaro* to the Great Tits in front of her window. It is the song near the end of the third act, in which the countess awaits the return of Susanna, and wonders why the love she felt for her husband has transformed from happiness to tears: 'Dove sono i bei momenti / Di dolcezza e di piacer? / Dove andaro i giura-menti / Di quel labbro menzogner?' (Where are the good times / Of sweetness and pleasure? / Where have they gone, the oaths / Of that deceitful tongue?). Rosa read that the warblers were disappearing from Germany as forestry, gardening and agriculture destroyed their nesting and breeding places, their hollow trees, the fallow land, thickets and shrubs, withered leaves in gardens, and it caused her pain when she read that. It was not because of the song they sing for people, but the picture of the silent, inexorable extinction of these defenceless little creatures which hurt her so much she had to cry. She wrote to Sophie asking if she remembered how she had telephoned her, asking her to come at once to the Botanical Gardens to listen to the night-ingale in the morning where they were hiding in the shrub-bery, Rosa and Karl, sitting on the stones beside a little stream. Sean read in Berlin to launch our book, and now he is dead. Susan sang and a scream of swifts flew overheard.

Radishes, today, *nonidi*, and two seed packets, 'French Breakfast' and 'Cherry Belle', still waited for sowing in the wooden poor bowl from an Irish church on the desk in the kitchen (Marita, said her reading was disrupted by this, wondering if there really was a desk in the kitchen, and then she stopped reading completely, but yes, it is in the window recess, for the kitchen is a room of many functions, especially when it is very cold outside). It was too cold, too wet, too wretched a day. In a room in a basement in a school, sixty people were held and twelve of them died in the room, the elderly. Their bodies had to be stacked in a corner of the cramped room where none but the dead had space enough to lie down and then they were taken out in the morning to be placed on the bare frozen ground. There were other rooms in the school; there were more people, dead and alive. There were more bodies by the roadside. Carla baked Easter biscuits, unshowy biscuits, she said, to keep at bay the waves of sadness. Currants and candied peel, crisp and spicy. Three ounces each of butter and sugar, an egg yolk, mixed spice (use your judgement), 6 ounces of flour, the currants, the peel, a little milk. Cream the butter and sugar, add the egg and milk, the flour, the spice, the fruit and peel. Roll out thinly, bake for ten minutes at 350 degrees, brush with the egg white and sprinkle with a little sugar if you like, return to the oven for another five minutes or so. Eat them when they are cool and try not to be sad, even though you are sad, impossibly sad, with a sadness like an illness, a disease. Traditionally (and tradition *is* something when all else seems to be lost or undone), these biscuits were baked to be given as gifts.

Time did that strange thing that time does if one is not careful, on the ball, keeping a close eye on that terrible old enemy. A week went missing, an entire week, and in fact, in startling, shocking even, fact, Palm Sunday was not last week but this week, as I realised when yesterday I saw a woman in the market holding her branch of bay, so Good Friday and Easter Sunday and then Monday, *Parfait*, were yet to come. I had lost my ability to measure time, to understand what day it is, even what hour. I counted words as if they were seconds. Time did not flow smoothly: I had moved to a domestic system that did not yet adapt to my new life, my new time routines founded on the demands of animals and daylight hours. I had written once about time and the Manufacture Oberkampf, citing the historian Eric Hobsbawm, and I thought he had once given a lecture he titled 'The Present as History', about writing the history of one's own lifetime, his own 'perch' (the word he used) constructed from his childhood in Vienna in the nineteen-twenties. He remembered the day Hitler became Chancellor of Germany, remembered the newspaper headline, remembered walking home from school with his sister, and he could still see the scene, as if in a dream. My *calendrier* was up the creek, my perch was down the river, and if the river, well, why not then the Bièvre, where Christophe-Philippe Oberkampf found his factory for the production of toile de Jouy was writing about the Bièvre and found a statue, a marble woman, reclining, for often women are rivers and often women *are* horizontal. Zoë wrote about the Bièvre, mourning its loss, the loss of a river that like time goes underground in Paris then emerges in what are now the suburbs: 'Not drowning but buried / the lost body always / hers always innocent / already filthy her / live arm absent from dead / arm lifting hydraulic / weight to feed the mills / diverted into sewer'. The river disappeared; stinking from the effluence emptied into it, it was buried underground. There is a photograph by Eugene Atget, taken in 1893, that shows the Bièvre flowing through the *13me arrondissement*, and now that view is under the rue Edmond Godinet. The river can be traced through Paris, followed in the names of the city's streets, after a mill, for example, or seen in curves of the streets; there are secret trapdoors opening to the river. Charles Marville's photograph of 1865 shows the tanneries along the river. The Bièvre fed the Manufacture du Gobelins, and it was said there was something in its waters that lent a special intensity to the red of the tapestries, but Rabelais said it was dog's piss that did that, and of course he would say that and that 'all the dogs came running of half a league round, and did so well bepiss the gate of her house that there they made a stream with their urine wherein a duck might very well have swimmed, and it is this same current that now runs at St Victor, in which Gobelin dyeth scarlet, for the specifical virtue of these piss-dogs'. In 1914 J.K. Huysmans wrote that the river Bièvre represented the most perfect picture of female misery exploited by a city; the river was like a girl from the countryside, worn out by the city, despoiled, imprisoned, suffering the bite of lime and caustic, and then in the evenings behind Gobelins, in a foul-smelling sludge, crying, fatigued, alone, trampling in the mud, by moonlight, under the minuscule arch of a little bridge.

Palm Sunday, third decade, *tridi Germinal*, was also the day of the first round of the French elections. It was the day of the Judas Tree, *cercis siliquastrum*, believed to be named for Judas Iscariot, who hung himself from its branches after he betrayed Christ. Carl Linnaeus named it in the eighteenth century, after *siliqua*, pod, for the flowers develop into purple pea-pod structures in the summer. The results of the election were as expected: Macron and Le Pen, with Melenchon a close third (if only the Communist Party had not been such idiots). Frédéric said that the choice should not have been too difficult under the circumstances. In Saint-Denis there was a good turnout for Melenchon, and my son was counting votes until eleven, exhausted. He was interviewed on a BBC news programme, the French child of English parents speaking for the French Left. The headline of yesterday's edition of *Ouest France* asked what choice for France. The second vote is on 24 April, and the result may repeat those of 2017 or 2002, or any of the times when the decision must be made to support a candidate in whom one has no belief in order to keep someone or something worse from power. For the Socialists and the Republicans, it was no longer an accident of history – they were wiped out, described as like ducks without heads that were still able to run for a few metres before they noticed they were dead. There might be a Left that is harder, more radical, yet to come. My son said he could not vote for Macron under any circumstances, though Melenchon urged that not a single vote should go towards Le Pen, that she should be given no voice. Nathalie Arthaud of Lutte ouvrière said Macron and Le Pen were both enemies of the working-class and she would cast a blank vote. Philippe Poutou of the NPA was more circumspect: no voice for Le Pen yet he would not advise a vote for Macron whom he called a pyromaniac fire-man. In her front-page photograph Marine Le Pen was smiling, as she had smiled and smiled throughout her relentless campaign, demonstrating her new softer image, fascist-lite, the more acceptable face of evil if evil could have a face that pleased, was pleasing, the face of a woman who loved her cats and disowned her father. Another photo-graph showed her clasping her hands as though in prayer, smiling in delight. Her spokesman, Louis Allot, promised a *belle surprise* to come in May. I read the results department by department, then commune by commune. Here, in our town, Macron, then Melenchon. There were three hundred and ninety-two votes for Le Pen, three hundred and ninety-two people about whom I would wonder, as I had done in the past, looking at faces in the supermarket, in the market square and at the baker's.

In *Ouest France* I read the obituaries, noting hopefully only those women who had lived beyond ninety: Janine, Simone, Annette, Henriette, Odile, Yvonne, Marie-Thérèse, Alexine, Thérèse, Charlotte, Anna, Germaine, dying in Dinan, Bon Repos sur Blavet, Dolo, La Chapelle-Neuve, Rennes, Le Haut-Corlay, Plancoët, Saint-Agathon, Saint-Brieuc, Dinan (again), Saint Méen-le-Grand, Daoulas. I liked the litany of names, of old women and old places. I wondered how meaningless this might seem to others, how bereft of interest. I am an old woman in an old place, I told myself sternly, yet with affection.

In *Ouest France* I added a few more headlines to my collection of modest yet notable moments:

> *He collects tins of Hénaff paté with pride.*
> *The cemeteries were cleaned by volunteers.*
> *The artisans were delighted by the Salon of wines and gastronomy.*
> *Divers are initiated into sign language.*
> *The celtic circle is on the way for the championship.*
> *The school children made a shelter for insects.*
> *The municipal camping will be renovated.*
> *At home, they share their favourite albums.*
> *Hit and killed by a car in the Loire-Atlantique.*
> *A motorbike rider severely hurt.*
> *A quad accident, the woman driver airlifted to hospital.*
> *Young people will discover the European Parliament.*
> *The body of a man recovered from the river Trieux.*
> *Against a background of alcohol, a disturbed night for the firemen.*

Mathieu made a book I like a great deal from those similar yellow headline posters placed in metal frames outside the *tabacs* where *Ouest France* is sold – where is the book now? I cannot find it. I think it is entitled *Une épidémie se profile* and it is faithful to the typography and colour of the originals from which these singular lines of poetry are taken, the weight of words such as *Girl hurt, the standing stone crushed her foot*, semantic collisions, such as *Rennes, fire in the old centre* and *Student life, Rennes in the Top Five*. Pure ready-made, he said, between art brut and conceptual art, but he did not mention other borrowed texts, such as Félix Fénéon's ruthless and economic *Nouvelles en trois lignes* of 1906, an anonymous column in *Le Matin* that distilled the most sensational news into three lines, each *nou-velle*, each *fait divers*, an account of violence, scandal and unrest, of suicide, murder, and fatal accident ... ah, *la belle époque*, sly and enigmatic, commonplace and tragic. Here are three, madness, money, and suicide, but I could open any page and select any one and laugh aloud:

Nurse Elise Bachmann, whose day off was yesterday, put on a public display of insanity.

Louis Lamarre had neither job nor home, but he did possess a few coins. At a grocery store in Saint-Denis he bought a litre of kerosene and drank it.

Epileptic, a farmer from Saint-Jean-les-Deux Jumeaux, Madame Robeis, fell head first into a jug of milk. Asphyxiated.

Saint Ida, and the plant of today was rocket, the existence of the salad leaf denied for years by Breton friends, even when I placed it in front of them, and then they might, with great reluctance and small shrug (you know how the French do that), have said, ah yes, perhaps it is good, which meant that they did not think it was, and now rocket is everywhere, tasteless and packed in bags in the cool compartments of every supermarket, lacking bite, pepperiness. I ordered seeds of wild and cultivated Italian rocket, and four kinds of basil, fennel (that I know will simply run to seed), mixed lettuces, soft, crunchy, and romaine, oriental leaves, cavolo nero. I determined to cut down this year, to sow fewer seeds, obliged by my accident, my ankle and foot still unbending, sometimes painful, though I managed to push down on the fork to loosen the ground where I intended to sow green and yellow beans next month when the soil has warmed, profiting from the sun, the new light, despite the chilly morning. I thought about work, for I am not supposed to work in France unless I am registered as a micro-entrepreneur, and I wondered what would be perceived as work if there was no payment in view or in intention. Ali was interviewed on the wireless on Saturday; she said she did not think of what she did as a career but rather as a way of being. I imagined myself saying this to the French and English tax inspectors. Ali spoke about Jacques Rivette's film *Céline et Julie vont bateau*, a film that influenced me greatly at a certain uncertain time in my life, which produced my work, my way of being. I loved, still love, the two women of the film who try to save a girl child from a haunted house and are trapped in time in a lovely loop of repetition: the history ends and the history starts again, and it is always the same story, one I avoid seeing again now in case I find I no longer love it. Of Saint Ida, if she is Ida of Louvain, she was very conscious of the beauty of the house of God and founded many abbeys. In the Bibliothèque nationale de France there is an illustration of her saying farewell to her sons. Goodbye, lads. There are other Idas: a Swiss hermit, a Belgian Cistercian nun, a French Benedictine nun; and there is our Ida, our small dog, part Dachshund, part Fauve de Bretagne, found as a puppy with a hind leg broken in three parts, who was breathing heavily at my feet, waiting for me to go out into the garden. I too was waiting to go out into the garden. I listened to the lies of British politicians on the wireless, their shamelessness, their arrogance. They lied about sexual assault, about rape and abuse and harassment. They lied about breaking the law during the pandemic, the law they made but not for themselves. They stand outside the law. The law does not touch them at all.

Each day (and today is that of a pigeon and Saint Maxime) during R.'s return to London I walked, no, hobbled, slowly up to the Metairie with the dogs four or five times, as well as struggling through a forest circuit leaning a little on my walking cane. Early this morning it was as though I saw myself from behind, in Wellington boots, wrapped in my dressing gown, one I do not particularly like, and an indigo blue jacket, expensive even in the sale but a poor buy nonetheless, its fabric pilling, since lost on a bus in Paris, damnit. I felt as if I had become Marcelle, whom I used to see walking in the same laboured way on the same path, accompanied by her little dogs Fifi and Samy, then only poor little Samy, until Marcelle could no longer walk, and we had to take Samy out, but he never wanted to come, not really, and his tumour grew and he could not walk and had to be put down but I refused to take him to the vet though in the end R. gave in. And when we were first here, Marcelle had Belle, rescued from the château, and Nora, then only Nora, and when Nora died, she could not be without a dog, so we got Fifi, whose elderly owner had died, from the rescue centre. The history of the village could be written in its dogs and cats. It could be written in barks and growls, in purrs and mews. It would be a fine animal tale, and I would ask Fabrice Luchini to read it, in the way that he reads the fables of La Fontaine. Marcelle always wore a thin shabby jacket; she would never wear the warm cream wool coat I bought her to replace it, and then she stopped going out at all, even refusing the wheelchair I was given and tried to give to her. All she wanted to do was lie in bed, grieving and angry, her legs swollen and her knees so twisted, so misshapen. Once she put a plastic bag over her head, in a clumsy attempt to either end it all or draw attention to her misery.

Passover, *pesach*, begins tomorrow. I reminded myself, the end of leavened bread for a week. Every corner of the house should be cleaned. Some will set the *seder* table with bitter herbs or horseradish, with green onion and salt. Lives were embittered by hard service. How little I know of all this. Mélodie, Marcelle's granddaughter, wrote to tell me she had a pigeon nest in the little garden of her new house. Yesterday evening I saw a tawny hare sitting up in the field behind the Metairie, unnoticed by the dogs. She stayed for a while, minutes in fact, sniffing the air, then bounded away into the forest by the château. The days are made up of small events, animal and plant business, important matters for them. Mushrooms send electrical impulses to each other, fungal word lengths though they may be saying nothing, or they may be like wolves howling to preserve the integrity of their pack, while trees extend their roots to support other trees. I have become enracinated. Sometimes I wanted to howl. No, *often* I wanted to howl and sometimes I did. It was no fun becoming animal. Fuck you, Deleuze and Guattari. Fuck you, Derrida.

There have been days of lilac, anemones, and pansies, and for once, Romme, who committed suicide in Year III, a *prairial* martyr, and his calendar commissioners were completely correct in their observation of the natural world and the time of flowers, no doubt with the help of André Thouin, who at the age of seventeen became the head gardener of the King's garden and later, in *brumaire* of Year IV, the chair of horticulture at the Musée d'Histoire naturelle, where he created the library. The white lilac, 'Madame Lemoine', planted for Marcelle who was also Madame Lemoine, was about to burst into flower in the garden, and the pale mauve lilac (I do not know its name) was already flowering, though I almost did not see it, hidden behind a hibiscus that has become huge. I cut branches, stripped off the leaves, pounded the ends of the stalks with a mallet, and brought them into the house, where their scent permeated the library. But not today, no, today Romme was not accurate, for there are no blueberries here, unless in exported punnets from South America, from Peru and Chile and Mexico, or from freezer compartments of the supermarkets. I worked diligently over the weekend, digging up the thuggish acanthus that every year overwhelms some areas of the garden, descendent of a plant I brought back from Rome over twenty-eight years ago. I pulled up the *arum maculatum*, curse it, about which I have complained vigorously already, the plant's sheath surrounding the flower spike that will become the stalk of red berries, the spathe and spadix that gave rise to its more common name for the resemblance of the fleshy stem, the flowers enclosed within, to male and female genitalia, the lords and ladies of symbolic copulation.

Greffoir, a little grafting knife for the last day of *germinal*. Jean-François once showed me how to graft an apple tree, the careful split of the root stock, the making of a wound into which to insert the scion, the shaping of scion and root stock and their clean clefting, binding them together with wax wrappers, merging the pulpy layer of the cambium. It should be done in early spring or late winter before the buds pop. I have never done it and doubt now that I ever will. The British prime minister is expected to address the Commons today, to apologise for his actions, and we are told it will be 'full-throated' but with few details about the gathering for which he received a fixed penalty notice and other events. There will be more lies. There will be no shame. Single men travelling alone from dangerous and poor places will be sent to Rwanda for 'processing'. There is no pity. There is no shame. Where are the social bonds? Where are the honest people, *les honnêtes gens*? In Maréchal's *Almanach*, Rousseau shared a day with Diogenes and Christ shared his with Isaac Newton. Plutarch was followed by Moliere, Michelangelo, Copernicus and Galileo shared the next day, Voltaire, Spinoza... There were courtesans and philosophers. His calendar was burnt by the royal censor, called blasphemous, impious, that he was mustering a vile troop of unbelievers. He declared a Year I. My ankle and foot was swollen and I was told to rest by the physiotherapist, but when I rested, I was too restless and too much turned about in my mind. *Vider la tête*, yes, to clear, to change, to empty the head. To make way for new voices. To hope we may hear them. To hope we may learn to feel shame.

FLORÉAL

P*rimidi*, *floréal*, the first day and one of roses. It should be remembered (who will remember, if not I?) that in 1789, two months before the fall of the Bastille, Chamfort, secretary of the Jacobin Club, who preferred to die a free man rather than as an imprisoned slave, said to Marmontel, the *encyclopédiste*: 'I see that my hopes sadden you: you do not want liberty at the cost of gold and blood. Do you really think you can make a revolution from rose-water?' In a speech in 1793, at a meeting of the Jacobin Club, Danton declared: 'I will no more tear out a page of my history than you will the pages of yours, which are destined to immortalise the annals of freedom.' Later, waiting for his death, Danton laughed and said that when men were fools, they should be laughed at. He said to Desmoulins and Phillipeaux, 'I pity you all, if you do not quickly recover your reason: you have seen nothing yet but roses.' He met Tom Paine, saluting him in English, saying he had tried to do for France what Paine did for England, less fortunate but no more culpable. He said he was being sent to the scaffold, 'and what then, my friends, I will go to it gaily'. Camille Desmoulins was distressed, no insouciant acceptance of what was to come for him. In Büchner's play, Lucille, his wife, is traumatised, driven out of her mind. She rambles, she sings, she runs away from the prison. In a speech she announces that if she closes her eyes and screams, all the commotion in the world will cease.

Throughout 2008 I collected French postcards, filing them under the theme of women and roses. They were usually from the period between the end of the nineteenth century and the 1930s. Then I carefully removed everything but the woman (leaving her face, hair, her rosy flesh) and the roses she holds or is arranging. I cut her from her ground. The image was then reproduced in the same size as the original card, the women now floating, bereft of context, groundless. My father was first in hospital, then in a home for those who had lost their minds. I visited him when I could, though he barely knew me. We sat in the garden among the straggly rose bushes, and he would fall asleep, hunched into a wheelchair, head lolling. I worked on my women and roses as he slept. When he woke, he would smile at me, showing the gap in his mouth where his artificial tooth should have been, the crown that was lost by the staff of the home though they denied it. He no longer knew what a book or a newspaper was. Very carefully he would fold up *The Guardian*, making of it as small a wad as possible, then insert it under the waistband of his trousers against his skin.

There have been days of oak and fern, and tomorrow, hawthorn. Once, for a year, I recorded the passing of each month in a photograph of a burn on wrist or hand, acquired in the ordinary course of my day-to-day life. But when I started the work, I stopped burning myself accidentally, and so was forced to burn myself deliberately in order to have the work completed within the year – ah, the logic of work. The photographs are round, each held in a rose-pink matte (the closest approximation of the packaging of the scent *Allure* by Chanel), each an exquisite detail of pain and time passing, difficult to identify at first as a nasty little domestic wound. Under each photograph, embossed in letterpress in a colour called *sanguine* – blood-red in heraldry and it means also to be positive or optimistic in a bad situation – is the name of each month of the French revolutionary calendar. I asked Sanja to write a response to the work. She commented on the density of reference points – in addition to the revolutionary calendar which frames the entire work, there were references to the domestic sphere, bodily pain, consumer culture, femininity, luxury. She felt that these various references embedded ultimately incompatible orders of time. Consumerism, conventionally understood, belongs to an evanescent time captured by the very nature of perfume, a transient sensation, while bodily wounds reflect a traumatic past that may or may not have fully healed, invoking the metaphor of a 'haunting past'. The diary format harkened back to a religious source in the Book of Hours, closely related to the liturgical calendar with its divisions of sacred and profane time and the monastic organisation of the day, and she remarked that one of the inspirations for the revolutionary calendar was the 'floral clock' devised by the botanist Linneaus: every hour was associated not with prayer but with a different flower – offering an 'aromatic' – materialist – treatment of time's passage. She noted how my accidents became acts, demarcating time's passing on my body, and so replaying the problem of how to construct a parameter for the passage of time usually experienced without intention, bound to the biographical contours of a life. She wrote that the French revolutionaries dreamt of returning to a transparent time in which, apart from these natural changes, nothing marked the hours, and all the temporal markers of a social, hierarchical life were abolished. Did not my attempt to mark time on the body as a kind of tattoo replay once more the (impossible) attempt to combine subjective and objective measures of time, she asked. The interior felt experience of duration (the intention, act, memories of pain) with the external objective measure (the photograph, archived, classified in the social form of a calendar)? I am quoting her more or less, of course, and hope she will forgive me.

While making the work I was invited to teach at the art school in Bourges. As I was describing this work-in-progress, I rolled up my sleeve to show my latest wound. There was no pain, so I had not realised the burn-blister had burst and that it was scarlet and yellow and really quite disgusting, such abjection. The students gasped in horror, and I felt a sudden and unexpected shame in displaying my sores. Vaunting pain. Saint Catherine would have disapproved. All those women mystics who sought to make themselves interesting. Such show-offs. Especially that Saint Angela of Foligno: a small scale of a leper's sores was stuck in her throat, and she tried to swallow it. Her conscience would not let her spit it out, just as if she had received Holy Communion. She really did not want to spit it out but simply to detach it from her throat. My body is full of wounds. I can describe the circumstances of each one. Such embellishment of pain. My afflictions are shared. Some saints covered the stigmata, like Saint Gemma, whose wounds regularly appeared each Thursday and disappeared on Friday, who with the help of her guardian angel would go to bed. Or Saint Mariam, whose stigmata appeared on Wednesdays and lasted until Friday. Gemma's came as flames touching her hands and feet, Mariam's came as she thought herself to be gathering roses for the Virgin's altar, and their thorns thrust into her, swelling her hands and feet.

For the first time since last autumn, I travelled to London. There was a great deal of catching up to do there, tasks to undertake, problems to resolve, family and friends to visit and to care for... there was still more gardening there. There was broken plumbing, a collapsed shed, rising damp in the kitchen; there was vigorous acanthus growth, yes, there too, from Rome, and a bay tree that had become enormous, shading the kitchen window. It was once a tiny plant bought in Paris in one of the plant shops along the Seine, a short walk from where I was living with my small son. May Day came and went, and back in France R. bought a sprig of lily-of-the-valley from an enterprising little girl whose mother had set up a table for her in the village. He encountered Françoise in the street by the baker's; she had done the same as a child, she said, adding that she had always made a surprising amount of money from the sale of her flowers, which rather dampened his sentimental enthusiasm for the gesture. I was still in London, and there was no May Day celebration, but only more clumsy gardening, digging out the recalcitrant roots of acanthus, then (happily) putting in a clematis, some herbaceous plants, mint in a clay pot, and repotting all the geraniums. In a little terracotta pot in the shape of a woman's head (almost a Medusa), I planted a pale pink fuschia. It was exquisite. It sprang from her head. On my subsequent return it was almost dead, for David does not water enough, and finally, it gave up its ghost, leaving Medusa empty-headed. I worked with my bare hands, which quickly became scratched and sore. In Ukraine people were putting on gardening gloves to clear the bodies of the dead. There was no space for the dead in the city morgues; the dead arrived every day, and many were found in mass graves or open forests or on the streets. Many were piled on top of each other in refrigerated trucks, and people came to put the names of those they had lost on to the black bin bags enclosing the dead. Often it was impossible to identify the corpses, too decomposed or too brutalised, faces smashed beyond recognition, disfigured or burnt; sometimes there was no head. People screamed and cried; they cursed. They nodded their recognition of a tattoo on a shoulder.

In our London garden the foxes (there are three, perhaps more) came every evening to be fed, and one, the young vixen, I thought, remained for hours, looking in at me through the kitchen window. Outside, she would come very close to me. She would sit by me as I weeded, watching me attentively. I did not want to tame her. It would be too dangerous for her. I read an old essay by Eric on the history of May Day. He noted that Pétain's Vichy government declared it a Festival of Labour and Concord, co-opting the day from the labour movement, class consciousness, and class struggle. Many years ago, Terry hung a banner at the entrance to his army camp on May Day: Workers of the world, unite. He claimed it would prevent him from being sent to Northern Ireland. May Day was a day to stop work, to refrain from work on a working day, choosing what to do in the company of family and friends, a symbolic strike, a declaration of workers' power. It was a day of struggle for some and a commemoration of martyrs for others. Not working also meant celebrating. There were garlands, flower-decked bicycles and carts; there were roses and poppies, and in France there was the *fusillade de Fourmies* of 1891, symbolised by the eighteen-year-old Maria Blondeau, who danced in a demonstration at the head of the young people protesting, swinging the branch of flowering hawthorn that her fiancé had given her, until the troops shot her dead. There was the dream of a new day. Starvelings might arise from their slumbers. The dust will be spurned to win the prize. The earth shall rise on new foundations. Labourers from fields will join hand in hand with workers from factories. There was a holiday without – outside – a calendar. In Year II the Liberty Tree replaced the maypole, the may of joy or of complaints but a dead tree, nonetheless. A living tree, tall, long-lived, and imposing in circumference was planted, signifying liberty, equality, and fraternity, flourishing in place of naked wood, firmly rooted, and providing beneficent shade, planted, pruned, and watered. Jean-Jacques Rousseau wrote about the ancient oaks under whose leafy canopies and shady feet the first festivals took place, but I could not remember any more than this and indeed, was uncertain if it was Rousseau after all.

The day I returned to Brittany I read a report of the sighting of a wolf on the Monts d'Arrée, Meneziou in Breton, in Berrien. The young wolf was filmed on an automatic camera, placed by Emmanuel Holder to film the passage of game, wild boar, deer. He did not expect to catch a wolf. The film was very short, ten seconds. The grey wolf, a young male, passed through a clearing, among the trees. Holder said it was a very emotional moment, especially as the wolf museum is nearby, and not far away there is still a wolf trap in an embankment dating from when wolves were established in the area. It was the first sighting in over a century. The young wolves disperse, travelling alone, leaving the pack in which they can find no place in order to find new territory for themselves, seeking a mate. They can travel hundreds of kilometres, a long journey, a solitary one. A woman who keeps goats saw the wolf pass her window, yes, with her own eyes, she recounted, at her bay window, and she could hardly believe the sight, it was like a dream, she said. A Freudian wolf-dream: *Suddenly the window opened of its own accord, and I was terrified to see that some white wolves were sitting on a big walnut tree in front of the window* – in the sketch Sergei Pankejeff drew for Freud, the wolves look more like little foxes. In October 2021 a dead wolf was found in Saint-Brévin-Les-Pins, in the Loire-At-lantique. Jean-Marc and Yvette took us to the Monts d'Arrée a long time ago. I did not know why we have not been there again, to the strange wild place where in the old stories the gates of hell are thought to stand, so we might stand ourselves between the worlds of the living and the dead. There is a scene, another story, a long musical sequence without dialogue, that breaks into Christophe Honoré's film *Non, ma fille, tu n'ira pas danser*: a procession clad in Breton costume makes its way to a chapel on the Monts d'Arrée, but there's a girl who prefers to dance, she wants only to dance and not to marry, and so descends to hell. In my head I heard the high voice of Tina Charles, singing that she loves to love but her baby loves to dance, he wants to dance, he's got to dance, and so there's no time for their romance, he won't give their love a chance. But she's spinning like a top and they'll dance till they drop. In the film a boy tells the legend of Katell Gollet, Catherine *la perdue*, the lost girl, to his mother, another lost woman. Katell said she would marry any man who could make her dance for twelve hours and many young men in the county tried their luck. She exhausted them. They died of exhaustion and never saw the next day. Oh, those feeble men. Her uncle locked her up in a tower, but she escaped to dance once more, opening the gates of hell, some say accompanied by the Devil himself, who danced her to hell. That is one version – there are others, there always are, and shame, shame, shame, shame on you, if you can't dance too. Your feet want to move, so don't stop the motion if you got the notion. You can't stop the groove. Go out find a dancing man.

There is a calvary in Plougastel-Daoulas that depicts the story: it shows her naked, pierced by the trident of the Devil as he drags her to hell, like the spear of the archangel that pierced Saint Teresa, another ecstasy of a mystic woman. Pain and jouissance. Teresa saw in the angel's hand a long spear of gold, and at its point there seemed to be fire. He appeared to her thrusting it into her heart, piercing her very entrails. When he drew it out, he seemed to draw them out also, and to leave her on fire with a great love of God. The pain was so great that it made her moan, and yet so surpassing was the sweetness of this excessive pain, that she could not wish to be rid of it. Her soul was satisfied now with nothing less than God. The pain was not bodily, but spiritual, she said, though the body had its share in it.

At the end of Honoré's film, a child falls through a glass window – when I saw it in the cinema in Dinan, the entire audience gasped and then there was a deathly silence. The mother was suffocating. There is a song, a child's song, *Sur l'Pont du Nord*: there's a ball, a dance, on the bridge, Adèle wants to go but her mother won't allow it, *non, ma fille, tu n'iras pas danser*, she sends her daughter to her room to cry, to wait for her brother in his golden boat, how wonderful to have a brother with a golden boat, and he takes her to the dance on the bridge, and she is wearing her white dress with a golden belt, he takes her in his golden boat:

La première danse Adèle a bien dansé
La seconde danse le pont s'est écroulé
Oh ! dit la mère j'entends le glas sonner
Les cloches du Nord se mirent à sonner
La mère demande : Pour qui les cloches sonnaient
C'est pour Adèle et votre fils aîné
Voilà le sort des enfants obstinés

The first dance Adele danced well
The second dance the bridge collapsed
Oh! says the mother I hear the death knell ring
The northern bells began to ring
The mother asks: For whom the bells were ringing
It's for Adele and your eldest son
This is the fate of stubborn children

Glas or tocsin, clang or touch or strike or sing, to ring, willingly, the biggest bell when afraid, with hasty or redoubled strokes (blows). But there were flowers too, another refrain, the language of flowers, in *Glas*, when Derrida wrote of Saint Genet (not one of *my* saints), the flower of rhetoric, the figure of figures and the place of places, the flower absent from all bouquets – it was a question, a proposal of 'what if'? Or it collapsed. Shattered like a glass window. It was *his* book, not mine. And Jacques wrote a letter to Jean in 1971, explaining why he could not speak up for George, for George Jackson accused of killing a prison guard in Soledad, for to add his voice would collude in the silencing of Jackson, his exclusion and submission, and 'yes, of course, but...' Jacques wrote, in philosophical displacement, and when Jackson was killed in prison, his letter remained unfinished. So many unfinished letters and others not even begun. Jean withdrew from writing books for some years, but when he died there was *The Prisoner of Love*. He wrote it while he was dying and when others had died, the displaced, the exiled, the beloved: *moss, lichen, grass, a few dog roses capable of pushing up through red granite.*

In London, during my two returns, I found that I was unable to write, although I had recourse to the wilderness of the terraced garden there, sadly neglected, overgrown with acanthus, such a symbol of recurring life, of resurrection and immortality, spikey flower shafts blossoming. Bear's breeches. Artifice. Crown of thorns. Grace or sorrow (symbols are so easily ascribed). Spine. Too much about acanthus already, as Allie thought, perhaps, but there *is* so much of it. I did think about what I might have written as I wrenched these recalcitrant rhizomatic roots from the earth, thick white tubers. Writing never comes easily to me. Writing fails me or I fail its incessant hissing demand. My impulse was to do nothing. Death drive, I said to Siddhartha on the telephone when he called from Berlin. He did not laugh. To be still, I said. You are never still, he said, and it was not a question. I missed him. I miss him. I did not tell him this. There was some more taming of the garden and then again more, and I planted two more clematis, which later died, mournfully and mourned.

Malcolm took Adrian and me out for lunch, and at one moment during the meal, Adrian held my hand in his hand very tenderly and I was moved to tears by his gentle gesture. He and I both drank a glass of a *fiano* on skin, a white wine made like a red wine, fermented with the grape skins, maceration, skin contact, *ramato*. The food was pleasant, but I disapprove of restaurants that oblige one to pay for bread and the small parsimony of three egg halves rather than two eggs for the devilled eggs with black sesame and trout roe. Later that day I had tea in Lincoln's Inn Fields with Anne-Marie after watching her beautiful odd film in Sir John Soane's Museum. We spoke about the tumour on her spine, the time and luck of her diagnosis and treatment, about fatigue, about voice and chorus and women and the absent presence of Eliza Soane, dear friend, dear friends, voices heard, while he, Sir John, could no longer hear his beloved wife. Tom wrote an essay about the film, a lovely essay, a careful essay, thinking about haunting, thinking about mourning: 'Days and dates sound like a litany, an attempt to fasten the incomprehensible within a structure of order or sense: Tuesday November 21st ... Wednesday November 22nd ... Thursday November 23rd ... But the event of death overflows, resists our attempts to understand. Even architecture becomes chaotic in the end. The sound of silence is a woman's voice lamenting loss.'

What has passed unwritten, unremarked? Meeting Tim for the first time, yes, in the café in Montparnasse, a glass of Sancerre, and going over the final edits to his book, amicably, without disagreement but the vexed question if the use of italics and quotation marks was over-egging, a long conversation about translation with this kind and interesting man. It was a short flowering this month, but as much as I could do. I can list this, what I have missed. Mushroom and hyacinth. Chamerops. A rake and rhubarb. Sainfoin and wallflower (rod of gold, *baton d'or*) and honeysuckle. The silkworm (yes, the bombyx, points of view stitched to the other veil, stop writing, full stop, period, and don't lose the thread, a warning note to self even if it was not I who wrote this, not at all, but one who kept silkworms in a shoebox, which is a bit of a primal scene or a screen memory, and in short, where something hangs by a thread) and comfrey (from which I have made a foul-smelling 'tea' to treat the powdery mildew on my roses and tomato plants). A hoe and sea lavender. Fritillary and borage. Valerian and carp (I remembered the frozen carp brought back from Prague in her suitcase by Alexandra, which we ate with Pavel in Manchester one evening, poached *à la juivre* in white wine with sugar, onions, raisins, carrots, peppercorns, and bay leaves. I stayed up most of that night reading a novel by Michel Houellebecq, and while I remember the small austere room in their Georgian house, I have no memory of the book, other than a dim feeling of slight distaste. Some cooks, those from the Alsace, add a few broken gingersnaps at the end of cooking to thicken the sauce for the carp, and then chill it, but we ate it hot that night without the crushed sweet biscuits.) Spindle and chive. Bugloss and wild mustard and a shepherd's crook. The hook of the crook, by hook or by crook, a sign of care, is used to catch sheep by the leg or neck; there are crooks for legs and crooks for necks; one needs a leg crook to snare a goat. I bought a new cane, an old Swiss alpenstock, with a small metal etiquette of a pair of chamois and the handle a polished black horn. There was a spike on its foot, a fierce piercing little thing, designed to grip the mountainside; I asked for its removal, which later I regretted. Such a useful thing, a spike on the end of a stick.

PRAIRIAL

The days passed, like the seconds, the minutes, the hours. Then the weeks, and so the months passed too, and soon it would be a year, and so on. Year after year. Life after life. *Floréal* became *prairial*. I missed the passing over from flowering to meadow. I missed alfalfa and day lilies. I missed clover and angelica. But I returned in *prairial*, yes, I came back in the ninth month, I returned to a meadow in the Spring quarter, and today was the day of the duck, oh dear little *canard*, which is also an unfounded rumour, a fabricated report, a false story, and three drakes in the canal this morning were mounting a female, repeatedly, savagely, dragging her under water. *Mal*, bad mallard. Zoë's poem for this day ends with *days running off like oil of whose back*. The news from Ukraine has been unbearable. In Mariupol the remaining group of Ukrainian soldiers holed-up in the Azovstal steel works, a fortress of underground structures in the city, surrendered to the Russian forces, abandoning the labyrinth of bunkers and tunnels. They had no way out; they were surrounded, they were brutally besieged by artillery fire, bombardment from the air, and missile strikes. Supplies of water, food, and medical supplies ran out, and then the women and children were evacuated. A woman said she and her husband had sheltered in a basement in the works, expecting to be there for a few days that turned into two months. It had been impossible to say how many people were there, in the constant comings and goings. Some shared food, blankets, clothing while others did not. The woman said everyone was different. She said she wanted only to rest now. Those who remained to fight were taken to camps in Russian-controlled territory. There were reports that they preferred death by combat rather than to lay down arms to the Russian army.

Rosa wrote to Sophie that she really hoped to die at her post, in a street fight or in prison. In nature she saw so much cruelty that she suffered greatly. She described returning from a walk in the country, where she suffered the voiceless tragedy of a beetle lying helplessly on its back as ants ate it alive. Rosa took her handkerchief and tried to flick off the little brutes, carrying the poor beetle to a safe distance on the grass, but two of its legs had been gnawed off and it was, she felt, a very doubtful boon she had conferred on the creature. She ended this letter, written on 2 May, by saying that she would write again soon, and Sophie should make her mind easy, for everything would turn out right, and for Karl too. On 23 May she wrote to Sophie about lilac and blue tits, their cry of *zeezeebey* (so lovely to say this aloud), and it was sweet to her when a hasty *zeezeebey* sounded from beyond the prison wall. She was not she wrote, at all equanimous; it took only a piercing wind to reduce her spirits to the most profound gloom. In fact, she rarely had much inclination to talk. Weeks passed without her even hearing the sound of her own voice. Sam wrote of her as a *Sonntagskind*, born on the Sunday thirteen days before the start of the revolutionary government of the Paris Commune. Sam said that from her prison cell she could hear the birds singing 'for the abolition of the very days of the week, for the liberation of prose and song and script and language and nature'.

I thought of nuns singing the divine offices unseen from behind their screens: invisible, celestial. I thought of Saint Teresa's warning of the conflict between the choir offices and the modesty and spirituality of the convent life. She said that the voices should be of those persons who practiced mortification, that the impression should not be conveyed that they were anxious to be thought well of by those who heard them. So strict, Saint Teresa, so quick to admonish those who sought to draw attention to themselves. The Tridentine Church was consistent in its approach to musical enthusiasm: control, restriction, prohibition. Enclosed.

While I was away the dear old dog Falcon was put down. His lovely head would not rise again to lay his black snout on my lap. He would never again catch a hedgehog in the lane at night, mistaking it for a ball as it curled up in his soft mouth. I cannot write of this without crying. Florentine asked me to write something about him. I will. I will but not yet. Instead, I would write about sleep for Anna, but not yet, tomorrow perhaps or later, later, when grief passes or grief thins. All the beetroot of last year was pulled from its bed today, the leaves given to the poultry. Some was still good to eat, or good enough. I made a hummus, with roasted beets, chickpeas, tahini, lemon, garlic. Last night and then again today – the day of lemon balm or *mélisse*, a plant of virtue and compassion – I heard Nazanin Zaghari-Ratcliffe interviewed. She was forced to sign a letter at Tehran airport; it was a false confession. Britain's lead negotiator told her the Iranians would not allow her to board the plane unless she signed. She spoke of the exchange of skills in prison, people teaching what they knew, from leatherwork to yoga to philosophy. The women would cook together. People gave what they had. Every day, she said, one little thing in her house throws her back to where she was, forms a picture, a memory. She did not think she had managed to close *that* (this is how she said it), no, she did not think she would be able to.

All morning, the day of oat grass and Saint Sophie. The saints must make their return, and why not today, Sophie following Didier, Donatien, Émile, and Rita, the last the saint of impossibilities, of desperate causes, to whom one turns when all else fails, whose foot (a statue) in the church in Rome is covered with silver, worn down by the mouths of those who have kissed it, the infertile women longing for children. Rita was a baby sleeping in her cot when a colony of white bees swarmed around her and the bees put honey in her little mouth. I wrote about sleep and my garden for Anna's magazine. I did not know if it would be what she wanted or expected. I stopped now – it was enough, I thought – and would return tomorrow to add a few lines about emergent dahlia tubers. I distracted myself by reading a post from Adrian about his preference for honeycomb towels, *nid d'abeille*, those in smart Roman hotels or bought by his mother or by him in the via de Gubernaio, or by his French mother-in-law, or the very best quality khadi towels from India acquired in what he hoped was a post-colonial gesture. Due to my reading, I was left with the uncomfortable feeling that my own towels had been subjected to the most stringent criticism. I have a pile of Turkish cotton towels, bought in Istanbul, and some are honeycomb, and no-one in the house likes them much, preferring the kind of terry towels with deep pile that are such anathema to Adrian. Someone I do not know commented that honeycomb towels brought together memories mixing space and times, eliciting a melancholic sense of irrecoverable loss. In Sri Lanka Benjamin and I bought a pile of such cloths. I gave most of them away. One remains on a battered nineteenth-century French armchair in the sitting-room in London, its red stripes faded to pink. Once, with me in Dol de Bretagne, Denis and Adrian bought Jacquard tea towels, which I wanted to like much more than I did. Saint Sophie was the usual Christian martyr, daughter of a rich Roman family with three daughters, Faith, Hope, and Charity, whom she refused to give up to the emperor Hadrian, and he killed them all, even the mother, for they would not renounce their religion and it drove him mad, yes, he was furious, same old same old. Saint Sophie is evoked against the late frost, like the *saints des glace*. Sophie the cold. After the *saint des glaces* has passed, the dahlia tubers may be planted out safely in the earth.

Only one dahlia tuber had put forth leaves and I was worried. From those I left in the ground over winter, only one appears to have survived, a pink and yellow cactus variety. Smothering blankets of horseradish were shooting out from where I remembered a beautiful 'Chat noir' dahlia to have been. It flowered late into the autumn, with spectacular deep red velvety flowers like sea urchins. It is toxic to dogs and cats, as are my tulips, daffodils, oleanders, irises. I have planted an unintentional poison garden; I have staged the big sleep. Even the milky sap of my euphorbias may cause skin blisters and eye irritations in human beings. I dream of my garden when I am away from it, awake, or when I sleep, even if that sleep is fitful and I cannot call it dead sleep. Dreams sleep deep. They are tubers. From the ground mysteries rise. This is a mystery and a dream, indefinite, like the heart, beating, leading away from death and towards self-forgetting. I pulled up and stripped the last of the spinach, which tonight would be braised in butter and olive oil, then sprinkled with golden raisins and pine kernels. Martagon lily marks the day in the calendar, a lovely plant sometimes called 'Turk's Cap', which it resembles, and politicians continued to bluster and lie, swerving responsibility. The last two lines of Zoë's four-line poem for today: *wear tomorrow's foreignness / where you become me I you.* It is economic, this poetry, but it is beyond my means, and I was envious. More, not less: bluster, persiflage. Yesterday children were shot in a school in Texas by an eighteen-year-old boy – on the news programmes, parents remembered their children, words breaking, hearts broken, weeping, speech failing. More bluster from politicians amid the grief.

The young black cat went missing this morning, or so I thought. Orphée usually joins the dogs on their first morning walk, sweetly oblivious to their constant rejection of his sprightly advances, as he leaps and mews with delight at their presence, Hera snapping at him, Ida skittling away. Later I found him asleep in my studio on top of a box containing framed drawings of women embracing snakes, returned from exhibition in London. I have not been in the studio of late – the same drawings from last year are on the wall, though rearranged and amended this year. There has been no demand for them, not even from myself. In the autumn I will return, I promised myself (and so I did). There was a dead magpie in the kitchen, a mouse neatly laid next to it. Upstairs, a mouse was squashed under the bathroom door. There was a skinned mouse in the car, under the passenger seat. This seemed inexplicable. Each morning I count corpses and dispose of them. In Ukraine people dig through debris for the bodies of the dead. A Russian woman recounted how her sons, both conscripts in the army, were sent to Ukraine despite what was promised. In her car, driving futilely, she searched for them. An officer told her they were in the field; what field? she asked, there is no field and they are not there. At last, she found them over the border and took them home. Today, wild thyme, *serpolet*, low-growing, spreading, antiseptic, diuretic, antispasmodic; it enlivens the spirit, a sovereign remedy for the melancholic. There is mourning and there is melancholia, both are responses to loss, though in the latter, one does not know what has been lost or knows only that something has been lost as an object of love. Freud made a distinction between the world and the ego, but Walter Benjamin did not, summoning melancholy to understand the sadness of mourning. I do not understand loss as a condition of possibility nor of detachment. What is it to be half-alive or half-dead, to be half-buried? To be unable to rest? I know about *that*. I missed noting or accounting for the feast of Ascension, the last meeting of Christ with his disciples after his resurrection and before his body went to heaven. He ascended while his mother was assumed: he was dead, then alive, and he got there himself, while Mary was dead, then taken, active son and passive mother, but each arose, body and soul, to heavenly glory. In William Blake's painting Christ is turned away, facing the light, arms outstretched and raised.

An agricultural tool was listed for today, *décadi*, not a plant or tree or animal or fruit: a scythe, for cutting down and reaping before threshing. It cuts in swathes, low to the ground. I decided I would not mention death or even Death again, as it would be far too obvious. However, death does tend to slip in or to slip by, going unnoticed or misrecognised, or death is surprised by finding its victim in the wrong place at the wrong time, in Aleppo, for instance, instead of Damascus, or in Baghdad, not Samarra. Death works carefully from its appointment book, prepared weeks in advance: time and place stated. I went out early to a *vide-grenier* in Saint Benoît des Ondes, returning rather empty-handed and disappointed (only two heavy linen tea towels with red stripes and a monogram in cross-stitch purchased), my fancy caught only by a remarkable bench with a narrow curved wooden seat and back on cast-iron legs in the forms of branches but the man, sporting a black felt broad-brimmed Breton hat and accompanied by two delightful small black dogs, mother and daughter, wanted four hundred euros for it; I would, I think, have paid a hundred, but did not even propose this. China's new book arrived in the post – more ghosts, a haunting spectre once again. Mira is quoted, opening a chapter, on love and hate, one because of the other. No time, no time, there was a cake to make for Mélodie and Hugo who were coming to tea, a cake of four quarters: butter, sugar, flour, eggs, vanilla, lemon zest. And a swarm of bees to re-hive while the sun was warm. Fabre d'Églantine said that the priests assigned the commemoration of a so-called saint to each day of the year, which exhibited neither utility nor method. It was a collection of lies, of deceit or of charlatanism. He thought that the nation, after having kicked out the canonised mob from its calendar, must replace it with the objects that make up the true riches of the nation, worthy objects not from a cult, but from agriculture – useful products of the soil, the tools used to cultivate it. We reap just what we sow. *There is going to be judgement in the morning; we're gonna be mourning in the morning.*

Fêtes des mères: at a *vide-grenier* in Lancieux there was a most charming small sailing boat for sale. Her name was *Mona*, and she came with a trailer. An elderly man was selling her, sitting quietly in a striped canvas folding chair. For a few moments I thought about how lovely this would be, forgetting that I have not sailed for over fifty years and even then I was incompetent at best. I was thinking of Lulu, Lulu Peyraud of the Domaine Tempier in Provence. Richard Olney wrote a cookbook with her in 2004, describing the life on the estate and the menus over the course of a year. She had a sailboat for thirty years in the port of Bandol, and at first she took all the children sailing with her, then the youngest, Véronique, was born, and the other children, the boys, grew up, and for years, whenever she had a free moment, she sailed with Véronique, and then Véronique grew up, so Lulu sailed alone. And it was a marvellous escape. She was a hundred and two when she died in La Ciotat in 2020. She said she was just *un petit bout d'une femme*, a little bit of a woman. She said she did not want people to imagine that she never did anything but cook. A spring menu might include a salad of green beans and fresh shell beans, roast pork loin with sage and little round white onions, which could be replaced with black olives, a gratin of squash with coriander seeds and mint leaves, a salad of curly chicory with a garlic vinaigrette, reblochon and goat cheeses, strawberries, a great glass bowl of them, with sugar and whipped cream to the side. Her civet of hare always had lots of thyme. She associated her dish of chicken with apples and calvados with her precious moments of sailing, for she could prepare it, set the oven, and was free to go off while it cooked. Véronique said her mother taught her how to set a table for the pleasure of the eyes. She thanked her mother with all her heart: *ma maman*. The fruit of this day, *primidi*, was the strawberry, and in the garden I must pick them every day, which should not be onerous but a pleasure. The gariguettes were coming to an end and the mara des bois, fragrant and with the flavour of a woodland strawberry, will begin in July and, with luck, continue fruiting until the autumn. There are tiny wild wood strawberries where Fidèle is buried. I remembered eating them on Rhodes when I was a sullen child, always standing apart from my family as though in shame, my own shame, not theirs, a foreign child, a changeling (left on the doorstep, they joked, or at least so I thought at the time).

Duodi: Saint Ferdinand (which one?) and betony: betony, hedge-nettle, bishop's wort, an all-healer with the virtue of calming, alleviating anxiety and depression, it grows in the fields around the sea at Lancieux, where there are polders and Daniel's grandmother once had a house, which was sold when she died in the care home and her beautiful spaniel was put down when she was admitted because her son, Daniel's father, would not take it in, and she said to me, ha, she knew her son, ha, yes, she did, ha. Betony used to be planted in the country churchyards for it kept away ghosts, unwelcome spirits. I continued clearing around the compost heaps, bindweed, nettles, couch grass. The lilac bush Rosie gave me was dead, but I cut it right down, almost to the ground, optimistic, for who knows if the dead might not yet arise. An earthquake struck and the curtain of the temple was torn and the tombs were split open and many saints arose and went into the city, and people saw this with their own eyes. For some time I had thought to make another attempt at an asparagus bed, this time behind the compost, where the soil is rich, and I will add manure and then sand or grit to lighten it. Then, next March, I will plant the crowns I will order in the autumn, hoping that there will be enough to eat from them in two years, spreading out their roots, purple Violette of Albenga. Tonight we would eat the first small new potatoes roasted with green asparagus from Spain and manouri cheese I found in the organic shop, happily, a salad of *feuille de chêne* from Guillaume, and Erica's mortier cheese, like a morbier but for legal reasons she cannot call it that, which has double parallel lines of blue, then strawberries, more strawberries. Francis and Florentine's new dog, from a refuge in Moldavia where she was kept chained, bolted this morning in their street in Saint-Denis when a car backfired and cannot be found. We were all beside ourselves with anxiety. Anxiety has become a perpetual condition. We are beside ourselves. Out of control.

Last night, a sighting of the dog. This morning, too. But she was too scared by the city to come close, too wild to respond to calls, could not be pursued but must be lured. A storm was forecast for the end of the week. Four years ago, the same time, our house was flooded for the second time. How anxious this made me, knowing I would be in Paris on Friday. The calendar day said pea, but the peas are still only tiny pods containing tiny slips of peas, and I wondered if the whole pods could be added to tonight's risotto, with last year's broad beans, the rest of the asparagus, small white onions, and garlic chives, and I decided yes, they could and I would, and after Zoë, include today's green shell. The television presenter Patrick Poivre d'Arvor has sued for defamation sixteen women who accused him of inappropriate behaviour and sexual harassment and assault and rape. He said they were bitter and jilted. He said that he was just a serial seducer. He said the women have been motivated by vengeance, because they had not enjoyed the regard or even a simple look of a man they had once admired. He said seduction was important and that it included kisses on the neck. He challenged anyone to look into his eyes and tell him anything else. French seduction, French gallantry: almost every eighteenth-century novel contains a scene of force or rape in the encounter between a man and a woman. Advances, incitations, manipulations, suggestions. In a group we were reading *ou pire*, Lacan's nineteenth seminar, making a slow, laborious, close reading of it and its translation, word by word. Therein Lacan says that a little girl thinks only of playing behind a fan, tucking her face into a niche and refusing to say hello, but there you go, this is how it will be later, and Catherine Deneuve, among others who should know better, spoke up for the freedom to importune. Seduction might be an answer to anxiety, I read, troubled dreams, uneasy fictions.

There was both too little and too much to write each day. The discipline I sought to instil in myself, the daily practice like a sporting exercise, nudged too close to my last book and I wanted this one to find a different form. The form was determined, of course, by the passing of the days, the new calendar with its plants and tools and animals, the honest people who make their appearance, some of whom are phantoms. Tony's book *The Fountain in the Forest* takes its chapter titles from the revolutionary calendar and with more than a nod to the OULIPO he includes – in bold type – all the words of the answers to the *Guardian* quick crossword puzzle from March to April 1985 and the ninety days between the end of the miners' strike and the battle of the beanfield, with the violence of police against a gathering. There is a murder and its investigation – the policeman has a doubly royal name; there are other deaths to follow, and symbolic killings. The politics of the book are worn like a heart in its pages, on its sleeve. Today: the day of acacia, sometimes called wattles. An infusion of acacia may stimulate the appetite when hunger is suppressed through worry. Gum arabic is produced from the resin under its bark by tapping; it was used in embalming in ancient Egypt, an adhering agent for the flaxen wrappings, and in paints, inks, dyes, and cosmetics. Blown up the nose it stops nosebleeds, *poof!* And they are gone! It was used in the binding of the pigments of medieval manuscripts. And it was traded in West Africa by the French and British colonies in the eighteenth and nineteenth centuries, leading to a gum trade war and the French expansion of its colonial empire in West Africa: Senegal, Mali, Niger, Burkina Faso, Mauritania. The French called it their *Mission Civilisatrice*. The histories of colonisation and occupation are reflected in the trade of plants, part of imperial designs, commercial values, like the human bodies measured exactly against their exchange value. Economic botany: the domination of others in a colonial setting. Today: the day of Saint Justin, of whom there are at least five, two martyrs, a missionary, a bishop, and a confessor.

I was in the studio to pack books in preparation for a book fair and roughly paint the name of my press with violet ink on brown paper bags, the ink leaving stains on my fingers for I am not a neat worker. The weather was grey, unexpectedly, but the light in my room was bright and it was a pleasure to be in there rather than in the subfusc of my study. I looked at the objects around me and desired to return to my fables, my collecting, the assembling of elements. On the wall, clipped to a supporting wire, was a child's jacket, made from black velvet, a little dusty. It is lined with a faded black and white striped cotton. The sleeve cuffs have little darts; the front panel crosses over to the left, to the collar or neck, closing with metal snap buttons on the shoulder and downwards. I found it hard to describe, as though I lacked the correct vocabulary for garments. I did not yet know what role this little coat will play, if any, but I was moved by it. My son telephoned to say there had been more sightings of the lost dog; he was heading to where she had been seen this morning. He had been to the gypsy encampment by the motorway, without success, and now was enlisting the young runners of the drug dealers in his search, promising a reward, and they were all quite excited though they were confused by what kind of a dog she was, repeatedly asking if it was a pit bull as though there were no other breed, and perhaps for them there was not.

Today, a day of an animal: the quail. Pascal used to sell them in the Saturday market in Dol-de-Bretagne. Once my son and I asked about them. Pascal assured me that they were easy to care for and we were sorely tempted. They need only shelter and food and water; they are hardy, robust. But they require washing monthly, to be held firmly by the legs as they are dipped into a bowl of warm water with some soap or shampoo; then they must be properly rinsed, and thoroughly dried with a towel and a hairdryer. Somehow this made them even more tempting, but I foresaw the monthly arguments about whose turn it was to wash the quail. I got up very early as I wanted to treat the chickens against scaly leg mite and blood-sucking red mites. They were caught in the henhouse, one by one, complaining vociferously; their feathers were dusted with a mite repellent and their legs painted lavishly with olive oil, which I am trying in place of more expensive treatments such as *huile de cade*, made from juniper. Only two had any sign of scale damage from the leg mite, but I fear that the Coucou de Rennes may have bumblefoot, a bulbous swelling under her feet that can only be dealt with by surgery, and my heart sank. I got out a jar of marmalade from the preserves cupboard, once my pride and joy, to take to Ricardo in Paris, along with a carton of eggs, a small gesture of thanks for his hospitality over the weekend to come. There was one good hispi cabbage remaining and it would go with pasta and anchovies and garlic tonight, perhaps also breadcrumbs. Among the leaves I stripped from it for the poultry was an enormous orange slug and I was delighted that the black duck snapped it up at once. I was tired of thinking about food and looking forward to being away from cooking for a few days. I felt I would also be away from writing my almanach again, though I would be among honest people, save for one or two, especially one whom I dreaded seeing. I remembered a poem by Alice Notley, and then could not stop thinking about it: she is strangely unhappy, her centre is a wild curious pain, and she does not find something transfigured and infinite, but filled with rage or despair; it was a source of work and gentleness and cruelty, but I think the order of these words is wrong, and in any case, one cannot tell the story of a poem any more than one can tell the story of a dream, and by one, I mean me.

So there have been days of pinks, elder, and poppies while I was in Paris where time passes differently, though plants and trees and animals are not unobserved. On the metro the beautiful pale-yellow dog of a man who was begging rested her greying muzzle on my hand, then lay on my feet. She is very tired, her master told me, *she does not sleep at night as she is guarding me while I sleep.* We had fallen easily into conversation around the dog, he, Ricardo, and me. We spoke about the virtues of adding olive oil to dog kibble, and he recommended the yolks of eggs against moulting, saying when they lived in a house, she moulted more. There was torrential rain that evening, and they would sleep against the ramparts that night if no other shelter could be found, he and his gentle, anxious, watchful old dog. In the countryside our house narrowly escaped flooding by the same storm, the waters rushing down the path from the fields, entering my neighbour's cellar again. The traces of mud remained on the tarmacked surface of the entry to the courtyard, and this morning Orphée rolled about there until his blackness became greyness. So there have been days of honest folk: Ricardo, of course, Susan, James, Vincent, Archie, Sam, Matthieu (less snobbish than when I first met him), Thomas (who had tiny pink eyes yesterday after the party, or rather, too much party), Tom (more settled, happier, intense), Anthony (who showed me photographs of his and Coralie's baby, Lucille), Juliette (about to depart for Japan to work on frogs), Fabienne (about to depart for Montréal to work on who knows what but I knew it would be formidable). Opposite the bus stop, I noted the old Marché des chevaux, the black horse's head flanked by words, including *double poneys*, the masonic temple declaring the rights of man, and beneath, the equal rights of women. I almost bought two crystal champagne *coupes* for Florentine in a *vide-grenier* by the mosque, but suddenly felt it would be an unfortunate birthday gift under the circumstances. The lost dog was sighted once again, but could not be captured, and the situation worsens between them. There is blame and there is anger, and I cannot, must not, intervene. On the bus to Montparnasse to catch my train home, I fell into conversation with an elderly woman, well, older than I, who was delighted to find I was English so she could speak the language she learnt many years ago when she met an English girl, a student, and followed her to England, to Surrey, to Cobham, to live with her and her parents, working in Tesco to learn English. She told me that she believed in paradise and that there was no trouble there, never any trouble at all in paradise. Ho hum.

Today I picked peas and new potatoes from the garden and collected the white onions that had been scratched up by a cock and hen who, mysteriously, had found their way into the potager once again despite the reinforcement of the fence. I thought about a béchamel sauce with cream, and then potatoes and peas to be added to it, strewed with snipped chives and their flowers, buttered cabbage with caraway and dill, a garden salad, with more herbs, yes, that would be supper. There was good cheese. There was rosé wine from Nîmes in the fridge. No truffles, no champagne, no Yquem. I had finished reading the autobiography of Richard Olney, which ends with the last meal he cooked for others, as his brothers said, eaten in his kitchen by his brothers, six days after his death, five days after his cremation. They ate brochettes of lamb's hearts and kidneys, the remains of the tomatoed pilaf found in the refrigerator; they drank a bottle of Château de Beaucastel 1986 from the cellar. Silence.

The blackcurrants were ripening, and soon, redcurrants, white currants, and then blackberries, soon, soon, always yet to come. The raspberries had begun and would continue to the autumn, red and yellow. Lime tree and cornflower. I used to collect the lime flowers from the tree at La Metairie to dry for tea, a Proustian infusion, woody, honeyed, catching the throat with delicate harshness. Patrick said it was the crumbs of the little scalloped madeleine dunked in the tea, the sensation of that, which made Proust's narrator shudder, filling him with extraordinary pleasure. His mother saw he was cold and offered him tea. He did not usually take tea, but changed his mind for no particular reason, and the sensation he experienced was unbidden, unexpected, it came from outside himself. He drank a second mouthful, then a third, and then it was time to stop as the potion was beginning to lose its magic. It was, Patrick said, a narrative device to start the novel. I live with someone who is losing his memory, little by little, slipping away or being snipped away. I can see it, hear it, disappearing. It is more frightening every day. In *Speak, Memory* Nabokov wrote, confessing (his word) that he did not believe in time, and the highest enjoyment of timelessness was when he stood among butterflies and their food plants. *This is ecstasy, and behind the ecstasy is something else, which is hard to explain. It is like a momentary vacuum into which rushes all that I love.* I wished, wish, it were that simple. I wished, wish, it were less painful. Mourning or melancholia? On the wireless I heard three English ambulance volunteers in Ukraine interviewed. They collect elderly people from their homes, people who are frail, unable to walk. They take them to safety, away from their homes, their country. One of them, a woman, said that for a Ukrainian, to leave the earth of their country is death. She said she always picked a flower to send with the person leaving. She did not say where she found her flowers. I coiled the tender stems of tomato plants (rose de Berne, noire de Crimée, cornu des Andes, green zebra, marmande, ananas, and Louis-Georges said it was odd to read the French names) in the polytunnel around their spiral supports, winding each gently around its spiralling *tuteur*: guardian, protector, prop. Under and in front I picked out basil seedlings in tiny clumps. Essential oil from basil alleviates depression, anxiety, stress. Holy basil, Saint Basil.

And then I went to London for ten days, where again I could not write, where the passing of the days was marked in other ways from necessity. This did not mean that cornflowers, camomile, honeysuckle, bedstraw, a tench (sometimes called the doctor fish), jasmine, vervain, thyme, peonies, or a handcart (to go to hell in) were forgotten, but they were not written, not at their time of passing. Days slipped by me. I wondered how to catch up with time, or if time had caught up with me. I cleared some of the garden in London, but I fear it is not tended enough in my absence. I wanted to make time for it. I watered my mother's garden, with particular attention to the newly planted clematis. She can no longer fill or carry a watering can, and even to stand in order to water the garden with a hose is impossible for her now. Her right leg blocks and she cannot will it to move. She stands, fragile, trembling. Her world diminishes a little more each day. I cooked supper for her, drank wine with her, kept her sitting at the table talking.

I went to hear Erica read; it was many years, we could not count how many, since we had seen each other, and though we do not really know each other, we greeted each other warmly. She had broken her foot – we commiserated, equally warmly. She read well, getting into her stride quickly and surely, with attention to time (something the other readers that afternoon did not do, reading for too long, with the exception of a poet, who did not read for long enough). She started with her book's opening, an obituary, on-going, for her mother, written with her mother, but what is included is what will never appear, the eccentricities, the madness, the rituals; she describes a life of detail, in detail, in the wry voice of the daughter who knows her mother must never read her book. Later that day, at supper with Adrian and Denis and their guest Diana, I admired their garden, a little labyrinth of roses and underplanting, ravishing. I found it strange to imagine Adrian digging and told him so. He declared his great love of digging. Denis was not happy with the red climbing rose at the front of the house, thinking it to be vulgar. Supper was a an extravagant Ligurian stew, a soupy tomato sauce with lobster and monkfish, accompanied by braised dandelions, aubergines with pine nuts and vinegar, followed by strawberries and a rhubarb and orange cake made by Denis, all delicious, an open world or a world opening. Coming to life. *En route*, it was the same route that I took many years ago to my psychoanalyst several times a week – it was a little shocking, a little unnerving, as unnerving as the man on the bus who had vomited curry down his chest and shorts, who said he would advise me on which bus stop to descend. I used to cry almost every time I left the analytic session, and once I said I felt I could not go out into the street weeping, but my analyst said, rather coldly under the circumstances (I felt), that it was Finsbury Park and everyone was crying, and it was true. I used to meet the next patient in the street and have a little chat (we were doing the psychoanalytic training together) – he always showed me his black notebook with his questions for the analyst written in capitals. Once I asked the analyst if he ever answered the questions. I cannot remember his reply. I learnt that my analyst had died in 2021, then wondered if I had confused him with another. I told Diana about the lost dog and as she is a psychoanalyst, she said to listen: *he dropped the leash*, hmm.

The British government planned to deport asylum seekers to Rwanda this week, regardless of the serious human rights abuses that continue to occur there: repression of free speech, arbitrary detention, ill-treatment, and torture, to send thirty-seven people, from Syria, Albania, Vietnam, Iran, and Iraq. It is policy aimed at those who have entered England through what the government calls 'illegal, dangerous or unnecessary methods', on small boats or hidden in lorries, when they could have claimed asylum in another safe country, such as France. Legal challenges reduced the number of those to be deported to seven men. Two said their phones were taken from them, they were separated, driven to a military base individually in the back of a van, their wrists tied with Velcro straps and guarded by three or four men. One said he panicked; he could not stop himself from crying, and on the plane, a Vietnamese man was biting his tongue so as not to cry out and an Iranian man was weeping. The European Court of Human Rights ruled that one of the men, from Iraq, faced a real risk of irreversible harm if he were sent to Rwanda. The judgement set in motion more legal challenges, and finally, all the passengers were removed, the plane was cancelled minutes before take-off. Undeterred by this setback, the Home Secretary insisted that preparation for the next flight would begin at once. The minister for Justice said the policy was part of a wider package, as though he knew there is no justice in this world. I listened to their wretched reasoning; there was no compassion from those who would implement such a measure, such a 'policy', and it was unthinkable, it should be unthinkable, but it has been thought.

MESSIDOR

While *messidor* is the tenth month of the French revolutionary calendar, the first month of the summer quarter, it is also a period of transition between the style of Louis XVI and the style of the *Directoire*, characterised (I am told) by its painstaking imitation of Antiquity and the importance given to rural and patriotic motifs. The first two days are days of rye and oats, the third is the day of an onion ('the onion?' asked Katharina). On *primidi* we drove to Caen, to the Institut Mémoires de l'édition contemporaine, to visit the exhibition entitled *Singuliers*, a presentation of signs, traces, and textures. The vitrines are arranged according to categories. Under *Tact, chosen object*, is a notebook of Jacques Derrida, without any personal notation yet bearing signs of use, the marking of four pages (at the bottom of each page a quotation from Hölderlin's *Hypérion* is printed; it is a picaresque epistolary novel, the narrator writing from his native Greece to a friend, Bellarmin, who lives in Germany). Under or in *Vide*, it is written that blankness is everywhere, written traces, drawn traces, marks inhabit each page of three notebooks, two drawings, the space of the page as present, as important, as any trace, informing, forming the trace. Then there are: *Folds, modulation of space*; *Simple, a single page* – there is Rousseau, *Doubles*, Rousseau again, and Jean-Luc Nancy and Schopenhauer, and it is for the latter we have come, subject of my son's thesis, his furious scribblings, *gribouillages*, more neglected little things. There is *Traced, drawing-memory*; *Daily, to repeat writing* (I am all for that, for sure); *Saturation*, the horror of the void, more Schopenhauer, and a notebook of Martin Bodmer, the Swiss bibliophile, whose extraordinary collection is accommodated in two neo-baroque houses in Cologny, near Geneva, their cellars now connected by a two-storey underground structure designed by Mario Botta. There is *Obstination, the spectacle of philosophy*, five manuscripts of Philippe Lacoue-Labarthe, whose handwriting is the tiniest, the most meticulous, I have ever seen. There is *Marquetrie, the construction of a diary*, Julije Knifer, the Croatian artist, who painted a single motif, the meander, a serpentine black line on white or white on black from 1960 until his death in 2004, a useless gesture, emptied of all meaning. It was, he said, a point where he arrived at the end, beyond which he could not go, and he told his daughter Ana it was life. There is *Workshop*, the shocking (or explosive) manuscript of Isaac Newton (detested by William Blake, his contempt concealed), from Bodmer's collection, and in *Signs*, the choreography of the written, Henri Michaux, ideograms, an archaic alphabet. I have forgotten some categories and a few names, more than a few, and while I could have found the little booklet accompanying the exhibition, I had misplaced it, and as I had been running up and down three flights of stairs all morning, no. But, yes, there was *Colour*, light!, and that was Goethe, of course, and *Childhood*, freehand, Yann's work from 2006, for which he asked a class of primary school children to copy the grid of a Clairefontaine exercise book designed to teach handwriting, freehand, and then had a thousand five hundred copies printed, on each page, pages seemingly empty, the hesitation, the wavering, the movement of each childish hand visible. I am often jealous of Yann's work, his cleverness. He never says hello to me, never recognises me, even in proximity of the same room, the same group of people. One cannot force friendship. And still, I am made uncomfortable, indeed, I am diminished, when I am unseen by Yann. Increasingly, of course, I am invisible everywhere. This is not self-pity, but fact. That it is fact does not prevent me feeling sorry for myself.

Despite the grounds of the abbey, its lovely courtyard, IMEC does not admit dogs, even small ones, and we took turns to walk the dogs outside and in the Canadian war memorial garden. In June 1944 the German Panzer division occupying the abbey captured eighteen young Canadian soldiers, and in violation of the Geneva Convention, executed them, bludgeoning or shooting them. There were other summary executions. A month later the Canadian Regina Rifle Regiment took back the abbey, enabling the liberation of the left bank of Caen. The news from the war came: Russian investigators had opened more than a thousand cases into 'crimes against peace', 'blood crimes', committed by the Ukrainian government, trials for the fighters, such as those captured at the steelworks in Mariupol. The head of the investigative committee said these were not simple street sweepers, drivers, and cooks, but military commanders. The weather changed as we returned home, the wind rising, and then followed rain.

While I was in London, the village flooded again, but did not reach our house. The mayor had not replied to our letter. Crowbars (for breaking open the drains), waterproofs, boots, torches, were made ready by R. The storm passed and despite my absence, our house survived the night. I saw that Lisa was writing about flooding of the Bievre, the floods brutal and strong, of cruel character, rising in one instance as high as three storeys and drowning a dozen sleepers in their beds, then, oh lord, that her house was flooded, rugs laid out to dry in her garden, a scene I remembered from here. The farmer had once again planted corn in furrows that run in the direction of the path to the village, right up to the edge of the hedgerow, where two trees have died from his deracination. Gianni, who had been an engineer in the Swiss Alps, said the hedgerow planted after the last flood was not adequate, that it would not shore up against disaster. But then again, nothing would, in the end, in the end times.

Onion day, and I took up those white onions that remained, laying them to dry. They were doing splendidly until the chickens got out and scratched them up. Some had a little white rot, caused by a fungus that stays in the soil, though if the first layer was peeled away, they were edible. The red onions seemed fine, as did the shallots, and they would stay in the ground until next week. Then they would be laid out on a wire rack to dry in the attic, the air circulating around them. The onion may be used to treat problems of digestion and loss of appetite, for the heart and blood vessels, for angina and hardening of the arteries. Patricia was operated on last week and news came from Yves: a triple bypass, five hours in the theatre, five days in reanimation due to complications. The worst was over, he hoped, but she was very fragile. Gavin's heart operation is next week. I worked several hours in the garden, cutting back, trimming and pruning, harvesting broad beans and potatoes, rhubarb and the first purple gooseberries (compote and cake, I thought). The dahlia tubers were not doing at all well, not emerging. I was extremely disappointed. The *almanach du facteur*'s trick of the month was how to keep fruit for longer: a cork cut in two and placed in the fruit bowl absorbs the moisture of the fruit, preventing blackening and rot; for red fruits, one should dilute a dozen drops of white vinegar in a little water and dip the fruit – after drying, the fruit can be kept for up to two weeks in the refrigerator. It was the longest day, midsummer; the almanach said it was the day of Saint Rodolphe, the bishop of Gubbio, an ornament of the Church as indicated in my book on Catholic martyrs.

The day of speedwell, *véronique*, is also that of Saint Alban, the first recorded British martyr, scourged and then beheaded. His head rolled down a hill and a well sprang up where it came to rest, miraculous healing water. The veronica in the garden was hidden under the rampant pink Japanese anemones, with which I was ruthless, without pity, unrelenting, tugging them out roughly. I left the white ones. An earthquake struck a mountainous region of Afghanistan while most people were asleep in their beds. Twenty-five villages were destroyed, the unstable houses made of mud or wood collapsed, were buried, entire families died. There was heavy rain. Survivors and rescuers dug out bodies from the rubble. There were bodies wrapped in blankets everywhere. A farmer cried: he had found forty bodies, most of them young, very young, children. A woman said she and her children screamed, her neighbours screamed. Some families had vanished completely. A tea infused from speedwell purifies blood, relieves congestion and coughing and asthma and alleviates the symptoms of lung disease. In his seminar on anxiety, Lacan said that respiration is not cut off, or if it is, it is cut off in a way that does not fail to generate some drama; respiration is rhythmical, respiration is pulsation. Breath: marked by the cut. What is it to be silent, breathless? Silence, to be silenced, might feel like death. In a French hospital the psychoanalyst Catherine Vanier whispered to premature babies throughout the night, speaking them into life through their histories. She insisted the mothers speak to their babies, that they spoke the truth, voicing their fears, concerns, anger, not empty speech, and the voice would allow the transfer from ventilating machine to mother, to world. A voice in the dark... then breathing, in, out, and taking in air, then a cry. We exhale when we speak. Open mouth, framing a body in relation to another, an Other, and there is no speech without breath.

The artist VALIE EXPORT made a work in 2007 in which a laryngoscope was guided through her nose by a doctor, Erhard Suess, assisted by her partner Robert Stockinger. Four monitors displayed her glottis as she spoke. She said that she had hardly formed a sound and already it was gone, leaving its trace in the perception of her voice by the 'others'; that power and powerlessness were compositions of the voice; that her voice was the trace of her individual body as it was that of her social body; that it sewed the parts, the sewing patterns of her ephemeral identities together, but it was not her own. It spoke for itself, she said.

I tried to assemble my thoughts, and this did not allow restful sleep, despite my vigorous activity in the polytunnel in the early evening as rain drizzled endlessly outside: all the tomatoes staked, the earth weeded (my fingernails were still black the next day, despite all the scrubbing that left my fingers raw), basil seedlings planted between the tomatoes, the tiled path swept, and the pepper plants and parsley seedlings taken out to where they were to be transplanted. In the market I bought some plants of a long pepper, *doux des Landes*, from the man I have known for thirty years. The pepper is an old variety with a fine skin from the west of France, where it was selected and protected by the Bernardine Franciscan Sisters. I did not know if it would be hot enough this summer for peppers outside; they had been a miserable failure last year, as were the aubergines, and I longed again to be further south, among vines and olive trees. The Sisters were an order of silence, giving up speech and sight, abstinence of the tongue and the use of the eyes, abstinence from curiosity. They did not look at others, keeping their eyes always on the ground. They wore hoods and capes and never showed their faces, though once a nun lifted her hood during a visit to the convent in 1854 from the Emperor Louis-Napoléon, the last monarch, and the Empress Eugénie, who asked to see her face. The Sisters planted pine trees in the sandy dunes, and the Sisters are buried in the sand in raised tombs that must be constantly remodelled. Each grave is decorated with a line, a cross, of scallop shells. They cultivated the fields, looked after the animals, worked at the forge, made implements in their workshop, embroidered. They could speak in their confession. They could tell the doctor of their ailments. They could speak once a year through a grating, to a family visitor.

Their dowries maintained an institution devoted to the reclaiming of fallen women, penitents. Once, the French government ordered that the Sisters' white hoods should be cut away so the sun might touch their faces (too many of the Sisters were dying, it appears, from the lack of light); the Sisters replaced their old habits, their new hoods and capes were black. The convent housed the polished skull of Mary Magdalene.

Today: the day of the mule, *mulet,* a gentle creature, clever and strong and usually sterile. The mule whinnies like a horse and brays like a donkey, a breathe in *hee* and a breathe out *haw*, but it also whimpers when excited or anxious. When Francis and Florentine lived for a few months in Lecce, he rented a donkey so they could walk in the mountains. It took some effort to find one, but eventually the owner of a riding school was amused by the request, and they collected his donkey. The walk was not a success, for the donkey was reluctant to walk with them at all. Robert Louis Stevenson's donkey Modestine was equally obdurate during his journey from Le Monastier, where he had been recovering from a respiratory illness, to Saint-Jean-du Gard. Modestine cost 65 francs and a glass of brandy; he described her as being not much bigger than a dog, the colour of a mouse, with a kindly eye and a determined underjaw. She refused to climb hills and shed the saddle bags, trembling under their weight. She was on heat and nickered at all the male donkeys they encountered. Bridget reminded me that Stevenson was not always kind to Modestine, that he beat her. In the end, he had to sell her, and they shared their last meal of black bread together, Modestine standing by him in the moonlight and eating out of his hand.

6 *messidor*, *romarin*, rosemary, remembrance: I was surprised to find myself crying as Simon and Garfunkel's

Bridge over troubled water was played on the wireless, a record choice of Rita Tushingham, who described how at night she falls asleep with a crystal clutched tightly in her hand. She once told me to shut up, quite loudly, quite rudely, in Patisserie Valerie in Soho – I had not been aware that my voice was so loud, nor did I know that she was so nasty. Another time, on a bus, a young man (I was young, too and very sad, speaking to my travelling companion about my great unhappiness) leant over me as he passed to descend and savagely remonstrated with me about my compulsion – his word – to share my grief with others. Embarrassment (shame): the loss of one's bearings, judgement. Lacan defined embarrassment as the experience of no longer knowing what to do with oneself, losing everything, being exposed in a radical confrontation with the failure at the heart of being, as being beyond inhibition and impediment.

Today was the *fête* of Saint Jean, of John the Baptist. In the past, fires were lit and there was singing and dancing, the young people jumped over the flames and sometimes there were fireworks. This happens less frequently here, but twenty years ago the next village always had its solstice celebration. In our village we used to have a summer party, but since Marcelle died, we no longer gather as we did. She loved a party, a glass of champagne, even or especially coffee taken together was enough as a mark of friendship in a relation that could at times be trying. *Oh, le café!*, said her granddaughter at her funeral. For a few years each house took it in turn to host a party. The habit has gone, on our part; nonetheless Marion and Benoît persist, and Ronald and Nelly invited everyone five years ago, an evening from which we crept away making a feeble excuse as the quiz he had devised for entertainment unfolded interminably, questions on Racine and Corneille, for example, and on the English monarchy – I drew my hand across my neck, the sign of the guillotine, and Serge caught my eye from across the room, and we laughed.

In Dol market we bought four mackerel, small and silver and fresh, fished last night, to fillet and fry, with a sauce *Bretonne*, egg yolks, a dash of tarragon vinegar, a tablespoon of *fines herbes* – tarragon, chives, chervil, and parsley, melted butter stirred in slowly like making a mayonnaise. It is a sauce that does not coat and must be served in a sauce boat. The fishman has his own boat. There were fine plaice, too, I saw. We bought a straw hat from a man from Senegal, who called R. a good boy and me a good woman, trying to also sell me, the good woman, a basket, which I did not want and did not buy, so I was not such a good woman in the end. It was the day of *concombre*, so there would be a cucumber salad, too, and the saint was Prosper, as I hope we may all. The US Supreme Court voted to overturn the Roe v. Wade ruling, striking it down, eliminating the hard-won constitutional right to abortion. Many states immediately enacted abortion bans and clinics stopped offering the procedure. Everyone knew this was coming, feared it. The path of a woman's life, her control over her own body, is now less free. There will be no exemptions for rape or incest. It is only the beginning of the story, only the start of terrible things to come.

The dogs raced across the marshes, made giddy by the rising wind; we got back to the car as the rain plummetted down, which it continued to do for the rest of the day, heavy showers followed by short intervals of sunshine. I could not face preparing my accounts, so instead cleared out the linen cupboard, making neat stacks, folds to the left, then read Susan's very funny novel with enjoyment and guilty pleasure, until I forced myself to work in the garden, sowing new sorrel and peas, mixed salad leaves, and transplanting parsley. Someone, *someone*, left the gate to the poultry run open

– two hens and a cock took full ebullient advantage of their liberty and I was downhearted. The Aracauna can still fly over the fence – I saw her, yes, with my own eyes – and so her wings must be clipped again, sharp scissors taken to her plumy flight feathers.

In the studio for a brief time, I painted the underwear of women in the last copy that remains of the edition *En toute intimité*. The tones of pink range from the palest nuance to a shade that is almost ochre. The book was for Elizabeth. It is a story of theft, of the kleptomania that is the crime of capital. Of labour, of the means of production. Of women crazy about their body, those 'wanton' women, those mad women. MARCHANDISE. 'In the twelfth century [...], very delicate things often appear among these commodities. Thus a French poet [Guillot de Paris] of the period enumerates among the commodities to be found in the fair of Lendit, alongside clothing, shoes, leather, implements of cultivation, skins, etc.' Of a social relation in the garment's relation to the stuff of which it is made (this may seem obvious, a trivial thing. It is those trifling things, those tiny, exquisite details that are of the greatest importance in the production of value). Use-value, exchange value. Breathless, head thrown back, eyes moist, half-closed, lips parted, the glimpse of a tongue. I have read the text, or extracts of it, with Emma, with Alice, and with Anna, who danced it, choreographed by Laurie. The drawings themselves are framed (the book was an afterthought); Gianni owns one or two. I started to draw a goldfinch after Carel Fabritius – mine will have the head of a woman, and there will be no chain holding it captive on its perch. I remembered that Fabritius was killed in explosion in the Delft gunpowder magazine.

Shallots (now drying on a linen sheet on the floor of the guestroom), absinthe or wormwood (a tiny drop of Louis-

Georges's homemade absinthe remains in its little bottle labelled 'Drink me' and one new year, unwisely, Francis and I did. And Louis-Georges should be more present in this book, I thought, as he is often on my mind), and a *faucille*, a sickle, for harvesting, reaping, cutting forage. *Octidi*, at lunch at John and Julia's, Amaury spoke of the different tones, the varying timbres and characteristics of organs (depending on where they were made). The one he liked playing the most was in Strasbourg, an organ made in Alsace. He has been called back to play in the abbey on Mont St Michel. Once he was a monk and then he fell in love and then he was a monk no longer. We talked about the work of the *souffleur*, who was once a person working a handle up and down, pumping away, and is now more usually a machine of labour, an electrical turbine, compressing air, sending it into the closed system of ducts, the windlines. *Nonidi*, a Russian missile struck a shopping centre in Kremenchuk and *décadi*, the search for survivors continued, volunteers, firemen, police, military personnel shifting through the rubble, laying out corpses in plastic bags. Eighteen bodies had been found so far; twenty-one or thirty-eight people were still missing, but they could be among the bodies found. It was estimated that there were between two hundred and a thousand people in the shopping centre.

In America the overturning of Roe v. Wade opens the move away from federal constitutional rights to the control of the states. Republican senators have questioned Griswold v. Connecticut, which struck down a state ban on contraceptives; Obergefell v. Hodges, which required states to recognise same-sex marriage; and Loving v. Virginia, which invalidated a state anti-miscegenation law. There was new violence. Maréchal once said, in 1788, that to women and kings one must speak in fables. In 1798 he said that to people and to kings, to children and to women, one could only speak in symbols. There are the fictions of the priests, the authority of other men (husbands, fathers, judges); like Jules Michelet, they do not like 'the blind and inescapable "law" of nature represented by the domination of the female principle and the primacy of physical reproduction'. There are stories and there are histories: some are spoken from imaginings and dreams, until only the *souffle*, the breath, remains, something that survived nowhere. I was too angry, too restless, but this has become a constant condition: I rage. There is a legend that a kind goldfinch flew down to pluck the cruel thorns from Christ's crown and a splash of blood stained the bird's head red. Sometimes there is a painting of a goldfinch on the soundboard of a harpsichord; *in life I was silent, in death I sweetly sing.*

Coriander, seeds drying now in the guestroom, and artichoke, and I have written enough about the artichoke elsewhere so this book cannot be that book, rewritten, repetitive – I do not want to echo myself in the way that I echo others, reproducing their words in a new order and timbre. Once I said I spoke as and for others. What grandiose impertinence. The rain persisted and a wet cat, Céleste, sat on my white linen shirt while I typed, leaving grubby traces. I was deferring organising my accounts, totalling profit and loss, thinking about turnover and where the money goes. My father had an answer: he would sing (tunelessly, he could never hold a tune despite his love of music) that *money talks, I can't deny, I heard it once, it said goodbye.* Some sixty euros waved gaily at me this morning as I paid Ricardo, the lovely Spanish vet, for giving Ida her annual vaccination, squeezing out her anal glands (I cannot, I just can't), and snipping fur from inside her ears, and for shaving the matted fur from Bevis, also checking his heart and kidneys. Indeed, he deserved more money than this, as Bevis had to be wrapped in a towel and held down by three people. Every day I washed Bevis gently with a face flannel, like a cat's tongue, as I used to do for kittens severed too early from their mothers. For motherless ducklings, one must rub them with a silk cloth to stimulate their preen glands. Once, Bevis, after whom the cat is named, sat patiently at the desk in R.'s studio with a duckling in his lap, caressing it with a silk handkerchief.

Raining, cold. A fire lit on 1 July, 12 *messidor*, and I was beset by obstacles. Rosa wrote to Hans Diefenbach that she felt like a frozen bumblebee, in March 1917, and that she would lie down next to the frozen bee and warm it with the breath from her mouth, bringing it to life. She was reading, no, re-reading some novels, if one might call them so but she thought not, of Gottfried Keller, and she thought they were old tales of long-gone dead people and things except perhaps for *Der grüne Heinrich*, which I have not read despite my best intention. W.G. Sebald set out from Fribourg (to Manchester) with *Green Henry* in his suitcase, along with Robert Walser's *Jakob von Gunten*, a disintegrating copy, which I have read but almost forgotten (how may I write a memoir if I am without memory?). Walter Benjamin wrote that Walser's characters came from insanity and nowhere else, leaving madness behind them, heartrendingly inhuman and superficial, or something like this, I half-remember, and then, that Walser wrote about ash, and that if one blows on it – and this is one of the interesting things about ash – it does not fly off in all directions; it is wretched, submissive, helpless, impotent, worthless, and so on. And yet, wood ash is very good for the garden, for chives, garlic, leeks, and lettuces (though very bad for parsley and asparagus and can lead to scab on potatoes), and my fire will help the soil tomorrow morning. Edwina used to hold her fallen frozen bees in the palm of her hand, though she knew she should not.

Oh, my almanach, oh my calendar, I will return to you, she

said, being far from her ground, the *terroir* of which she was not native but nonetheless felt rooted there, sometimes tied down by the twisting and constant demands of animals and plants, the necessity of care. She was away again in London, then in Hastings, where her mother was suddenly in hospital, because of a fall, a break, one that echoed her own, a shadow of her own shattering. For the first time she was alone in her mother's house, a house in which she had no belonging, no belongings. She had to imagine her mother's life and that caused her to imagine how her own would be if she reached her nineties. She understood more now about what it is to be unable to move, to tremble, to be locked in fear, when each step must be considered before ventured. The fall, she thought, the unexpected slipping or sliding, not a leap, not at all, no joyous bound once possible. Though actually, of course, her mother had never been very keen on walking, simply the means to get her from one place to another rather than a pleasurable activity, to reach a chair, inside or outside, and to sit reading or talking, not leaping up, for instance, to pull up bindweed strangling a rose or to snip off a dead rose or to gently blow away the tiny black or greenish-bronze pollen beetles inhabiting the canopy of a rose, preferring those with yellow, white, or pink flowers. The beetles come inside the house on the flowers, if not shaken or tapped out of the blooms, then crawl towards the light of the window. The roses can be protected by encasing them in muslin bags or old nylon tights, but she did not feel it was worth the effort this would require. Late one evening, putting out food for the foxes, she recalled a line from a poem by Barbara Guest: *you go in your orphan feet / crossing the tiles.* And so she did.

What have I missed? I have missed currants and hairy vetchling. I have missed cherries and a park, which can also be an enclosure. I have missed mint and cumin. I have missed the haricot bean, though this morning I picked a colander full of them, thin and green, snappy-skinned. I have missed alkanna, the dyer's plant, guinea fowl (delicious roast with *vin santo* and grapes, rubbed with garlic and rosemary or sage). I have not missed sage (very good with potatoes and cream, baked, then parmesan added towards to end, uncovered to brown), and I bought fifty leek plants, to put in the ground later, making a hole with a dibble, inserting each leek, then watering them in. The ground was very dry on my return. I picked the first courgettes, and there will be cucumbers soon, far too many, so bread and butter pickles call. I have missed the explanation of why one must never cut dressed salad with a knife. Of the saints, I have missed Florent, Antoine-Marie, Marietta, Raoul, Thibaut, Amandine, Ulrich, Benoît, Olivier, Henri or Joël. Today was the *fête nationale* and soldiers, firemen, police, gathered in Dinan for a procession with the fanfare. There will be fireworks in the town, the village, on Saturday and a *bal Populaire*. There were fireworks last night – a rehearsal? – and Hera trembled and panted, crawling onto my lap. She could not settle. The sounds were distant (I could barely hear the bangs, the explosions, no more than tiny echoing thuds), but she was acutely sensitive to them. The British prime minister, a rogue, a liar, resigned at last, without grace, without remorse, and a pack of scoundrels followed baying in his wake, proclaiming their integrity and right to power. A woman who survived trafficking was targeted for removal to Rwanda, forcing her to leave against her will instead of offering her protection. The detention centre that holds her does not provide legal advice to its detainees. Forty people received a notice of intent to remove them to Rwanda – most of them survivors of torture and trafficking. This unpleasant land, mine, not mine. Shame. Guilt.

Since January these women have died in the old people's home in the town, which looks on to the cemetery, *et in arcadia ego*: Hélène, Paule, Marie, Jane, Angelina, Yvette, and Ada. Unlike the newspaper, the commune's magazine did not give their age. When I visited Marcelle in the home during her brief sojourn, I always found her slumped back on her bed; I tried to get her to sit up, to return to herself, I more distressed than she, but her self was gone. I would take the kitten to see her, or rather, for her to see the kitten, and that was something that brought her back into the world for a moment: the touch of white fur, a pink nose. My mother went to hospital last week, the day before I left France, but I think I have reported this, yes, I repeat myself or one like myself for the moment. She is immobile and – tested positive for Covid, though she was not told why she was being moved until she asked, insisted – now has a side room to herself, where she is no longer obliged to tolerate the woman who constantly asks for news of her cat, calling excuse me, excuse me, and who at night complains that my mother's reading light shines into her eyes. Neither body nor pain can be controlled, any more than one may control oneself, but bodies are the continuation of self, both spirit and flesh, in pain and in patience, particular, individuated. The redcurrants must be picked and turned into jelly.

I became sixty-seven, ah yes, overnight, *septidi*, garlic, Saint Donald, but in England, Saint Swithin, and if it were to rain on this day, it would rain for forty days, but it is relentlessly hot. Fires broke out in the Gironde, red weather warnings were issued. The animals lay flat on the tiled floor, in the cool of the kitchen. I closed the doors, lay down myself. Even the evenings were hot, continued to be hot, despite a little breeze, a soft warm current of air. I was on my own, and could eat what and when I liked, sleep under a single cotton patchwork quilt. Tare is followed by wheat; the wheat is running out because of droughts and heatwaves and wars. The Russian Army stole the grain from territories they had seized, the Ukrainians said. The Russians denied it. Grain exports were blocked. The Black Sea ports were closed. Then today *chalémie*, shawn, which I read as calumny, but no, it is but a musical instrument, one with a double-reed, like an oboe, *hautbois*, with a conical flaring wooden body, called a *pirouette*. It has a bright soft tone. Reed is *calamus* in Latin, and *chalémie* has nothing to do with false witness, misrepresentation, vilification, unlike those bidding for the leadership of the Conservative Party whose debate I heard.

On Saturday night the fireworks started again; Hera clung to me, again panting and trembling, continuing even after the display ended. Her entire body shook and shivered, and I could not calm her. Time flickered back and forth, the problem when I did not write every day, faithfully, consistently, and often words failed me even when I did settle to the page, to the daily entry, the account of this and that. I was reading Georges Perec's *Lieux*, a birthday present from my son. Perec described it as a monstrous idea, nonetheless exhilarating. He chose twelve places in Paris, streets, squares, crossroads, linked to memories, events, the important moments in his life. Each month, he described two of these places: the first time, in a café or in the street, in a neutral way, listing shops, architectural details, micro-events; the second time, anywhere, at home, at the café, at the office, he describes the place of memory, evoking the memories linked to it, the people he knew there. He did not have any clear idea of the result when he started, but he wrote to Maurice Nadeau that he knew that lost time, the time he gave to this project, was both its structure and its constraint. It was not a restitution, but a measure of the flow of time, of the time of writing, which for him until now had been a dead time, a time for nothing.

THERMIDOR

Primidi, the first day of *thermidor*, the eleventh month, a day of einkorn wheat or spelt. There is a quick bread that can be made in a matter of two hours with spelt flour, lot of grains (sesame, linseed, pumpkin, sunflower), dried yeast, no kneading; spelt reacts quickly with yeast. Originally Fabre d'Églantine was going to name the month *fervidor*, from burning, then named it instead from *thermon*, the heat of a Greek summer. Trotsky used *Thermidor* as metaphor and analogy. I intended to read Albert Mathiez again, for his Marxist interpretation of the Revolution, his admiration of Robespierre, on the parallels he drew between the Jacobinism in power between 1793 to 1794 and Bolshevism, but it was too hot, far too hot, fervid indeed. In the speech Trotsky made in his defence to the Central Control Commission in 1927, he said – and it is a long extract that follows, with two gestures made by the speaker, waving his hands up and down:

> During the Great French Revolution many were guillotined. We too had many people brought before the firing squad. But in the Great French Revolution there were two great chapters, of which one went like this (*points upwards*) and the other like that (*points downwards*). We must understand this. When the chapter headed like this – upwards (*points upwards*) – the French Jacobins, the Bolsheviks of that time, guillotined the Royalists and Girondists [...] And then there began another chapter in France, when the French Ustrialovs and semi-Ustrialovs – the Thermidorians and the Bonapartists from among the Right-wing Jacobins – began exiling and shooting the Left Jacobins – the Bolsheviks of that time. I should like comrade Sol'c to think this analogy through to the end and, first of all, to give himself an answer to the following question: in accordance with which chapter is Sol'c preparing to have us shot? ... When we did the shooting, we were firm in our knowledge as to the chapter. But comrade Sol'c, do you clearly understand in accordance with which chapter you are now preparing to shoot?

One must always think through an analogy to the end, especially to the end times. I found a tick embedded in my arm, a tiny nasty thing, the size of a pinhead, no larger, and I extracted it with great care, noting its legs wriggling and hoping I had removed the foul head. Despite the heat I managed to transplant turnips and kohlrabi, parsley and dill, and move some romaine lettuces though I doubted they would survive the transfer, and then the sky went dark and there was thunder and rain, but not enough rain, I feared, and so I withdrew to the house, languid, listless, head aching, for the afternoon. The lettuces were completely flat by the evening, and the turnips fared little better. I still had hopes for the kohlrabi and parsley. The wet bandanas I tied around the dogs' necks to cool them down seemed only to irritate them and they discarded them quickly. This morning there was an enormous dead rat on the kitchen floor. Gingerly I picked it up by the tip of its tail and slung it out from the back door across the road into the field. When I opened the front door, which some would consider to be the back door, into the courtyard I found a smaller dead rat, whose corpse I also disposed of in similar fashion. I wondered if they were related, part of a greater rodent family, the one that proliferates under the hanger where we keep the straw for the poultry; mother and child, dead and divided. Occasionally we trap them in humane traps and release them in the forest, where they must take their chances, but sometimes we are reduced to poisoning them, though it is not without sadness.

Duodi, the day of common mullein or *bouillon blanc, verbascum thapsus*, which is poisonous to fish but may be used to treat coughs and tonsilitis, bronchitis, chills and fevers, swine flu, migraines, gout, colic, hoarseness. Its oil, extracted from leaves or flowers, is a remedy for earache and eczema, but it produces a sensitive skin reaction, an irritation, in some people. It is good for getting rid of ear mites in dogs and cats, too tiny to see but producing a dark crusty substance made of dirt and wax and the secretions of the mites. The tick bite on my arm was itching, reddened, but this might have been due to my scratching at it, imaging its head still to be embedded. I dreamt last night that we had another storey on our house, one with four rooms, which I recognised from the house in the country in which I lived for two unhappy adolescent years until I ran away from home. In one room there was a wasp nest by the door, and I put my foot through it. The wasps stung me around my neck in a circle and I woke up scouring at it as though it were real, so now I had an unattractive necklace of abraded skin. On my other arm I had a raised rash from nettles. Itchy welts.

Anna replied to say she would be happy to sing at the launch of my book in Berlin in September, Brecht/Weill's *September Song*. She wrote from Siena, where she had a premiere that night. She was singing from *Porgy and Bess*, 'Summertime'? the programme did not say, only 'ballad', then Ada Gentile's *Come il ricordo* and Marcello Panni's *L'eco dell'eco*. The echo of an echo. I am that, was that, will be that. Saint Catherine of Siena ate the filth of the sick for whom she cared, as did other women saints. She ate the eucharist, bitter herbs, cold water, spat out food or vomited it after swallowing, taking it in to let it out. No extrojection without introjection. She drank no wine herself but miraculously, could fill a cask for others to enjoy. She told her biographer that she had never tasted anything sweeter than the pus from the putrefying breast of a dying woman. In a vision she drank from the wound in Christ's side, where she slaked her thirst. There, she said, she found such sweetness and such knowledge of the Divinity that it was a wonder her heart did not break, that it was a wonder how she was able to continue to live in her body with such an excess of ardour and love. To eat and to hunger had the same meaning for her, both were painful, both were joyful; she was nourished by fatigues of the body and anguishes of desire, the sources of salvation. *The living is easy, the fish are jumping, the cotton is high, and one of these mornings you are going to rise up singing, you are going to spread your wings, and you will take to the sky.*

Saint Victor, and then Marie-Madeleine, honeydew melon and rye grass. The rye planted in the field across the road was gathered and baled, six nice round bales. Last year the young farmer leasing the land from the chateau planted hemp, but it was not a success. When Paul was still a farmer, he brought me a round bale of straw one year and it seemed to last forever, its centre rotting slowly and heating up, steaming. I found a farmer near Rennes who makes small rectangular bales and Francis crammed a dozen in the car at Christmas. A ceasefire was announced to allow cargo ships to collect stranded grain from Ukrainian ports on the Black Sea. No merchant or civilian vessels will be attacked, nor port facilities. The time was running out if the harvest of last year were not to start to rot. Hélène and Jerôme have opened their restaurant at their market garden. Patrice knows the cook, Caroline. I ate some of her snacks at Marie and Sophie's opening at the Mediathèque last Friday, an exhibition of their wolves, gouaches and sculptures, which presented another world. Patrice suggested we all eat together at the restaurant soon when he called by to bring me a bundle of fifty leeks from Dinan market, though I knew we never would unless I were to arrange it and I knew that I would not. I made him Lebanese coffee with cardamon, showed him how to plant his own leeks (with the dibber!), gave him three pots of jam, a barba di frati lettuce, which he persisted in calling rocket no matter how many times I told him it was not, two fat golden courgettes, and six fine eggs of various colours from dark brown to light blue, which I felt he should have admired a great deal more than he did.

How diligent I have been, how I have laboured. The painting of R.'s old studio is done, and it remains only to sand and oil the floor. Gareth messaged to say he would visit after all at the end of August and build bookshelves in the old studio in return for his stay. His new book of poems has just been published, poems about woodworking, labour, craft, autism, including a glossary of woodworking terms, turning wood and words. I edited Allie's lovely essay, which moves from girl to showgirl to goddess: the goddess says yes to things that please her and no to the things that bore her. Quite right too, I thought, but with regretful recognition that I would never be a goddess.

I have never been good at saying no. I have two essays for publications to write and not a single good idea. Tony's invitation to make a booklet for his Piece of Paper press lies in front of me and I had a glimmer of an idea, I did have an idea, and if I said it often enough one would come, a simple writing spell, most effective when uttered shortly before a deadline. I painted an iron garden table and three chairs in arsenic green, and the dogs acquired green smudges. I found another tick, this time behind my knee. In the garden the last of the gooseberries were picked and the bushes pruned, though I did not achieve the desired goblet shape. When I moved on to getting rid of the suckers from the base of the fig tree, something stung me – painfully – on my arse through my overalls, and then I felt enough was enough for the day.

A ram and Saint Brigitte, who is a saint of little interest. John the Baptist carries a lamb, of course, its gender unspecified. I thought of the painting by Hans Memling in the National Gallery in London, the saint extending his right forefinger as though to tickle the lamb under its furry chin. The lamb has a slight smile. There is a small collection of sheep figures on the shelves above the child's day bed, once Francis's and other small children have slept there since he outgrew it, and behind the stove in the library, more lambs of God. *Agnus dei*, who takes away the sins of the world, the lamb with a red pennant with a white cross (or is it the other way round?), have mercy upon us. The shallots, harvested last month, were dry enough to tie in little bundles with red jute twine. The coriander seeds were stripped from their stems, as were the dill seeds. These were pleasant hours to spend calmly in the courtyard, shaded by a nice parasol. Copies of my book *Abécédaire* arrived in the post and on opening it, I found two errors, neither of them mine; I felt churlish after I pointed them out to Susan, also mentioning the rather disappointing quality of image reproduction. Elijah said the book would sell like hotcakes in Berlin, something I rather doubted. I booked three restaurants for our visit to England next month, which would be our first (and only) holiday for three years, since we visited Francis and Florentine in Lecce and ate one evening at Le Zie, where the *signora* cooks and her name is simply *la signora*, spoken with hushed deference and reverence. Francis asked if he could see the *signora* in action and was called into the kitchen to the envy of other diners, *dove si trova il ragazzo che vuole vedere la signora cuoca*. It was one of the nicest meals I have ever had: little fritters (which *la signora* demonstrated to Francis in the kitchen), finely sliced carrots in oil and vinegar (surprisingly delicious), a bean purée with wild chicory, stewed octopus, and I forget... pasta, lamb with potatoes. One had to ring the doorbell to enter. Ah, said the waitress, *siete Francesco che telefona per prenotare un tavolo*. She hovered about him, clearly very taken with the handsome foreign boy who spoke such good Italian.

I thought about the meals for next week, to keep simple, to use what is growing here. I waste nothing. I noted that the tomatoes were beginning to ripen, and thought of *panzanella*, the tomatoes crushed with good bread, with good olive oil and salt, perhaps some anchovies, some basil. The mystics tasted the body of God, and they were astonished by it. The sacrament is flesh and blood, it is bread and wine, it is a body and the church. Once Francis and my godson Émile did not swallow the host but returned to the pew, hiding the discs in the palms of their hands. Furtive and sniggering, they unfurled their hands to show me. Isn't there a story by Graham Greene in which a man asks a boy to steal a communion wafer for him and the boy refuses and the man cries?

Last night I woke with the sudden thought that the ballad Anna sang from *Porgy and Bess* was in fact 'Bess, you is my woman now'. But rather, I think, it was a medley made up of themes from Gershwin's musical. The Quantum Ensemble played this, violin, clarinet, and piano. This morning, this day, Saint Christine and horsetail, *prêle*, or snake grass or puzzle-grass, which stops bleeding, heals wounds and ulcers, and is a living fossil. It enhances bone and skin and hair. Despite the qualities of horsetail, it is a pernicious invasive weed, spreading deep underground from neighbouring properties or land. I walked to the village market with the dogs this morning to buy oranges, plums, lemons, radishes, aubergines, and carrots. I tripped over a tree root when returning and fell flat on my face. The dogs were quite anxious, hovering over and licking me, then rushing away and back. Mostly I felt foolish, but I also realised how easy it is to have an accident, so stupid. I lay there for a while thinking this. The horrible *guardien* of the chateau has barricaded the path that leads to our village; already he prevented the descent to the chateau grounds when the path is flooded, installing plastic chains and several notices of private property which Rosie and I continue to ignore, for property is theft, as Proudhon says, not Marx. The footpath has been subtracted from the commons, from productive use by others, the walkers, the ramblers, or those, like me, without a car, taking a quicker route to the *bourg*. The footpath is common land, and we have been denied our right to pass. Pierre-Joseph Proudhon was the son of a peasant family, self-educated, anarchist *par excellence*, and he wrote that property was not only theft, but despotism. This is not the argument I would use when I go into the *mairie* next week to complain about it. Probably I would not cite Marx either, but of course I could.

Raoul Peck's film *Le Jeune Karl Marx* opens with the massacre of peasants collecting wood in the forest, presenting a primal scene of the philosophy of Marx. In the vote for the title of law, 'even the pilfering of fallen wood or the gathering of dry wood is included under the heading of theft and punished as severely as the stealing of live growing timber'. Marx commented: 'It would be impossible to find a more elegant and at the same time a simpler method of making the right of human beings give way to that of young trees.' He argued that the gathering of fallen wood and the theft of wood are quite different matters. Growing timber must be separated from its organic association in order to appropriate it, which is an outrage against the tree and thus also against the owner of the tree. However, in the case of fallen wood, nothing has been separated from property, for the wood is already apart from property as the owner of the tree possesses only the tree and the tree no longer possesses the branches that have fallen from it: 'The wood thief pronounces on his own authority a sentence on property.' Once I made an exhibition founded on Marx's articles, and several commentaries thereon, in particular Daniel Bensaïd's book *Les dépossédés*. There was a forest scene. There were animals. There were stuffed animals liberated from the branches on which they had been fixed. The dead came alive. Collectively, the animals of the forest rose up with an instinctive sense of right, gathering the alms of nature, their roots positive and legitimate. They resisted that their customary rights should become the monopoly of the rich. They assembled and asserted their rights. They owned nothing but themselves.

Days of mugwort, safflower, and yesterday, blackberries, growing behind the polytunnel, where when weeding I found a flat dry dead thing, a chicken, it seemed, though we had not lost one, I thought, until much later, months later, I realised it was one of the black hens and felt very bad that I had not noticed her absence. Today the tool of the calendar was a watering can, and I arranged mine on the terrace outside the old studio we were renovating. I stood back to admire them, a fondly foolish expression on my face. Today marks six months of war in Ukraine, and I read in the newspaper about a woman who was selling flowers and wondered who was buying them and what the flowers were.

There was another dead mouse in the library, or rather, its head and some internal organs, rejected. I tried to write about Robespierre for Tony's pamphlet, and managed only a hundred words, most of them existing elsewhere already. I wanted to write about him as though he were alive, elegant, dapper in his sky-blue silk coat, his shoes with silver buckles, feathers in his hat and flowers in his hand, walking with his dog Brount, but he, like his brother, like Saint Just, like Couthon, was killed on this day, *10 Thermidor*, *décadi*, to be buried in a common grave. He knew how to knit and to sew. Two of the cats, Nana and Aristide, who usually did not, came onto the bed before dawn, settling themselves respectively on my stomach and legs, purring quietly. Lenin called Rosa's cat Mimi a majestic animal, saying she was a magnificent creature whose like he had seen only in Siberia. Mimi snarled like a tiger when he tried to approach her, whacking him with her paw. Rosa said she liked looking at Lenin's ugly mug. Mathilde Jacob sent Rosa a photograph of Mimi, which made her laugh, for the image had caught her perfectly. She asked Mathilde to kiss Mimi on her little eyes. She hoped Mathilde would be a good educative influence on Mimi. She made the brave decision not to bring Mimi to prison with her, for the little animal was accustomed to gaiety, so happy when Rosa sang to her, when she played hide and seek with her across the apartment or caught the light through a prism, the cat pouncing on the rainbow arcs. In March 1917, she told Mathilde that tulips, hyacinths, and violets were flourishing. She felt that she was not a real writer for she never found writing easy; she wanted to convey the living spirit.

The candidates for leadership of the Tory party tried to outdo each other on who would be the toughest to crack down on migration, one promising more schemes with African countries, like that with Rwanda, the other detention in cruise ships off the coast of England; both would limit the numbers of refugees. One would not be cowed, she said, by the European convention of human rights. The other said he would do whatever it took, that no option should be off the table. They were, they are, grotesque.

NOTES FROM FOUR DAYS AWAY

Arrosoir, watering can. My watering cans were once again lined up on the terrace of the old studio, which is almost finished. They had an order, and it was disrupted. I bit my lip. Waxing and polishing the sanded pine floor. Lunch at Bistrot Boris, mussels. Panic grass: it takes its name from the Latin, *panus*, a swelling. Christian showed me a drawing by Jean-Jacques Lequeu, an architect who never designed a building but drew buildings and bodies, who drew from his library. Christian said Lequeu's buildings are bodies and his bodies are architecture, an architecture of cavities, doors, corners, curtains, that he was a builder of fantasies: a woman's breasts swell from her bodice as she draws back her wimple to reveal them and the cloth bunched in her right hand has the form of a phallus. The drawing is entitled something like: *for we too, we will be mothers, for...* and the drawing was made in 1793 or 94, in the reign of Terror, prompt, severe, inflexible justice. *Salicorne*, glasswort, or samphire or sea asparagus, which I used to collect on the banks of the Rance. The water is too polluted now. Another dead rat, this time in the library. A sick hen. Apricots, a slightly burnt onion and tomato tart, forgotten for a moment, then too late, as my sister telephoned to tell me our mother had fallen from her hospital bed. A picnic by the Blavet, where a train passed on the railway bridge overhead, with all the travellers waving, and we all waved back self-consciously. Some aquatic plants from Julia for the new pond: water lettuce, *pistia*, a kind of fine grass with a white flower. A bottle of perry made in Lamballe from John. Arguments over supper: the usual things. A cat with worms – again. Basil. The first shipload of grain left Odessa. The weather was overcast. I sat in the courtyard talking after breakfast with Julie, who arrived last Friday, until mid-morning. I clipped Ida's fur, trimming carefully around her eyes and muzzle with a small pair of embroidery scissors that look like a bird, then bathing her. She became silky and resembled her younger self once again, like a little sheep, my darling lambkin girl. In the night she cried to go into the room where Julie was sleeping. The sick hen was despatched. I wondered if these notes would become anything other, but no, they would remain like this; what might be said in favour of the sketchy, the fragment, the incomplete, the outline. More arguing. I re-read the little book I did with Fabienne, what, five, six years ago, a month of exchanges about our reading, our writing, our interruptions, desired and undesirable. Therein I cited Jacques Rancière writing that for the workers of the 1830s it was not a question of demanding the impossible but of realising the impossible themselves, and that the workers withdrew from the forms which domination imprinted on their bodies and imposed on their actions. Adrian and Denis once wondered if they would have a garden like mine or one like Jacques's, with just a few well-placed shrubs – have I written that already? Jacques's workers, real people, not figures, are (and I remember this exactly, I think) 'perverted proletarians whose discourse is made up of borrowed words'. I loved that then and I love it now. I know this to be me. I borrow even from myself.

Back at my desk, in a warm study, some small breeze, the little currents of air bringing in odours from the courtyard, the kitchen, and I imagined that Simon had written about the breeze, but he had not. Was I thinking about breath? About the trauma of breath, inhalation, then exhalation, blowing... in and out, in and out. I thought of Laura writing that *every breath is born out of, and returns to, stillness*. Currents and ripples. The day is that of the ewe, lovely female sheep, and when my son was very small, he was delighted with his red boots lined with – and he would pause, breathless, lowering his voice to whisper in awe – *real sheep fur*, and also the day of Saint Julien. Julien telephoned to say he had administrative problems and so – and he spoke charmingly in English – he had spoiled time and so the new steps for the old new studio, which had been mine, would be delayed. Time is often spoilt. There are over thirty Saint Juliens, thirteen of them unknown. On this saint day, whichever Julien, though it may be Julien *l'hospitalier*, the summer catches fire or comes to its end, *s'enflamme où touche a sa fin*. There are no apples on our trees and the leaves are burnt, falling as though it is autumn. The hydrangeas were suffering and last night I started to cut off the dry and brown flowerheads. The hot weather continued although rain is predicted for Thursday. There was a ban on watering; potagers may only be watered between 8 o'clock at night and 10 o'clock in the morning. Private swimming pools may not be filled, and I did not give a fig about that. Flaubert tells the legend of Saint Julien in *Trois Contes,* the saint who killed a mouse and strangled a pigeon, then killed, massacred, a valley of deer, and was cursed by the stag, condemning Julien to kill his own parents, his parents who doted upon him. They lived in a château in the middle of a forest. And it is such an Oedipal myth, for he killed his parents, mistaking his father for his wife's lover, his mother for his wife, striking them with a dagger as they lay in bed, piercing their breasts, and there was blood on their white skin, on the bed clothes and the floor, and trickling down an ivory crucifix, and the murder was seen by his wife at the door, whom he took to be a phantom until she fled in horror. He ceded everything to his wife and after the burial of his parents, he left, ceasing to exist, taking the road to the mountains, wandering the world but shunning company, as he was repulsed everywhere – all fled from him, the horses in the fields, the birds in their nests, the insects on the flowers. Each night the murder of his parents began again in his dreams. He saw his reflection in a river and thought it was his father. A leper came to Julien's hut, to whom he gave his bread, his wine, his candlelight, his bed, and the leper told him to take off his clothes so he might have the warmth of Julien's body. The leper demanded that Julien stretch completely over him, mouth to mouth, chest to chest. The leper's eyes became as bright as stars, his breath as sweet as roses, his hair like rays of sunlight, and Julien was ecstatic. Clasped in the arms of the leper, who grew taller and taller, he rose to the blue sky, face to face with Christ, who carried him to heaven. Anyway, said Flaubert, that was the way the stained-glass windows in his church told it. Our Julien's father, an *ancien militaire*, has razed all the shrubs surrounding his neo-Breton house, so no-one can hide in the bushes.

When friends are staying, I cannot write, even to snatch at a few words here and there, oh lord, give me the economy of the poet rather than my tendency towards verbosity and constant embellishment. There is always too much to do, passing from breakfast to lunch to drinks to dinner to the next day and the next, with entertainment thrown in, including anxiety, anger, and raised voices as R. forgets increasingly, failing to register what has been said or done, asking the same question repeatedly, experiencing deepening confusion, unable to organise, withdrawing, holding his head in hands, pressing his hands over his ears. He had lost one of his hearing aids, but anyway he was refusing to wear them and when he did, did not insert them correctly. There were the days of marshmallow root, flax, almonds, gentians, and a lock, all untold, passing by along with the saints Lydie, Abel, and Gaëtan (also the name of a child who had watermelon for the first time on the beach with us many years ago) on Sunday, preceded by a Saturday of Transfiguration, when Christ took Peter, John, and James up on a mountain, where Moses and Elijah appeared and Christ's clothes became dazzling white, whiter than any Fuller's earth could bleach them. They were exalted, glorified.

In a *vide-grenier* I bought an Anglepoise lamp, two bronze Cupid curtain hooks, a *terre de fer* plate with pink thistles, a book entitled *Hystérique*, published in the magnificently named series *Déséquilibres de l'amour*. If I ever have another press, that will be its name, I told Arnaud when he remarked upon it joyfully. Today, Saint Dominique and the carline thistle, spiney and cottony, its flowers opening in dry weather, rich in nectar and beloved by bees. It is an emetic, purgative; pungent and bitter, warm and aromatic, it may be used to treat hysteria, venomous bites, including those of a rabid dog, dropsy, poison, nausea, the pain of hypochondria; it kills worms. Once Wenjue gave me a box of thistle tea she bought in Scotland. I have not seen her for a long time; she continues her work with the Chinese prostitutes in Paris, while in her work assuming audacious roles in the skin of others, in the pleasure of others or of herself, photographing herself in the moment of orgasm, in her *jouissance* or *douceur exquise*. I planted Savoy cabbages early in the day, then spoke with two young women online about the history of some public galleries in Cambridge in the 1980s, which they are researching – there will be a live discussion in October, and three old friends will also speak, and I will be obliged to think more carefully about the rash assertions and gossipy remarks I made this morning. History was catching up with me; history overtakes me.

Who died when I was not on duty? These women, all over eighty and some had reached their hundredth year or more (their great age my only rule for their listing) have died: Gil, *artiste peintre*, Blandine, *veuve*, Marie-Thérèse, *veuve*, Amélia, *veuve*, Emma, Fernande, Marguerite, Lucienne, Marie or 'Mimi', Annick, Marie-Léa, Yvonne, Valentine, Danielle, Marcelle... for each who has died, a list of those who have survived them follows their appearance in death. The dead pile up, spread out, and nothing was more real than their bodies. Marguerite Duras said, I think, that writing was the only thing stronger than her mother, whose madness was not her illness but her health. Writing was like weeping, she said. I spoke with my mother on the telephone; she said in hospital there was nothing to do, that nothing happened, that she was bored, that there was nothing to say. I replied that I had quite a lot to say, to tell, but she did not want to hear me and suggested I might wish not to call her every day.

Amour, *duodi* of the second decade, and the caper, and while I had 'goldfinch' noted in my diary, that bird would have to wait as I got all my ducks in a row in preparation for travel and made the last of the peaches from the field into jam, adding basil when putting the fragrant golden mass into jars. Sometimes everything has to wait, not least the poor people in England who have no dentist and are reduced to sticking in dentures with Superglue or performing their own extractions. As food, energy, and fuel costs rise, people are cutting back on food and other essentials; in winter, they will take refuge in warm libraries, it was suggested, assuming, of course, that they can find a library, as over eight hundred were closed in the last decade, a quiet disappearance of a resource that was targeted as disposable by the government. I read a poem by Fanny Howe: her enemy, she wrote, kept a bowl of anemones on her bedside table, a cruelty that killed her will to perform the duties of an invalid. The first *her* here was the enemy, the second and third, the poet. How difficult pronouns are. I wrote about Robespierre's coat at last, and the many portraits of himself with which he surrounded himself – and see, there is more trouble with reflexive pronouns, as is any reference to person or thing, returning one to oneself, marking the unusual and the different, the personal and the solitary. Then there were the reciprocal pronouns to consider, but the courgettes were waiting to be stuffed, with onion, garlic, tomato, rice, parmesan, and mint, and there were thin green beans to prepare, to be eaten with crisp fried capers and garlic, so my foray of thought on grammar ended for the day, the day of love. And slices of cold watermelon for dessert, I thought.

In this last *décadi*, I caught up with lentils, the yellow starwort, and today, the otter, but my catching up was no more than to think of the days, wrestling my writing into the shape of an A4 sheet for Piece of Paper press, simultaneously forming words and text boxes to fit them, such a stupid way to write. Therein I emerged, somewhat to my surprise, as the older daughter of the family with whom Robespierre lodged, a woman who with her sister lay weeping on the floor of their house as buckets of animal blood were hurled against the door by the mob when Robespierre went to his execution. His devoted dog, who lay under his writing table at night while the incorruptible worked, may have been a Great Dane. Of course, it was not the Great Dane who knocked over poor Rousseau on rue Ménilmontant on one of his solitary promenades, leaving him with his face bruised, rather than in the mortal danger reported in the *Courrier d'Avignon*, which deplored his fate of being crushed by the huge dog, rushing at full tilt. Montaigne was once knocked unconscious by a charging animal, a horse ridden by a groom, which came down upon him like a colossus. Rousseau examined his injuries on his return home, a split upper lip, a swollen lip and jaw, a sprained right thumb, his left thumb injured, and his left arm and knee sprained and very swollen. His attitude to his injuries was different from Montaigne's, though he appropriated, if that is the correct word, some of the content of Montaigne's essay 'On Practice' to reflect on the implications of his experience. For Montaigne, the *bouleversement* was close to death, while Rousseau was quite the brave little soldier about the incident. I have become as stoic as Rousseau, even though my right ankle continues to be painful and swollen. I cut back the grapevine on the terrace, and vigorously pruned and cut back plants in the adjoining bed, entangled two of the clematis in pots, mourning the loss of a third, likewise the loss of a camelia, though, ever optimistic, I left its roots in place, for who know what might rise again. From the garden, the first new chard, tiny leaves, for pasta, with garlic and ricotta, beets for a hummus, and cucumbers with onions salted and brined for bread and butter pickles. On the news, the broadcaster referred to the woman candidate for the Tory leadership by her first name, to the man, by his surname. Both bastards, I muttered, both swine. I lost my new cane, my lovely alpenstock.

Everywhere but in *my* garden, I see 'Pierre de Ronsard' roses blooming splendidly. My own languishes. My cucumbers have mildew, the yellow beans are over, and there is one, just one, pumpkin from the many plants whose leaves appear to be rampantly thriving. The quince tree, cut back severely last year, has the same fungal disease that causes its leaves to fall prematurely. Bevis, our remaining ginger cat, is dying – he has stopped eating, nothing tempts him beyond a mere sniff. Last week he revived, as he did last year, voraciously eating the various experimental expensive cat foods bought in increasing desperation, grudgingly accepting some fresh mackerel, refusing tinned tuna. But now he did not care for any nourishment. He ceased grooming himself some time ago. We were to leave for London this evening and Francis was left with the dolorous task of taking Bevis to the vet, who happens to be the Columbian vet Alberto, whom no one can understand. I picked up Bevis and set him on my lap; his paws felt cold, but he purred and placed his head against me. Grieving. I was grieving his death while he lived.

In Afghanistan girls are not allowed to go to school for secondary education. Some go anyway, and when the school inspectors come, they slip away. The younger girls are frightened; any day could be their last day in class. Schools are being closed, and the Taliban say it is temporary, as they said before, a closure that lasted six years. There are secret schools, private classes, volunteers teach, some of them the women who went to school the last time dressed as boys. Myrtle, colza, lupin, and cotton: the days passed, largely unwritten. I read Alan Davidson's book on Mediterranean seafood, which I thought I had lost. He has a light touch, a charming anecdotal approach, such as his account of the ladies in Livorno who abandoned their husbands to the cardplaying to argue over the preparation of a *cacciucco*, offering much conflicting guidance. Finally, he distils the following: a *sofrito*, olive oil, red pepper and garlic, fresh tomatoes, salt, peppercorns, parsley, then small and bony fish, cooked until they fall apart, the whole thing rubbed through a sieve, then fresh fish added to the broth, in sequence. I made *brik à l'oeuf* for lunch, with tunny and capers and an egg, and a tomato salad with cumin and red onion. I determined that I would not cook while we are in England; I booked restaurants accordingly and looked forward to supper at Vivien and Richard's new house, or at least, a house that is new to me. It rained again last night, and the air was clear. I would not write again for a week and burning heat would pass into the fruitful twelfth month.

FRUCTIDOR

This was the month the Republican calendar was abandoned and the Gregorian calendar was restored, following a report made by Pierre-Simon Laplace, mathematician and astronomer. It had endured twelve years, two months and twenty-seven days. It was also the month of a *coup-état* in year V, organised by the Directory itself to put a stop to the plotting and moves of the royalists, who had created 'Philosophical Institutes', to work towards restoration of the monarchy through the ballot box, keeping Republicans away and calling upon honest people. The Directory turned to Napoléon Bonaparte. Bonaparte wanted, he said, a strong and honest government. Don't we all, we said at supper on the first day of *Fructidor*; Vivian served figs with goat cheese, followed by tiny squid stuffed and braised, then Eton Mess. Richard said he had stopped writing the second volume of his history of the British Empire and the forgotten accounts of resistance to its formation. In the first book he showed the systematic oppression, the violence, of the imposition of colonising British rule; rebel slaves beheaded in Demerara and Jamaica, displayed mutilated defeated bodies, reprisals of brutality. Our empire. All empires. He reduced his library when they moved, getting rid of modern history.

Having arrived too early for lunch we walked through Fairlight on Sunday (six-row barley, by the way, for *quartidi* and Saint Pope Pius X, devoted to the BVM and opposed to any modernisation of church doctrine and the intrusion of the secular errors of nineteenth-century philosophy, no truck with any of that. He preached from the pulpit, a rare papal thing for popes usually preferred to keep their distance, and he lived in poverty, also rather rare for a pope). We saw detached bungalow after detached bungalow, one in three flying a Union Jack, one in three with a smug motorhome in the smug driveway, each smug house with its own smug name. It was a horrible place. It had neither centre nor heart. We ate good fish and chips, uneasily. I did not like being called 'guys' by the waiting staff. I also did not like the response of 'no problem' to any thanks or request – of course it should not be a problem but indeed how irascible I have become. We caught the bus to Rye and were delighted by our purchase of a homemade wooden box for carrying small bottles of beer, with a bottle opener handily fixed on its side.

In the news, horrors unfolded. We had wondered at the absence of people swimming in the sea; we found this was due to the risk from sewage, the discharge unmonitored, beaches marred by waste, while water company executives were paid huge annual bonuses that had risen by twenty percent from 2021, receiving an average one-off payment of £100,000, while foul water was pumped into England's rivers and seas. Where are the honest people? The staff crisis in care homes was reported; in facilities that cost £1,600 a week, residents were left in their rooms for hours, without water, waiting to pee, refused help to get out from a chair, woken at 4.45 a.m. to 'help staff', incontinence pads unchanged at night. Where are the honest people? The eleven men who raped Bilkis Bano and killed her three-year old daughter in Gujarat in 2002 were released from prison, welcomed home with sweets and garlands. A legislator who was part of the review committee that recommended the release said that the men's status as high-caste Hindus argued in favour of their liberty, Brahmin people, their family's activity was very good, their high-caste values were very good. Where are the honest people?

While we were in London, Bevis was indeed put down, as I feared, put to sleep, euthanised, as I dreaded, killed. He had an enormous tumour in his mouth and had lost a kilo in weight in a month. There was, Alberto said, no other choice. Francis called me from the vet's when I was on a bus; the people around me heard the conversation and they all commiserated on my loss with extraordinary and unexpected kindness. Bevis's absence was most present; I missed his insistent cry for food, I missed his body against mine, I missed his head against my face. He was with us for sixteen years, found by the side of a busy road near the airport that has since closed. We were down to five cats now. I looked on the Bon Coin for kittens, and noted a young black cat named Sumo, who was being given away because he bit when playing. There was a young female collie-husky cross, whose owner wanted to rehome her as the dog's mother had disappeared a few months ago and she could not bond with the daughter. There were quite a few goats, always tempting, including two extra-small kids, born this spring, advertised as calm and docile, with free delivery. There were too many Malinois, with absent owners who did not have time for the demanding or difficult dogs they had acquired under lockdown, and a Rottweiler-collie cross, photographed attached by a chain in a dirt yard, the owner claiming this was because his land had no fence. There were two Staffies crossed with Malinois, male and female, shown in a cage, the owners saying they were leaving for Réunion and did not have the means to take their dogs, Roxy and Rex, with them. Mel Chen, in *Animacies*, warns against conflating human ideas about the animal with the animal itself; we must, she writes, ask after a broadly construed register of sentience. Thinking and feeling through sentience may revise dominant animacy hierarchies by admitting a range of interanimation and unrecognised recognition. In *The History of Animals. A Philosophy*, Oxana Timofeeva argues for a history of animals, a historical materiality, however spectral. There are animals before the law, and then they are excluded from it, to become things once again. Since animals do not really own their death, they cannot really possess their life, and so they cannot be a subject of law.

Céleste returned after two days absence, slept heavily upon me, and again, I reminded her, as she purred, that she sounds of her own accord, vibrating inwardly and causing the air to vibrate; that her being is manifested, but nothing is said. In *Le Silence des bêtes: la philosophie à l'épreuve de l'animalité*, Élisabeth de Fontenay writes that animals make themselves heard even if they are denied the two types of *logos*, reason and words, though Porphyry, unlike the Stoics, believes them to have *prophorikos*, the uttered word that delivers to the outside the handiwork of internal reason. No-one has taught us how to translate what they say. Their language does not speak to us. What is the right of the one who does not speak to be there in the world, in the same way, and in the same world as the one who reasons in the clear language of the mind? What is the right of the one who cannot commit himself to any duty? We name them, and they know we have named them. Cats know their names, but sometimes, often, usually in fact, they cannot be bothered to respond to our call. De Fontenay cites Montaigne, that we live beneath the same roof and breathe the same air, that between us, there is a perpetual resemblance. On the wireless there was a short report on a Japanese study of the emotions of dogs. The researchers placed strips of paper under the eyes of dogs during normal interaction with their owners and just before they were reunited with them after several hours of absence. The dogs shed tears then, tears of joy. Hera and Ida, but especially Hera, howl with joy when those they love return, even if they have been absent only for moments. It was a day for sugar melon, a cantaloupe; the furry remains of the melon found in the depths of the refrigerator went to the chickens, who also experience a wider range of emotions than many people think and can recognise themselves in mirrors. Chicks can count, though I am not sure *what* they count.

Five days passed that seemed to be composed of conversation

and meals, and shopping for those meals or considering the garden produce for them. It is always like this when friends stay, and when they leave, I count what remains undone and attempt to resume where I imagine I left off. But the pleasure was great nonetheless, and Gareth built a set of shelves using the steps of the old miller's stairs that once led to the attic and chestnut for the top shelf, waxed and polished. I did not know him really when he came but felt we had been friends for a long time when he left. Francis left for London and R. returned from London, much brighter than before. I counted the days of dogbane, also called apocynum or Indian hemp, which may be used to treat depression and anxiety, of liquorice, which can heal ulcers, and then on Saturday, a ladder, one of which was standing under a rose arch in the garden and which I could not face climbing to cut back the Blairii number two, a Bourbon climber producing fragrant double flat blooms of pale pink with a deep pink centre, with a sorry tendency to blackspot.

Sunday was the second *primidi* and a day of watermelon and Saint Augustine, who saw jealousy in a baby, a child who was not old enough to talk but when he saw his foster-brother at the breast grew pale with envy. It is a first (a primal) scene in his *Confessions*, and in the following chapter, Augustine writes how then he ceased to be a baby unable to talk and became a boy with the power of speech. Still subject to the will of his family, nevertheless he began to understand the relation between word and thing in the world, between object and sound, and moreover, to express his wishes, to speak his desire, whatever Wittgenstein said about the limitation or circumscription of Augustine's description. And it appeared to start with fraternal rivalry. Lacan tells the same story of *invidia*, that makes *the subject pale before the image of a completeness closed upon itself.* We visited two *vide-greniers*, and most satisfyingly, I bought:

1. A forged iron table with a handle to carry it, and two levels, the bottom with a rack for six bottles.

2. A gueridon with a marble top and curly legs, some signs of woodworm.
3. A white maid's apron with a red laundry monogram on its ties. Disappointing on further examination at home.
4. A sturdy blue cotton carpenter's apron. Satisfying.
5. A small amateur oil painting of a landscape view that includes a stretch of water with a rowboat.

But I did not buy:

1. Two wooden boxes, hand made by 'Yann', depicting a Breton man and woman, carved and painted, with a slash in each cheek like a Heidelberg duelling scar, the bragging scar, the *Schmiss*, a dubious badge of honour that showed men as good husband material, for reasons of class privilege and stupid courage. Or the carved slash was like a tear, falling from their eyes. But Gareth did buy them and gave them to me, somewhat with regret. Serge said they were for napkins at a certain epoch.
2. The delightful little box in the form of a book, but Gareth did buy it, and later, when I polished it for him, I broke its hinge and was sorry.
3. A beehive and swarm for 250 euros from Monsieur Le Sommier, who was eighty-seven, a former teacher of chemistry who had, he told me, always dreamt of teaching English. The queen, he said, was of a race of exceptional sweetness and docility.

We saw the *doris* boats shored at the *grève*, the sandbank of Ville Ger, and their departure or return across the river to the Cale. I remembered that the French word for strike is *grève* after the Place de la Grève in Paris, where people would go to seek work, loading and unloading boats on the Seine, for example, the cargos of wine and wood and grain. This place is now the square of the Hôtel de Ville, where in winter we used to skate on the rink installed there and where the *sans-papiers* evicted from their squats demonstrated. In 2013 it was renamed again as the esplanade of Liberation. I think in English these little boats are called dories, shallow-drafted, sharp-bowed, planked with straight boards. The *terre-neuvas* sailed their boats before departure to Newfoundland for the cod-fishing and salting to the inlet at La Souhaitier to be blessed. The dories were piled on the bridge of the sailing ship. Jean-François was one of the last *terre-neuvas*, signing on when he was eighteen to raise money to study at the École des Arts Décoratifs in Paris. R. took Gareth to visit his atelier where the immense Renaissance-style bed he had taken twenty years to carve for an aristocrat was covered with a blanket, still there, for the aristocrat had been obliged to leave his château in Brittany for a castle near Verona and now was waiting for the completion of his *ribat* in Tunisia, where the workmen were taking the building materials for other jobs and his architect said, it was *comme ça*. And the count is virtually *sans domicile fixe*, said Jean-François, though his lack of shelter is probably far from that of those who are forced by circumstance to inhabit the streets, living in precarity.

The first ship carrying wheat from Ukraine to the Horn of Africa docked in the port of Djibouti this morning. The MV Brave Commander carried 23,000 tonnes of grain destined for Ethiopia, drought-ravaged by four failed rainy seasons, crops destroyed and cattle killed. It was doubtful how the grain would reach Tigray as humanitarian deliveries by road and air were suspended amid the fighting between the forces of Tigray and Ethopia, but grain might reach Amhara and Afar. Many more ships have carried grain to Europe, fulfilling existing business contracts. Yesterday was the day of fennel, which has bolted in my garden as I knew it would – I left some in the hope that where it appears it might still form a bulb and pulled out those plants that will never do so. Zoë's poem struck me, one line, more than half the poem's five-line form: *even if it's always too late and the last time around never quite worked the stopped season isn't dead but waiting*. Today is barberry: *stopping is a way of stepping through*. I made black bread with wheat, rye, and walnut flour, with seeds of poppy, sesame, and sunflower. The pears from Antoinette were about to rot so I made a sorbet with them, a simple one, the pears puréed with sugar, lemon juice and zest, apple juice – I should have added some grappa but forgot, distracted by fatigue. Yesterday I had seen my house in a new light after – due to – Gareth's visit, and it had seemed charming, but today I was in pain, and the house and its surroundings looked dull and shabby to me. Rain was foretold. The light fell during the afternoon and the air was very still, *waiting*.

There was no rain. The day was of the walnut, *noix*. I picked the new peas for *risi e bisi* this evening. There were figs from the tree to eat with soft goat cheese and new honey. The roses over one arch were pruned at last – it had taken three days. I moved on to the arch with the honeysuckle, clematis, the 'Handel' rose, ivory bloom trimmed with a rosy red. I read a poem by Anne Sexton, titled 'The Poet of Ignorance', in which she has a body but cannot escape from it, she does not know how, and a huge crab is growing inside her chest, a great weight, and she goes about her business trying to forget it, but it grips harder and the pain enlarges. Behind my eyes I often have the feeling that a blanket of sheer red rage is descending to blind me, and then I speak in tongues. The wildness of anger. Rosa Luxemburg wrote to Mathilde Wurm that she had become as hard as polished steel and would rather be stuck in prison than fight beside Tilde's heroes, those creeping cowardly petty souls, and that it was lucky that world history was not made by people like her friend as we would still have been stuck with the *ancien regime*. Tilde and her friend Dora Fabian were found dead in their London flat – a double suicide was supposed. Tilde fled Germany for Switzerland in 1933, then London; her property had been confiscated and she slept on trains.

Who else has died? Jeanne at ninety-three, for one, and another, Marie-Luce at ninety-five. And then Annick, Marie-Therese, Josette, Renée, Raymonde, who reached their nineties. Eugénie and Anne achieved a hundred years, the latter to join her tender husband Louis and her equally tender son-in-law Lionel; for the former, no flowers, no rite of souvenir, the family requested. Some younger deaths: Angélique, only thirty-four, leaving behind her husband Anthony and her children, and Aurore, thirty-nine, a brutal death. The granite statue of Jeanne Jugan was unveiled and blessed in the Valley of Saints in Carnoët. She is seated, opening her hands to the wretched to offer them bread. Next to her is a frog, for if one directs light on a frog, it cannot turn away its eyes from the source of light and Saint Jeanne told her Little Sisters of the Poor that they should be as frogs before God, looking at no other light. I wondered if Juliette knew about this. The festival of the *andouille*, a large sausage made from the digestive tract of a single pig, onions and seasoning mixed with chopped slices of the pig's stomach and small intestine, returned to Guémené-sur-Scorff. A cloudy stink of urine wafts from the sausage when it is cut open. A white wolf, a female, escaped from a festival in Beignon, and was wandering in the forest of Brocéliande; she is tame, no more dangerous than a stray dog, her owner said. A woman stabbed her companion in Plougonver and the man was severely wounded.

This – my – almanach would be put on hold, while I wrote a catalogue essay for Scott, who told me to write what I liked, that he had no interest in the museum that had commissioned him, which he felt, like all museums, silenced or suppressed its objects. This he took literally: he would make resound the noise-generating objects that were silenced in their display. I was trying to write channelling Samuel Delaney and *Game of Thrones*, then found the museum had a *Game of Thrones* theme. I was not deft at this kind of writing, but I was imagining a group of insurrectionaries who had made their way to the museum where they would arm themselves for a last battle, after China Miéville, I thought, after the Paris Commune, I thought, after the Invisible Committee. A cock called noisily at the gate to the courtyard and was followed by a handsome male pheasant, who took flight over the houses. Is it possible to write two things at the same time without them colliding, cock and pheasant? A cock and bull story? *Coq à âne* passing brusquely from one subject to another... a series of silliness, contradictory, burlesque (that would be good, and I thought again of Allie), and then perhaps I could work in the trout that marks the day, a trout's tale or tail, a flexible girder steering the fin.

Sextidi, and oh joy, at last, after more than two years I had my Renault 4L back from Denis, who has made a grand job of its restoration. I forgot how to drive, and I flooded the engine. It is only the first step that counts, *et cetera*. In fourth gear the engine sounded choppy. In the fields by the river six egrets stood among the cows – each bird appeared to have its own brown cow, how now indeed. I met Françoise with her collie-Labrador cross Sparrow, *le voleur de fromage* and the nibbler of hens. He was excited to see Ida and Hera, but Hera was having none of his advances. Françoise and I shared our plaints of how our adult children became adolescents again in the family home. She told me of the family meetings she organises at which she shows them photographs on her phone of their sins and omissions – the tidemark round the bath, the wet towels thrown on the floor, the dirty coffee cups in their rooms. She said she had been the same at their age, but I had not. I was always quite tidy, given to the making of careful arrangements and with a tendency to accumulate. A woman walking her perfectly reasonable-looking large dog on a lead approached, shouting hysterically at us to call back our dogs, to put them on their leads. For Christ's sake, I said. Our dogs ignored us completely when we called them back, of course, no discipline, *mauvaises graines*.

It was my son's birthday, but he did not answer any of the

ways I tried to call him. My sister said he was probably in the British Library, but frankly, at 8.30 in the morning I doubted that. Lemon this day and Saint Ingrid, and there are all the martyrs of September, too, too tedious to list. I sold a drawing, my woman goldfinch / *charbonneret*, who looks like Joan Collins (apart from her bird body, that is, but then, who knows), as so many of the women in my pictures do, surprisingly, another agent of divine punishment, another mean food-stealing woman. Ingrid was a Swedish princess; she founded a cloistered convent, a contemplative order, no harpies there, just little brides, their union with God contributing to the salvation of the world, practicing penance, walking barefoot, silent. To make *citronade*, take two fine ripe lemons, slice them thickly, and place in a jug with 50 grams of sugar, mix well with two litres of hot water and allow this to infuse. When it is cold, press the pulp from the lemons into the water and keep cold. Add mint if you like.

There were three roe deer in the field behind the house. They stood very still, alert, looking at me looking at them. Suddenly they turned and bounded into the woods at the edge of the château's land. The hunting season started on Saturday. There were hunters everywhere, in red or orange gilets, some with horns to call their dogs, but not yet here in the village. I hope the family of deer in the forest survive. I hope the wild boar who leave the traces of their hooves in the earth survive. I hope the hares in the fields survive. The hunting is kinder now, or at least, organised and calm, no longer do packs of dogs run into the gardens and across the roofs of the outbuildings; no longer do I have arguments with half-drunk men whose guns are unbroken despite the law requiring them to do so.

Teasel and buckthorn, and then today Mexican marigold, which cures a queasy stomach and soothes toothache. The roses and honeysuckle and clematis arches were tidied. The potatoes were lifted. My arms last night were red and sore with nettle rash, my fingers were studded with tiny thorns. R. was stung by a bee on his lip, which swelled alarmingly, and he felt quite faint. He took *apis mellifica*, under duress on my part, five pills every fifteen minutes for an hour or two. He said he wanted to give up beekeeping. Other tasks achieved: planting out curly endive, removing a dead rose, taking up the cucumber plants that have succumbed to mildew, making bread, writing to Juliette, then to Tim and Hilary with false promises. Not achieved: any advance on the essay for Scott, which reads as lumpen and unconvincing.

The latest news: *gym douce* has resumed in La Landec, the comîce Agricole in Évran attracted a large crowd on Saturday, the library in Langrolay will soon have some new books, Antoine Bourseul has returned to Plancoët from his stay in Germany, the painter decorator Olivier Laroche has reopened his business in Matignon, in Fréhel the tennis club enregistered a dozen new inscriptions, two women were injured slightly in an accident in Corseul when the woman driving lost control of her car and it went into a ditch (firemen and gendarmes were at the scene), and there were twenty *exposants* at the *vide-grenier* in Plelan-le-Petit, where I bought a pair of blue worker's trousers for R. for three euros, a blue jug shaped like a pumpkin for one euro, and a home-made wooden shelf for two euros. I also met a delightful old Vietnamese pig in a field, who trotted over to me, calling *nunk nunk* and luxuriated in having his snout scratched. Poor old boy, now outside as having outgrown his pet size for the house, like Sylvie's Gaspar. If I had one, he would live in the house and sleep on the sofas and beds whenever he wished.

When I re-read or imagined others reading at some time in the future, I thought about the events that are absent, even though they were momentous, world events. Readers would think, I thought, that they had not been noticed by me. My mother has been fading. I spoke, no, I speak to her, every day but she has less to say, and even though usually the very name of the woman who was yesterday elected as the new leader of the Conservative Party is enough to send her into a paroxysm of rage and loathing, she barely remarked on it. In Britain the anti-union laws are among the harshest in the world. This woman, this terrible stupid woman, has proposed an attack on organised labour, that workers would not be permitted to strike unless the strike ballot shows not only the support of fifty percent of those voting but also fifty percent of those eligible to vote. This woman would not have been elected as a member of parliament in 2019 if this law applied. Actually, there would not be a single elected Conservative MP, and perhaps not even a Labour one. Postal workers voted for strike action. The firefighters are set to ballot. I was reading E. P. Thompson's book on artisan and working-class society from 1780 to 1832, how people took part in their own making, the production of a culture and political consciousness. Then I read Joshua Clover, writing that the source of the strike is the transformation that moves bodies and capital into the sphere of production, opposing production and circulation. There are so many lessons to learn on a picket line, because of the picket line.

In the book exchange by the chapel of La Souhaitier, I found a copy of Alain Robbe-Grillet's *Pour un nouveau roman*. Its previous owner had assiduously highlighted the first two essays in green and yellow felt pen, then given up. One of the passages in green: the great writer, the 'genius', is a kind of unconscious monster, irresponsible and deadly, even slightly imbecilic, from whom messages are sent that only the reader can decipher. I remembered the films of Robbe-Grillet, which I saw in Venice, I think, their odious smug misogyny, their violence inflicted upon young women, the coldness, the cruelty of *Successive Slidings into Pleasur*e, which contains very little pleasure at all, and at the end, the last line, the detective inspector, played by Jean-Louis Trintignant, said that we had to start all over again. Christ, no, I thought.

Today is a day of the wild rose, *églantine*; Fabre d'Églantine, the author of the nomination of calendar's days and months, went to the guillotine with Danton on 16 *germinal* year II, convicted of corruption and the destruction of national representation. One account said he cried on the way, for he had been unable to finish writing a poem; another said he hummed the song *Il pleut, il pleut, bergère*, as he mounted the scaffold. It was a song from his opera comique, *Laure et Petrache*, of 1780, and poor Marie-Antoinette became the shepherdess, the storm from which she should bring in her sheep to shelter became the forthcoming revolution, the thunder approaching, the lightning. The sage advice of the *facteur*'s calendar is to use chalk for the removal of grease stains from a garment, rubbing the stain gently, and rinsing after ten minutes. A box of chalk placed in the wardrobe or cupboards will stop the development of damp and bad odours. Draw a line with chalk and ants will not cross it – they have a horror of chalk.

The essay was done at last and sent and now revised. Scott was pleased with it, and I was relieved. Writing never comes easily to me, as I keep saying, as though the words will produce ease. I read his kind remarks several times, rather with astonishment, delighted that he had caught the whiff of the Invisible Committee, joining other sources: Marx, Kropotkin, William Morris, Prosper Lissagary, a conversation between Louise Michel and an unnamed Zouave, Elié Reclus... others unnamed, including commentators on the Peterloo massacre. He saw – as I had hoped – the tension between use-value and textures, that the description or appreciation of objects and surfaces was part of a circle of violence. He said that the museum would hate being presented as a resource for insurrection, but after all, it *was* a space containing thousands of firearms.

My perennial mild depression returned as the weather changes. I was slack, languid, given to the desire to lie on my bed and read, the book falling limply from me, I was not reading at all. I was halfway through clipping the box hedges when the rain came down. Today is *noisette* and of course the hazelnuts are still unpicked, as they were last year, and it may be too late. I found a dead pigeon behind the greenhouse. I feared bird flu, rumoured to be in the area, but it bore the marks of a cat, Luna, Céleste, or Orphée, no doubt. I managed to drive my car to Dinan with only a little trepidation. I bought salad plants, autumn Batavia, and if the rain ceased, which it showed no signs of doing, I told myself firmly that I would plant these and sow spinach and two kinds of Palla Rossa radicchio. The variety I sowed last month is doing splendidly, and it was better to sow directly into the ground than in seed trays as I did last year. In Da Ponte's painting of the wedding at Cana, there is radicchio di Treviso in one of the baskets of fruit and vegetables. Birds are supposed to have dropped the first seeds on the belltower of the monastery at the gates of the city, or it may have first been grown in the English garden at the Villa Palazzi by a Belgian nurseryman in 1870. I considered forcing or blanching the chicories, making the effort of tying closed their heads, covering them with straw to block sunlight, or digging them up, wrapping each head in newspaper and keeping them in the cold and dark. Yes. The newly elected prime minister said she supported and would extend the Rwanda scheme, that she would make it a priority. The High Court will deliver its ruling on the legality of the scheme in October. The first hearing is taking place this week. It did not stop raining.

When it did not rain: there were the days of hops, sorghum,

and the crayfish, and I took more time off writing to work in the garden, to cut back and shape a bay tree, seeded by a bird, to trim a Californian lilac, to finish the pruning of the box hedges, which I did mostly by hand with my cheap yellow-handled secateurs, two euros from Leroy Merlin, until my palms had blisters. I cleared the ground of acanthus and bay shoots around the bay tree, then moved on to the holly, also planted by a bird. And I took time off from cooking, working into the evening on Saturday, then having dinner at La Matz, where Caroline's menu of the week was focaccia with cherry tomatoes and rosemary, served with a tiny glass of juice made from tomatoes, a little spicy, perhaps with ginger. Then marinated mackerel and a salad of green and yellow beans in ponzu vinaigrette, lots of grilled hazelnuts; then grilled octopus, roasted sweet onions, a green pepper purée, spelt with chickpeas, a sauce of black olives, a sauce of *fromage blanc* with herbs and garlic; last, vanilla ice cream with lemon verbena, a roast apple on apple purée, a *financière* of hazelnuts. All was delicious. Helen, Jerome, and Marie were dining there also, with Sophie and Thierry. We chatted briefly though we sat apart. It was a pleasure.

What I refused to speak (or write) about was the death of the British queen, about which I had conflicted feelings. I did not want to join in any action to celebrate her death, yet I did not really feel she made too great a sacrifice as many suggested. Perhaps one simply cannot feel delight at the death of any person who has done little harm, despite what the person symbolises. Priyamvada asked for examples of the favourite media clichés of the moment. It is endless, the fawning, the forelock tugging, the blindness towards the social deprivation around us (or its denegation of any connection with royalism); there is only sentiment without political logic. In *On Kings*, Marshall Sahlins and David Graeber analyse not only the rituals of obeisance and deference but equally how the same ritual structures inform the rituals (and the politics) of regicide. When the symbolic rite of regicide is over, the victim stays dead. The queen is dead and long live the king, and I refused to care. I took the day off on Sunday too, to go to the Potato Festival in Ploeuc-l'Hermitage, which promised displays of over two hundred varieties of potatoes and two hundred tractors, which was not so, though later we thought there might have been two sites and that we had missed one. A tractor turned up the ground of a field and people grubbed up potatoes, of the variety BF15, bred from Belle de Fontenay, longer in shape, filling a paper sack for three euros, though the woman next to me tried to fill her own bag, pretending it was free, which she knew it was not as she had asked me. Other highlights were the potato sorting shed and the milking parlour, where a cow lingered at the threshold of the milking machine, refusing to enter or go back, in a stoic act of bovine resis-tance. We ate chips from a cardboard cornet, which in the car later Ida ate, then threw up. What a splendid weekend.

Now it is a day of bitter orange and R. left for England on the ferry from St-Malo this morning. The week stretched ahead of me, and I could do what I liked, when I liked. But I was, am, dutiful, and did the laundry, took as many bags of garden cut-tings to the dump as could be squashed into my tiny car, now driving with greater confidence, Ida and Hera in the passenger seat, Ida's paws up on the dashboard, and neither barking quite so loudly at any passing dog as they do when in R.'s car. I walked them at La Souhaitier, the sun on the water, the tide in, and the lovely collie who is left alone in a garden by the path kissed my face when I leant over the fence. I would like to steal him. I hate his owners. Emails and an invoice were sent, an invitation to read accepted, work chased, Wiebke's corrections done, the kettle descaled, and a navy-blue linen shirtdress bought in a sale arrived, the first new dress for a long time. I had stopped buying new clothes. How cheering a nice new frock can be, like a new lipstick. I ate good bread with crunchy peanut butter as the dogs had their food, and read Rebecca's book, the chapter on Winnicott and Mrs Beeton and the cooking of sausages, on the body in the kitchen, the body of the sausage and all that went into its production, pig, worker, butcher, cook, pan... butter ... a book on everything that Winnicott omits. This was the first September I have not had to return to my job at a university; that was, is, my new liberty, realised, for real, in real happiness, light on the water, on the day of Saint Apollinaire, the first archbishop of Ravenna or the bishop of Valence, both martyrs. The poet Apollinaire said he loved light above all else, describing drawing as the voice of light; he despaired that his frequentation of prostitutes (his love for all things tender and voluptuous) distracted him from poetry. I allowed anything and everything to distract me, full of self-justification.

Monique leant over her balcony this morning to ask the name of the yellow flowers in my garden and if I had a plant I could spare. I did not know what she meant at first. She described the form of the flowers, how they dip and fall, and I realised it was the solidago, which I wish I had not planted. It is also called goldenrod and is the calendar's plant for today. *Verge d'or*, I told her, and that there were small plants for sale at Magasin Vert, where this morning I bought a hydrangea paniculata, 'vanille fraise', and a purple-flowered sage, both reduced in price. I also filled with bulbs my special offer *sac magique* that arrived in the post to offer me a fifteen percent discount on the contents, and I could not resist the bargain: allium 'gladiator', two kinds of narcissi, tulips, stuffed in, crammed to the brim. The morning disappeared, vanished completely, after the car would not start, its engine flooded, the dogs had to be walked late, and my mobile telephone went on to VoiceOver, giving audible descriptions of whatever was on my screen, which took over half an hour to disable as I screamed with rage. Jean-Luc Godard's death was announced on the wireless while I was deferring work, sitting on a sofa eating more peanut butter on the good bread and finishing Rebecca's book, which in some ways I wished I had written and largely was glad I had not, for though I found a little of myself in it, it was also distant, like so many of the young people I know, their impetuous lives. Godard's death called for the mourning I could not, would not, make for the Queen. I hoped that queues to see his body lying in state would be kilometres-long and special trains laid on to bring mourners from across the country. I listed his films in my head, end of story, end of cinema. I thought about Christian, his great love for Godard, that I would write to him, two or three things about love, but in the end I did not, as I was uncertain if he was in Jerusalem or Berlin, and did not want to ask, for reasons that were obscure to me.

On France Musique this morning, *octidi*, I heard a woman singing a song about washing her pasta with tomato sauce to get the essence, rinsing the pasta with the sauce, rinsing away the sauce: something worthwhile still remains, a shadow of the tomato, a tomato vibe. She likes it that way, so kill her, she sings. She realises that her lover has never rinsed the sauce from the pasta, that he has never even put the sauce on the pasta in order to wash it off in the whole time they have been together, and she can no longer place any trust in him. Later, after writing a mediocre short piece for a poetry journal, I tried to find it again, but it did not seem to exist. Yesterday I read about Marcella Hazan's tomato sauce, Rebecca cooking it wildly, dancing. Everyone knows this recipe, one onion, peeled and cut in half, cooked with a big tin of whole tomatoes, San Marzano and five tablespoons of butter for about forty-five minutes, crushing the tomatoes from time to time, salt added at the end. It is advised to take out the onion, but I leave it in, blending it with the hand blender, and it is good this way. Online I found a surprising number of songs about tomato sauce and pasta but not this one, the only song

I desired. Perhaps, like Freud's beautiful butcher's wife, I sought only that my desire should not be gratified. But no, no, I really needed to find it and returned to my search more diligently, this time with success. It was by Jennifer Walshe and Matthew Shlomowitz. And that was enough for the day, I thought, going out into the garden to sow more spring cabbages and chicories.

Wednesday was maize, followed on Thursday by the chestnut, a *marron* not a *châtaigne*. A *marron glacé* is made from a *châtaigne*, not a *marron*, appearing first during the reign of Louis XIV, though that is argued. The sweet chestnuts started to fall in the lanes, but were still in their spikey green husks, and no one was collecting them yet. The Bach remedy derived from the sweet chestnut is addressed to the total despair of those who feel that they reached the limit of their endurance. In the Utter Pradesh six men were arrested for the rape and murder of two Dalit girls. The girls were strangled, their bodies were suspended from a tree by their shawls. This was intended to make their deaths look like suicide. The men came on their scooters and took the girls away from their home by force. The girls' mother tried to stop the men. She ran after them, but they beat her. She shouted and sought help in the village. The police said the girls knew the men and had gone with them willingly.

It was the last day of *fructidor*. It should have been a day of rest or of festivity, in the revolutionary calendar, that is. The month ends with a *panier*, a basket. I stripped the second harvest of coriander seeds from their stalks. I wrote a short essay to read for Julia's book launch. I was angry and tired and in pain. Fabre d'Églantine said the calendar must show the people the richness of nature, to make them love the fields, and to methodically show them the order of the influences of the heavens and of the products of the earth. A basket is a worthy object.

VENDÉMIAIRE

This was the first month of the new calendar. *Primidi* marks the foundation of the Republic. The National Convention decreed that every year would begin at midnight of the day of the autumn equinox for the Paris observatory. The first year of the French Republic began at midnight September 22 1792, and ended at midnight separating the 21 from the 22 September 1793. The second year began September 22 1793, at midnight, the true autumn equinox having arrived that day for the Paris Observatory at 3:11:38 in the evening. The Committee of Public Instruction was charged with having printed the new calendar in different formats, with simple instructional material to explain its principles and its use. Article XV states that *Professors, teachers, mothers and fathers of families, and all those who direct the education of children shall hasten to explain to them the new calendar.* It is the month of *vendange*, vintage, of the grape harvest, and the first day, *primidi*, is consecrated to the grape. The name comes from an old Occitan word for the grape harvest. I ordered six bottles of La Clape, a wine from the Languedoc, from the vineyards of Occitania. La Clape was once an island; the Romans called it Insula Laci. The white wines are made from many grape varieties, Picpoul, Marsanne, Clairette, Rolle, Boulboulenc blanc – the latter must account for forty percent of the blend. Geno used to laugh when he brought out a bottle of the Clap, as he called it. The grape harvest was good this year, despite the heat, the dryness; there has been little disease due to both. The president of the Organisme de défense et de gestion of the Clape region, winegrower at Château Pech Redon, was pleasantly surprised, acidity was low. In the pine forest of Izium, there was another harvest, that of over four hundred bodies buried there by the Russian army. Volunteers and officials clad in protective suits and masks dug the earth; some examined the bodies, others made notes. The bodies were taken to refrigerated containers. Some of the bodies were very small. Some had their hands tied. Some were wrapped in rags. Others wore military fatigues. There were signs of torture, the officials reported. The shallow graves were marked with wooden crosses, most of which had numbers. In London people continued to queue to view the body of the British queen. The line was closed yesterday for several hours, as it had grown so long. The temperature fell again last night. People waited in the cold. The bodies of Louis XVI, citizen Capet, and Marie-Antoinette were taken to the cemetery of the Madeleine, which closed in 1794. Purchased in 1796 by a cabinetmaker, Isaac Jacob, the Madeleine was excavated, until it was bought again by a lawyer, Descloseaux, who styled himself as the guardian of the royal remains. He made a shrine of it, planting cypresses and willows; he planted an orchard. The graves of king and queen were marked by lilies.

I was absent for a *décadi*. I returned to disorder, as always. Not least, there was the disorder of not writing while away, in London and Berlin, while reading, reading myself in both cities; in one, the short essay I wrote for Anna, in the other, entries from *Abécédaire*, the parts on maids or with maids, or even the briefest appearance of a maid, my nursemaid. The next reading would be wolves, then encounters with paintings, and later, poetry or poems or poets, then pain and morphine, then mothers and fathers, then flowers. But with the same introduction or the penultimate entry, I thought. Ah, the disorder of not writing, it is about losing the plot, when one cannot act normally or understand what is happening, when one becomes confused or crazy, when one starts to behave in a strange or silly way, when one acts in a disorganised, chaotic, or irrational manner. R. described his loss of memory as bricks sinking into water. I was angry with him, blind with rage, almost all the time, and shouting too much.

The days that I missed were many: sweet chestnut – *châ-*

taigne – that was when I travelled, taking two buses to get to the airport as R. came back with COVID; crocus – that was when I saw Lubaina's show and Brece's film, and was delighted to see Jaspar; a horse – that was when I spoke to Eleonora in Turin and found myself inviting her to London to work with me at the next book fair and when I met Sharon to discuss how we might speak together at the Freud Museum next year; balsamine – that was when I met Gill to talk about her day-book and we ate Portuguese custard tarts; carrot – that was when I read at the launch of Anna's journal and Frank lay on a sofa for his reading performance with an interior voice beside him or emitting from him, and I saw Sam, John, Joe, Monika, Kirsten, Oliver, and Giorgio was in the distance but I missed him when I left without speaking to him and he was upset, and I found out that Hilary Mantell had died and a Tory budget was announced giving a tax cut to the most wealthy; amaranth – that was when Joe visited and we discussed how he might begin working with me; parsnip – that was when I had to get up very early to get a bus to London Bridge and the first train to Gatwick airport and when I got to Berlin I was exhausted and had a headache but had to read, and Susan brought two bottles of champagne. I had to rally force to perform and Rares said it was theatrical but that was not a criticism, he said quickly, and it was Rosh Hashana, *Shana Tovah*, I said, and Kim said and Christian said, *L'Shana Tovah tikatevu, Gut Rom Tov*. I missed the day of the *cuve*, a vat or tank or reservoir – that was when I had lunch with Christian before he returned to Jerusalem, and was filmed by Julia reading for her book launch a few days later, and saw Siddartha, who had not come to my reading the evening before, which had upset me, though he said he had lumbago and I thought crossly that nowadays no one has lumbago, and had supper with Julia and Moritz. I missed the day of the potato – that was when I had coffee with Katharina in the little café near Savignyplatz, run by two elderly Sicilian men, one who speaks only Italian, the other who does not speak at all, and she spoke about the state she must enter in order to be able to write, and I was recorded by Laurie speaking about anger and women, and Sam collected me from Laurie's apartment and travelled with me as far as Schöneweide on the S-Bahn so we could talk about his book. I missed the day of the *immortelle*, the Italian strawflower, Helichrysum, which never fades, the pumpkin, and the mignonette – that was when I was spending those days with my mother, whose life now is confined to two rooms and a staircase, and she is bored and furious, and I spent five hours at the airport, flight delayed, also bored and furious.

Home, yes, home, to donkey and *belle de nuit* days, though the *belle de nuit* is the four o'clock flower, and today, today, *citrouille*, another pumpkin, one that is round and orange, the pumpkin of Halloween, all hallow's eve. Home to disorder, home to setting things right, home to raging... home to losing the plot again and again cutting back the wisteria on R.'s studio that was once my studio, the climbing roses, the grape vine, the jasmine, on the front wall of the house. One thing after another and then back to the beginning. But there was fish soup with saffron and cream, and a rhubarb crumble with a vanilla ice, and the next day there were oysters, and clams for the spaghetti with chili and garlic and parsley and white wine. So at last my almanach was up to date, plot recovered, with the vegetables and animals and tools at least, all the saints were missing, of course, but many honest folk were included in their place, even if only in passing, and to their names I should add Padraig and Erin and Florian and Sanja and Elijah. And in that time, I became a visiting professor in London, wondering how I would assume the role as much as the title (but it is no more than a title). In the field the cattle egrets gathered, following the tracks of the cows, grubbing the worms and insects unearthed by their hooves; they are small, sociable birds and the sight of them mingling with the cows was both funny and sweet – they do not like to get their feet wet. Rosie called by with a crate of apples, and tomorrow, *sarrasin*, buckwheat, there would be the making of chutney, with ginger and dates and apple cider, tomorrow, *octidi*, tomorrow, Saint Francis. My own darling boy and my grandfather and my uncle, names are passed down.

Twenty-eight years ago, we arrived in Assisi one evening. We were on our way to Rome, where we lived for three months. It was winter. We had driven from Brittany, crossed mountains, lost our way in a storm. It was snowing, the streets were icy, the town still. We were in time to see Giotto's frescoes in the cathedral. It was before the earthquake in 1997. It was before the restoration work that followed, believed by some to have compromised the murals. It was before the Scrovegni Chapel was struck by lightning in 2014. In the upper church twenty-eight scenes depict the life of Saint Francis. Giotto may not have painted them at all. There is the homage of a simple man, the gift of his mantle to a pauper, a miracle of the crucifix, the renunciation of worldly goods, a vision of a flaming chariot, the exorcism of demons, a sermon to the birds (everyone knows this story: the saint said oh my brothers and sisters to the birds, he exhorted them to show their joy as the creatures of God, and the birds stretched their necks, extended their wings, opened their beaks and gazed at him attentively), many other scenes from a saintly life and death. Francis, my own boy, was a baby then, swaddled against the cold. Last week he walked, my own Francis, my baby, from Perugia to Assisi. This summer we had planned the pilgrimage walk to Saint Jacques de la Compostelle, part of it at least, leaving from Rachel and Max's house in the south, but it was impossible for me. He said he found the frescoes to be somewhat underwhelming. I could not remember them, though I remembered the streets of Assisi in the snow, like a filmset.

Who died in my absence? Odette, Jeanne, Yvette, Henriette, Nicole, Michelle, Maryvonne, Françoise, Adrienne, and Simone, in Lamballe, Dinan, Saint-René, Dinard, Saint-Brieuc, Lanvollon, Rennes, Rostrenen, and Penguilly. And in Trémeur, the *doyenne*, Virginie, a hundred and one-years-old, elegant and with an iron will, and who remembered when the children walked four kilometres to school, wearing wooden sabots; she would have liked to follow her studies but she said that was impossible at that time for the daughter of small farmers and at the end of the obligatory schooling, girls like her had to work in order to feed their families. Who has died? In Tehran, Mahsa Amini, beaten about the head while in police custody for breaking hijab rules. Her head covering was too loose, the morality police said, she was unsuitably attired; they said they had not tortured her, that she had a heart attack, they said, and they always say this, don't they? In Karaj, Hadis Najafi, shot in the abdomen, neck, heart, and hand in a protest against the state for Mahsa's death. Who has died? Forty-one people. Or fifty-eight people. Or more deaths, uncounted. Bonfires were lit in the street and women took off their headscarves and burnt them; some cut off their hair, some danced; they cried death to the dictator, they chanted woman, life, freedom. Today it was announced on the news that schoolchildren, young girls, have taken to the streets in protest, discarding their head-coverings.

Tournesol, sunflower, and the sun came out intermittently. The leaves of the flower may be crushed into a poultice to treat sores, swellings, the bites of snakes or spiders. Ukraine was one of the largest exporters of its oil; its cost has tripled since the outbreak of war. My plans for the day went astray and I was not sure why. When there was no sun, it was grey, a little windy, discouraging weather for the planting of bulbs, five pots done yesterday, ninety tulip bulbs, and a hundred bulbs from last year to go into the ground and the pots on the terrace with clematis, ten alliums ('Purple Sensation', strap-shaped leaves and clusters of starry mauve flowers), some botanical daffodils ('Rip Van Winkle', an unusual raggedy flower, multi-petalled, greenish-yellow), more narcissi ('Cheerfulness', creamy-white, late flowering, double ruffled and strongly scented). Serge called by yesterday evening with a plastic box full of girolles, which he had found in our field – two days ago there were none, and we had looked frequently over the last month, disappointedly. It was the rain and the moon, he said. I ate them with *gigli*, shaped like a bellflower or lily, fluted and ruffled, sometime called *campanelle*, little bells. The girolles were sautéed in olive oil with garlic and parsley and some *crème fraiche* added, then parmesan.

In Italy, Giorgia Meloni appeared on course to become president. Her right-wing alliance, Brothers of Italy, took control of the Senate and the Chamber of Deputies. She held up a sign saying *thank you, Italy*. Earlier this year she made a speech to Spain's right-wing Vox party, saying, *Yes to the natural family, no to the LGBT lobby, yes to sexual identity, no to gender ideology… no to Islamist violence, yes to secure borders, no to mass migration… no to big international finance… no to the bureaucrats of Brussels*. She posted a video of herself on social media, holding two melons to her chest, winking at the camera, a surprising sudden turn in style from one who had made being an exemplary woman and mother central to her campaign. The French popular press reported that Isabelle Adjani had become a blonde, mysterious and enchanting; one article remarked, inexplicably, that she may have a career spanning more than fifty years in the film industry, continuing to captivate with her aura, but she is still a mother like any other, loving her two sons, they report.

Two days passed, wine press and hemp. Today, peach, but

the harvest is over. Serge brought round a jar of his wild peach jam, and Zoë wrote that *the day you were dreaming of was already here,* but it never is, I thought. The *pressoir, more blood in the economy,* she wrote, *the winepress, pressed down in the word made flesh.* Ah, yes, I thought, considering transubstantiation, wine into blood, bread into body, priest into sacrifice, like a hand in a glove, God seen through a transparent veil by the faithful, though that was not insisted upon in the elements of the eucharist, the rosy blood, the supper of the lamb, the unleavened bread of sincerity. The Fourth Lateran Council of 1215 said that to carry out the mystery of unity we ourselves receive from Christ the body he himself receives from us. In the crumbs and drops... concomitance, *corpus christi.* The flesh is food, the blood is drink. The anthropologist Alain Testart wrote that while women might offer a sacrifice, provide the animal, decide the reason for the sacrifice, address the divinity, a woman would never play the role of the priest. Women were excluded from the mystery of the eucharist, excluded from the place reserved for the transformation of wine into blood.

I worked on a reading list, at Anna's invitation, to accompany an exhibition in Düsseldorf: the theme was wildness, or at least that is how I chose to read it – a place beyond law (the palace), the mountainside to which I invited wild readers, the Bacchae or *my* Bacchae. I thought about Freud's criticism of wild psychoanalysis, that psychoanalysis could not be learnt from books, at least not without a very great sacrifice of time, labour (and success), since 'wild' analysts do harm, to themselves and to psychoanalysis, when in fact, effects determine causes, not the other way round. What happens when a reading goes badly? I dreamt I gave a very bad lecture, a terrible thing, and at the end G. appeared, kissed me, and laid his head on my lap. He was wearing an ugly sweater, also a terrible thing, more terrible still than my – any – reading.

Today: the first day of Sukkot began in the evening at sunset. Sunset: Festival of tabernacles, feast of booths. Some would build a shelter, some would gather the four species, *etrog*, a citron, *lulav*, palm branches, *hadasim*, myrtle, *aravot*, willow, and shake the branches, it has a pattern to follow, to the east – to the front, to the back, to the right, to the left, up and down – the four species are the heart, the spine, the mouth, the eyes – or they are the unity of a people. Maria wrote that she was waving and shaking, shaking and waving. Maria is a weaver and a poet, weaving and writing, writing and weaving. The structure, the *sukkah*, should have two and a half or three sides, made of anything that grows from the earth, severed from source; the branches for the roof, *skhakh*, should be loose, not bundled, so the stars may be seen through them at night. It is a pilgrimage, a harvest festival, the beginning of the rains, a time of celebration, a place to inhabit in remembrance, after you have gathered in from your threshing floor and from your wine press. From Year III the pastoral festivals were revived, along with fairs devoted to industrial progress; there were fireworks, temples (labyrinths of false ruins, the repertoire of antiquity, the sorcery of staging), music, forging sentimental social bonds (a new consecration). The painter Jacques-Louis David decided on the costumes, the movements of the crowd, describing the diverse groups as living gardens decked with flowers, with scents; the mothers left their husbands and sons, carrying bouquets of roses, accompanied by their daughter with baskets of flowers; the fathers and sons carried swords and held branches of oak. The new festivals took place on a *décadi*, by decree, save for that of *primidi* this month, for obvious celebratory reasons, and of *nonidi* of *Thermidor*, celebrating the end of tyranny.

In Tehran it appeared as if some fountains ran with blood, as if their pools were filled with blood. The waters were dyed, and it was said it was done by an artist or artists. It was once a way to honour the dead, in remembrance of martyrs. It was the day of Saint Denis, the first bishop of Paris. He was decapitated on the hill of Montmartre, where there is still a vineyard, though this one has not always been there, for it was planted in 1933 to stop developers building on the land. The harvest festival, *fête de vendange*, of Clos Montmartre, ends today with a closing ball in Square Louise Michel. Saint Denis carried his head to Saint-Denis, indicating where he desired to be buried, the site of the cathedral. Saint Denis is the saint of syphilitics, though this is seldom mentioned. There is a German prayer from the fifteenth century that asks the saint for protection from the French disease. During the revolution the National Convention ordered the destruction of the tombs and mausoleums of the kings and queens of France in the cathedral. The necropolis was restored during the Bourbon restoration. It was impossible to identify many of the remains, buried under quicklime in mass graves. They were confined to an ossuary. The effigies were gathered from where they had been dispersed, those saved by Alexandre Lenoir who had claimed them as works of art for his Musée national des Monuments français in the former convent of the Petits-Augustins on the left bank, a building that is now part of the art school. In the cathedral, *with my own eyes*, I have seen the heart of Louis-Charles, Dauphin of France, son of Louis XVI. Dead at ten from tuberculosis, in the prison of the Temple, the child's heart travelled; it went from hand to hand: removed in an autopsy by Dr Pelletan, preserved in alcohol, lost then found in ruins after the July revolution of 1830, placed in a crystal urn by Pelletan's son, taken into the possession of Eduard Dumont, offered to Carlos, Duke of Madrid, kept at Schloss Frohsdorf near Vienna, passed to Carlos's son Jaime, then to Jaime's sister Beatriz, and finally, passed to Princess Marie des Neiges Massimo, who gave the child's heart to the Memorial of Saint-Denis. The heart lies near the graves of the child's parents. From a strand of Marie-Antoinette's hair, there was DNA proof that the heart was her son's. Son's heart. *Soleil cœur coupé. Adieu adieu.* In the end. *À la fin.*

Yesterday: amaryllis, but as I was reading Julia's introductory and concluding thesis chapters, the day passed unmarked – I could not move from one mode to another, and weather was wretched and my anxiety had returned in full force at night, dry-mouthed, sleepless. Writing was prohibited – I forbade myself. It was a relief. I made *compôte* from the green apples Annick gave me, boiled the slices in a light cane sugar syrup, added some twists of lemon peel, such enchanting curls. The amaryllis flowered while I was in hospital last year. The bulb put forth leaves in the summer, long and glossy, but no flowering stalk, then the leaves turned brown when I left it unwatered outside in the sun. I cut them off, back to the knotty bulb. Suddenly the bulb has sprouted new leaf growth and I brought it inside, placing it on a sunny windowsill, watering it hopefully. A young woman pierced her heart with an arrow, a golden arrow, she pierced her heart for thirty days and on the thirtieth day, a crimson flower grew from the blood of her heart. The woman was gone but the blood-red flower remained, her gift to the man who rejected her. He opened his door and there it was, the heart-flower. It is a myth, of course, yet another one in which a woman dies for a man or for a god, turning into a flower, a shrub, a tree, but of course, I have said all of this before.

Today: *bœuf*, beef, but also a cow or an ox. The cow or ox is alive, but the beef is dead. The beef is meat. David Hayman described a dinner with Jacques Lacan in a Parisian restaurant, the daunting pyramid of beef he could not chew his way through. In Lacan's apartment, Lacan pointed to a passage in Hayman's book on *Finnegans Wake*: 'But by writing thithaways end to end and turning, turning and end to end hithaways writing with lines of litters slittering up and louds of latters slettering down, the old *semetomyplace and jupetbackagain* from tham Let Rise till Hum Lit.' Did Joyce mean symptom, Lacan asked Hayman. It was a hopeful question, for it would knot Lacan's thoughts on psychosis, the symptom as a knot, Joyce the saint (*saint homme*) and Joyce the sinthome, elaborated by Lacan in his usual baroque style, taking sinthome from Rabelais, who combined theology, writing, and medicine with the pleasures of the body, with obscenity. No, said Hayman, for neither symptom nor *symptôme* had any resonance for him there, it is *see me to my place and jump it back again.*

Incorruptible bodies were on my mind, those who did not rot, who were miraculously preserved, who were covered with quicklime without effect of destruction, whose hearts and bones were incorrupt, who remained fragrant, who emitted a sweet unearthly odour, who remained moist and flexible, who opened their eyes and changed position, who continued to bleed, blood flowing from their wounds, so many of them. Saint Claire of Assisi, Saint Catherine of Siena, Saint Rita of Cascia, Saint Bernadette of Lourdes, Bernadette Soubirous who saw the Blessed Virgin eighteen times, the patron saint of the sick... the latter was exhumed in 1909 (she died in 1879), buried again, exhumed again, buried again, exhumed again and at this third time dissected and her organs were found to be still soft and malleable, though her skin, her flesh, had turned brown under its waxy covering, sealed with wax, just like an apple.

Francis sent me a photograph of a cake from Saarbrücken, where he was attending a conference; the small square cake bore a text on white rice paper (it seemed so – the photograph was hazy), *Traumkulturen*, which I hoped was the name of the cake, a dream-culture cake. It was, in fact – and rather disappointingly – the title of the conference. He told me about an interesting presentation on Freud's objects, the keynote of the event, entitled 'Dreaming Things', exploring the role of things in Freud's practice and writings, the historical signature of things. I told Francis about Ruth's book, where things predominate, speaking things. I remember that she wrote that these evocative objects are not heirlooms, but things skimmed off the surface of everyday life, furnishing day to day existence, acting beneath what is visible as cues for thought and spurs for memory.

I spoke to Martina in Ireland, who was almost in love and went a little pink as she told me about this; she said she had waited twenty years (but it did not last, and the rosiness has gone, replaced by a different kind of embarrassment that she had entertained sentiment for a man who always wore a tie). She described the singing circles, the groups that go round singing from pub to pub. There were three days without entries to my almanac and these were days of the aubergine, the pepper, and the tomato – the last of which were in the garden and would come in to become a ratatouille *à ma façon*, with coriander seed. I listened to a programme about Trieste and James Joyce, who said he did not seek Flaubert's *mot juste* but rather, sought the order of words in his sentences. Lying on my bed, I read Ruth's book, flanked by two dogs and with a cat lying heavily stretched out along my legs, making it difficult to move, and she wrote about the gnarled potato Leopold Bloom carried in his pocket (*in the trousers I left off. Must get it. Potato I have.*) She wrote that the tuber serves as a prophylactic against rheumatism, but perhaps that was Joyce. Amulets, she wrote, talismans, and self and body enmeshed. There is a risk, she said, that objects may intrude into the space of remembering, and while they may remind us of other people or the persons we once were, that may fossilise us or others.

There were two days of lightness, following the dark and anxious day of *sextidi*, and my spirits lifted despite the rain.

The shift in my mood was unfathomable to me. Often it is unbearable, but it must be borne. Today, a day of barley, the mood changed. There had been bad news from Paris, which I felt I could not recount here, and Francis could not come to Brittany after all because of the circumstances. Today, there were hunters in the forest all day. Their sounds carried across the fields. Their dogs bayed. There were gunshots. There were the strange whooping cries the men make to call their dogs when a beast has been sighted or to summon the dogs back. Women appear to be excluded from the hunt, except, of course, for Artemis, and then the hunt was hers and hers alone. Since then, I have not seen the family of roe deer. But at dusk, three or four hare ran across the path to the Metairie, from field to field to forest, and my dogs pursued them futilely into the woods, returning breathless and sheepish, tongues lolling from their mouths in the silly and endearing way dogs have.

The saint's day yesterday was that of Teresa of Avila, who as a girl cared only about flirtations with boys, and clothes. When she entered a convent, she continued to charm but felt her charm kept her from God. She would not let the nuns of the order she founded bow down or kneel to a princess. The papal nuncio called her a restless disobedient gadabout who went about teaching as though she were a professor. What cheek some women have. In Rome, Bernini's baroque sculpture of this rather cheery and attractive saint represents the ecstasy described in her *Life* when an angel plunged his spear through her heart and entrails, many times, in and out, seeming to pull them from her body and filling her with the sweetness of excessive pain and leaving her all on fire. Pain, an excess that disturbs, pain that is trapped in the body without release. In Seminar 20, Lacan said that you only have to get to Rome and look at Bernini's statue to immediately realise that she enjoys [*qu'elle jouit*], there's no doubt about it. And what is she enjoying? he asked, connecting pain to the jouissance of women, attributing pain to the order of infinity. Those men... hah, they do not know what they are seeing or saying. Idiots. The next day was Saint Edwige, and the character of those named for her, it was reported, would leave no-one indifferent. The saint herself was austere and humble and there was nothing at all interesting about her.

Décadi. Who has died? Brian Catling has died. Conrad Atkinson has died. Alan Halsey has died. Simon's mother has died. Their ages are various; they are all older than I. Jonathan has not died but might as well be dead – he has Parkinson's disease and Parkinson's dementia, doubly incontinent, he can no longer speak or walk with any ease; there are hallucinations. Yet he was found naked in the bed of a ninety-year-old woman in the care home. That gave some cheer. Older than I, too, are the dead women I do not know, the octagenarians and nonagenarians and centenarians breathing their last, those who departed, slipped away, passed on, shuffled off their mortal coil, succumbed, kicked the bucket, snuffed out, gave up the ghost, and crossed over this week: Anne, Marie-Hélène, another Anne, Félicie, Marie *dit* 'Mimi', Marie-Thérèse, and we have the sadness to announce, *nous avons la tristesse*. Yes, I have the sadness. I suffer *tristely*. What have I achieved on this *décadi*, the last day of *vendémiaire*?

> I have cleaned the henhouse. But I have not cleaned out the duck and goose houses.
> I have put tamarind to soak and cooked the chickpeas. But I have not picked the chard that will join them in a stew.
> I have bought cat biscuits from Silvie in the market. But I have not bought biscuits for the dogs as I did not have enough money.
> I have been to a *vide-grenier*, where for two euros I bought a framed painting of the sea, glimpsed through a tree, painted by 'Josée', who wrote on the back that it is a view of La Briantais, where later I walked the dogs, looking for that same view.
> I have hung Josée's painting in the bathroom, moving several others to new positions to accommodate it, in our gallery of

amateur sea and landscapes. Their point is not that the work is well done, as I explained to the man from whom I bought the painting, but he did not understand me and made a joke about checking to see if it were a Van Gogh. But I have not put away the hammer and screwdriver, not yet anyway.

I have made a cake, with sultanas and *citronat*. But out of laziness, I did not put in tiny strips of lemon zest, and it was not as a good a cake as it should have been. A mediocre cake.

I have picked a crate of medlars and placed them to blet in the guestroom, and I have taken a basket of them to Serge and Claudie. But I have not cut back the nettles around the water tanks, nor have I pruned the hazels.

It was the day of the barrel, the *tonneau*, a vat or a keg, the useful object of the *vendange*, for the ageing of wine or some spirits and beers, for balsamic vinegar. The *tonneau* is made from oak, various species. The vat breathes. It gives up the angel's share in its breath. A libation. The maenads, the bacchants, priestesses of Bacchus, tended the vines, when not raging in their orgiastic frenzy. There are always duties to perform, even for the wild girls.

In the middle of the night, she woke with the realisation that once again she had lost time, that days had disappeared, were not noted in her *almanach*. She noticed that she had returned to the third person. Vegetables, fruit, a tool, and several saints were missing, though often she omitted them if they were of little interest to her. She could not locate them in her notes as she searched for what was absent. *Brumaire* was not yet, and despite her dismay, it was also (curiously) as though she had gained time as much as she had lost it. She remembered someone (who, she wondered) once talking about travelling by train to Paris then immediately back to London then again to Paris, perhaps continuing this *aller-re-tour* forever, losing an hour one way, gaining an hour on the return. Would time stop and one's life extend indefinitely, eternally, a stranger on a train?

BRUMAIRE

Primidi. On my writing table there was a sheet of paper. I did not remember writing the words scrawled there, though the handwriting was mine, a clutch of inky sentences:

dîtes le trop fort
écoute cherie
en catamini
passe à ton voisin
belote rire
nul so decouvert
autant bonne année
j'ai un faim de loup

What did this all mean? say it too loud, listen darling, on the sly, pass to your neighbour, belote laugh, no one knows about it, so good year, I'm hungry as a wolf. What is a belote? It is a card game with thirty-two cards, invented in France in 1920, trick-taking. The belote is a royal pair: king and queen of a trump suit. Ah, yes. These phrases were not from my unconscious, traces of automatic writing, the production of messages through mediumship, divination, channelling, somnambulism, the dictation of thought in the absence of all control by reason. No, these are the words on the amusing wafers, *gaufrette amusante du Nord*, like the board game, very old, first made in the biscuit factory of Eugene Blond in 1894, five years before Freud's dream-book was published, the inscriptions in the patois of Flanders on the crisp wafer layered with extremely sweet vanilla cream fondant. On each wafer, a little amusing phrase is written that will make you smile: the buyer is assured. And I did – smile, that is – remembering then that I had written down the phrases first so I could eat the wafers after, all of them, *mangez-moi*, which made me feel a little sick, and *plus quand est fou, plus on rit*, the crazier one is the more one laughs. The factory is proud of its production, assuring the customer that as soon as you open the packet, a delicious vanilla scent grabs your nostrils! The visual aspect is also up to scratch. The wafer is smooth, golden, and decorated on both sides. The top has a nice border around the 'funny' phrase that made this northern wafer famous. The underside is decorated with regular latticework all over. The communion wafer is not at all amusing, however, nor is it at all delicious. It sticks unpleasantly, gummily and resistant, to the roof of the mouth. Nuns used to make the wafers, but now they come from a factory, often with a monopoly in the country of production. The Vatican says that the host must be unleavened, purely of wheat, and made recently so there is no danger of decomposition (after all, it transforms into the body of Christ). The bread and the wine *are* the body and the blood. There were miracles of hosts that bled, announcing their violation through becoming flesh. I think the rules on the host are different for other faiths. Every day my breakfast is a matzo, called here *pain azyme*, a paper host. For dough to become matzah, it must have the potential to leaven but without leavening. It must be closely watched so it does not leaven. No more than eighteen minutes should pass between the making of the dough and its baking. It is the bread of poverty. I have noticed that bakers, the *boulangers*, are usually men, as are pastry chefs, in France at least, though there exists a militant group of women bakers. However, the *boulangerie*, site of production and of commerce, is feminine. The *boulangères*, which is taken to mean the wife of the baker, not a baker herself, sell the bread, the cakes, the biscuits, the tarts. I bought two lemon tarts in Pleslin on the way to Lydie's opening in Dinard. On the lemon filling, the compelling words *tarte au citron* were piped ornately in chocolate icing.

It was the day of the apple but there were no apples; instead, I collected fallen pears from a path in the forest. They are hard, do not ripen, rot quickly. Half of those I brought home were rotten inside when I peeled off their skin in spiralling twists. Those I salvaged were put to simmer with red wine (the remains of a very good bottle), sugar, strips of lemon peel, and cinnamon sticks. Later, I thought, I would return to the path with a basket, not for the pears but for the chestnuts, even though we always forget to roast them. Every day for the last month, from another forest path, I have dragged back long branches, leaning them against one of the hangers to dry out until I can chainsaw them into small logs for the smaller stoves. I was determined that I would not order a cord of wood from Gérard until December, better yet not until the next autumn. Peasant meanness: *radin* and *grippe-sou*, cheese-parer and penny-pincher, skinflint and tightwad, *pingre* and *mesquin*. The annual apple fête in Quévert, cancelled for the last two dreadful years, would take place in early November, its theme this year the pear in *effervescence*, which may be translated as bubbling, excited, high-spirited, fermented. There will be two lectures, on the making of perry and on the advantages of lateral grafting. There we first met Charles, who died four years ago suddenly, who taught R. and Rosie about beekeeping, who had spent his working life underwater in nuclear submarines, who had been abused in a Catholic orphanage in Brittany, who was not allowed to see his daughter or granddaughter by his crazy wife (she hated his bees). Our remaining hive was under constant attack from the Asiatic hornet – it is unlikely that it will survive the winter. The bees lined up courageously at the entrance. It was heartbreaking. Charles's death was heartbreaking. When a beekeeper dies, the bees must be told, they must be put into mourning, a piece of the funeral biscuit (sometimes ladyfingers, soft and spongy in the centre, crisp and sugary on the outside, sometimes round doughy biscuits wrapped in pairs in black paper, or ale-cakes, or shortbreads flavoured with ginger, caraway, molasses) must be taken to the hive. If the bees are not given news of the death, they will become sick and die, or they will sting everyone and leave. Saint Ambrose is the patron saint of beekeepers – as a baby, sleeping in his cradle, a swarm of bees flew in and out of his mouth, but he was unharmed. Ambrosia, also called bee bread, is the honey and pollen fed to the bee larvae. The forgers bring it back to the hives and the nurse-workers pack it into the comb cells with their heads. Saint Ida of Louvain tasted the word as flesh on her tongue when she recited *the word was made flesh* and it was like honey, sweet not bitter.

I bought the small squid called *encornet*, from the man who sells from the trawler that fishes out of Cancale. The squid or squid-like cephalopods were fished in the bay there – it was not the usual man, however, but perhaps his son. The usual man no longer works on the trawler following an accident ten years ago – once he rolled up his sleeve to show me the enormous scar on his arm. The squid were stuffed with onion, garlic, parsley, tomatoes, their tentacles and fins chopped up fried in olive oil, then breadcrumbs added to the fragrant mixture. The opening sewn closed, they were gently braised in a sauce of onion, garlic, oregano, tomatoes, and white wine. Athanasios insisted that I should have added pine nuts. Geno said they looked like boiled mice, that they were disgusting. But no! served with an aioli, they were quite delicious, following a salad of rocket, dates, fresh figs, and soft goat cheese, with a dressing of pomegranate and good oil. Apple day was over, and we ate some sweet pears with some pleasure, with a nice morsel of pecorino.

Sunday and celery, *céleri*, a branch of which went in the garden soup for lunch, with turnip, carrot, leeks, onion, potatoes, barley, lentils, and a great bunch of flowering basil. We picked more of the ton of medlars from the tree, piling them into wooden crates, and took them to the village market for Arnaud to give away. Blet is the same in French as in English; he said his generation did not know this fruit. I took a plant, a white chrysanthemum, to Marcelle's grave in the village, and cleared away the dead heather from last year's All Saints. Monique never mentions that I have left a plant for her mother – perhaps she does not know it is from me. Rita once brought three large chrysanthemums as a present when she and Jonathan visited, a few years before her death; I did not tell her they were intended for the cemetery, where no doubt Marcelle's body, like the others, has also rotted away, leaving only the bones and the scraps that cling to them. Later, Rita and Jonathan sent a dangerous Japanese grater from London. I have sliced my fingers many times using this mandolin and my sister refused to touch it. Rita died of her cancer. Once she dug out the roots of dandelions in my garden with a tiny kitchen knife, a *couteau de service*. The dandelions have, nonetheless, always returned in the same place – the return of the repressed or the real always returning? The grater has a lethal blade, and often thin slices of my skin and flesh enter the celeriac remoulade or other salad, my blood staining it red, but of course that does not matter when it happened to be beetroot. I cleared the last of the runner beans from their iron tripods, the stalks now twisted and dry. I decided not to dry the beans this year for next, their taste is dry. The rain fell then. More rain. Misted views from the windows.

Before I left again for London, I picked up more pears in the woods, on this day of the pear. And they are green and hard on the outside though they may have rotten centres, like the monstrous British government that twists and turns and lies and blusters and is unbelievable. I read the names of roses, all the wives, 'Ena Harkness', for instance, and all the other *madams*, *mes dames*: mademoiselle 'Cécile Brunner', sweetheart and mignon, 'Zépherine Drouhin', the *belle dijonaise*, 'Louise Odier', which does not like damp ground. Do not lay Louise on damp soil, no. I sowed broad beans, spring peas, the white and red chicory that grows in low whorls. It was the day of the pear, as it should be.

I had to work backwards, from the afternoon of my return, *quartidi*, possessed by only a blur of memory, in which the vegetables and fruit included endives (chicory), Jerusalem artichokes (only fit for pigs, according to my neighbours), water chestnuts. salsify, scorzanera (black salsify), beetroot. I could not read my handwriting for one day, the day I went to Cambridge for a round-table discussion that was not round but rather formal, and where the past evaded me. It was chaired by someone I nearly loved once or could have loved and did not – I did not know if it had been reciprocal from his reaction towards me, which was devoid of any warmth. I felt that I had little to add; an important person was absent, who had accepted to speak then declined; I feared it might be because of me, that there was another friendship that no longer existed. The tree, last weekend, was a *sorbus*, mountain ash, rowan, stringy gum, quicken and quickbeam, wicky and wicken and wiggen and witch, a lovely thing with rosy wood and grey-fissured bark, bearing false fruit, orange to reddish-brown, which animals like (sometimes the tree is called dogberry) and humans can eat after the first frosts. Planted by a door, it keeps away witches, generally a good thing, a portal tree between life and death, ingress and egress, and so it goes. I learnt of another death. There was a *charrue*, a plow, another day I missed noting, unpacking books, writing invoices, and I thought a *charrue* was a cart until I looked it up, which defeated my intention to consider the tumbril, tilting back to empty its load, arms or bodies, alive on their way to execution or dead, decapitated, thereafter.

Much was seen or read or thought, but quickly, it all fled quickly, for I felt I must catch up – and was barely observed when attempting recollection. When I said to Eleonora that I had not written a word while in London, and was unhappy about it, she asked coldly why I felt I should write (I sensed judgement and also I thought she had taken the packet of Marvis jasmine-mint toothpaste when she left, as well as choosing to sleep, Goldilocks-like, on my bed when I left for my mother's house. Later I found it was R. on his last visit who had taken the expensive Italian toothpaste, though he does not like this flavour or indeed, this brand of toothpaste, deploring the absence of fluoride, and I was glad I had not written an accusation, even one framed as a polite enquiry), and I could only reply that if I did not, I would die, and oh, that old death-drive once again, all organic things returning to an inorganic state, undoing, destruction. And linked to the suicidal tendency of narcissism, so perhaps that explained the candid coolness – and certainly, for sure, my repetition-compulsion, here we go again. My observations, well, a few, brief, succinct, for the days that passed unnoted, the days of a city and the days of visiting my mother, included the violence against migrants, a firebomb at an immigration 'processing' centre and the time it took to declare this to be a terrorist attack, outbreaks of dysentery, diphtheria, scabies, and MRSA at Manston, an image of a child held up to a wire fence, mobile phones confiscated, children classified as adults so they might be removed; the claims of the outrageously reinstated home secretary that there is an invasion of people seeking asylum, a claim challenged by migration experts. Or a report on the predatory police officers, staging unwarranted stops of women, an abuse of power they called 'booty patrols', pursuing women for sex, watching pornography on duty. I read about wolves at Donlon Books, while the street and pavement outside were dug up to lay cables; I read about encounters with works of art at the Small Publishers Fair where I also sold books, without charm, but the attention to customers from Eleonora and Joe, their different approaches (pouncing enthusiasm and quiet intention) more than compensated for my surliness. I read before Tim read, then introduced him and his reading, and in the introduction and the readings, I was as charming as I could be, which is sometimes very charming indeed, but I was tired, very tired, and then the next day had to face my mother's sullen resentment of her situation and her refusal to make more of an effort, had to engage with the problems of her medical care, arguing, trying not to raise my voice in anger while repeating the matters, the issues, insisting on their resolution, and above all, wanting to sleep, sleep... I passed through Paris, eating Senegalese food with my son, visiting the exhibition on Parisian women citizens, the women activists from the revolution to the 1970s, at the Musée Carnavalet. On display was a black silk purse, supposed to be that of Louise Michel, a marvel to me, striking to my heart, embroidered with the dates of revolutions, 1789, 1830, 1848, 1871. *Holy shit*, wrote Lisa, *where is that?* I passed Ricardo's flat on the long bus ride to Montparnasse and saw his lights were on and so I knew he would be at his desk, alone, painstakingly cutting strips of printed paper, assembling his collages from other images. For a moment, I considered sending him a text that I was outside but did not do so and I was not sure why.

In the museum there is Proust's bedroom, or rather, an amalgamation of three bedrooms, from boulevard Haussmann to rue Laurent-Pichet to rue Hamelin, a ghost room, a recreation, a fiction. There is an overcoat, his coat, as weighty in appearance and meaning as Freud's in London. It is double-breasted, lined with otter fur, a thousand times denser than human hair; Proust wore it constantly, even to dine at the Ritz on the Place Vendôme; it served as a blanket on his bed. It is mortified. I had forgotten the threads of Proust, tracing, forming, convergence in his cork-lined room. The walls of the house at Illiers, his father's house, were hung with red damask. His childhood bed was swagged with high white curtains. The cook, Françoise, made beef in aspic which he compared with a sculpture by

Michelangelo. Later, his secretary and housekeeper, Céleste Albaret, did not cook for him, no, though she did serve him two croissants and two bowls of café au lait at four in the afternoon, and she ordered his meals from restaurants, a little chicken breast perhaps, a small fillet of sole, no wine – he drank very little. Céleste became Françoise. Sylvain Maréchal, in his project of a law that would forbid reading to women, notes that reason dictates that women should be excluded from botany with the exception of vegetables and herbs, and that it is well known that cooks who do not know how to read make the best soup. Illiterate *potagères*.

My first day of return was a turkey, and that is also a dud, a flop, a disappointment, an ill-advised or stupid act. There was a lump in my cheek, a cyst, I thought, but the new doctor in the village told me it is no more than a *calcul* in a salivary gland, a tiny calcification. Perhaps my body is turning to stone, slowly becoming petrified. I would not be surprised. I remembered my maternal grandmother taking me to Mother Shipton's cave in Knaresborough, and the dropping well, its water petrifying the objects placed in it, giving them a stony exterior. Such magic, such witchcraft... Mother Shipton was Ursula Southeil (her name has various spellings), a prophet, a soothsayer, born deformed, hunchbacked and ugly, in a thunderstorm, cackling not crying as she emerged into the world and the storm abated at the moment of her birth. She lived alone with her mother Agatha in the cave, both ostracised, until the bishop had them removed; Agatha was sent to a convent, Ursula to a foster family, and mother and daughter never saw each other again, mother and ugly child divided. When Ursula walked in the streets, she was mocked, hag-face, devil's bastard, Satan's spawn, but still, people came to her to be cured by her herbal remedies. The doctor advised me to suck lemons. Hah, yes, it is a sour and negative mood, or it is an expression of anger or scorn when directed to someone, an imperative. This new doctor does not like me very much. I missed Bruno and I missed Yousef, our first doctor here, who came from Lebanon, who once, when I was ill, called by in the evening as he was worried about me.

While away I had been thinking about some syndromes, those called Fresoli, Cotard, Clérambeault. Persecutors follow one, repeatedly changing their appearance, strangers are familiar people in disguise, there are imposters; different people are one person who keeps changing, Places, events, and objects cannot be recalled. Or one has lost one's soul or is dead; or organs and parts of the body have disappeared. One might stink of rotting flesh in the delirium of negation, or starve oneself to death, for a dead body, one condemned to eternal damnation, has no need to eat, what would be the point. Even if unconvinced that one is dead, one continues to suspect it. It is as if one no longer exists. Or one is a walking corpse. Petrified. On a more cheerful note, from *thanatos* to *eros*, one may become convinced that another loves one, and that exalted other has a higher social status, sending messages through subtle means, the posture of the body, a car licence plate, an arrangement of household objects, special codes, ah yes, the secret admirer that only the lover (beloved?) can read, perceive, interpret, see love's true form. There is repetitive calling; there are unexpected visits and continuous attempts to send gifts or letters to the beloved. Yes, the traumatic object cause of desire, dialectical inertia, but nonetheless, clarity of thought and purpose may be brought to erotomania, and something survives, reproducing itself outside the delusion.

There followed a weekend of chervil and cress; the former grows abundantly, both seeded by me and self-seeded, fragile-leaved, delicately aniseed in flavour; of the latter, the last of the Turkish cress has been eaten. Rocket grows, now without the ravages of the flea beetle (I should use a sticky

trap), and there were still tomatoes, basil, and a few courgettes. The pumpkins were magnificent if not plentiful. The
apple tree, the *madeleine*, was been cut down, the wood
logged and stacked. The fig and mulberry were yet to prune,
but it is better to wait until February; the runners from the
base should be torn off rather than cut. From the market in
Dol, there were scallops, cooked with sage and smoked butter, and again delicious little squid, made into a stew with
red pepper, tomatoes, onion, garlic, white wine, and chickpeas. The next day there was a groundnut stew of pumpkin
and sweet potato, with spiced red rice from the Camargue,
a *bleu d'auvergne* with the first batch of the medlar cheese,
and a carrot cake with cinnamon and nutmeg. The rain fell
steadily. Summer clothes in the wardrobe were replaced by
those of winter. I wondered why I had so many dresses that
look the same, so dark and drab. They are costumes, after a
fashion. I read Gaurav's book, *Costumes of the Living*. He
wrote that all the clothes we would ever make would be
stitched from those we already owned, either growing old or
never worn. He wrote of his woollen place, but I did not
understand him then. Walking the dogs towards the forest
path, we saw in the distance a couple accompanied by a Dal-
matian dog; they were leading a small grey donkey on a hal-
ter. We could not catch them up for a closer admiration of
dog and donkey. I remembered Francis as a small child
holding a donkey on its bridle while its owner, a Dutch
woman, went into the pharmacy. She was on the pilgrimage
route to Saint Jacques de la Compostelle. We were staying
with Rachel and Max, and from their house the mountains
could be seen against the sky. This summer I had intended
to walk part of the route with Francis, but of course my accident prevented it. I do not know if there would be another
time. Had I written this already? Yes, of course I have.

Dentelaire and *grenade*, plumbago and pomegranate,
celestial blue and garnet red. The former, taken as an

emetic, expels nightmares; it is used to treat warts, wounds, broken bones. Taken as snuff, plumbago cures a headache. The latter, the seeded apple, the apple of Grenada, represents both fertility and a pause in fecundity. Persephone saw the dead and married their king, who was both a god and a place, who was reluctant to return her to her mother. He gave her a pomegranate and she ate its seeds, enough of them to bind her to him. A pomegranate holds over six hundred seeds, one for each *mitzvah*, each good deed (and no good deed goes unpunished). It cures ulcers and fastens teeth. The unicorn bleeds the juice of the fruit from its wounds in at least one medieval image. I made potato gnocchi, little puffy clouds flipped quickly over the curve of a fork to indent them while pressing firmly against the tines with the index finger in a perpendicular position so they absorbed the rich sauce of the last tomatoes, peppers, and courgettes that bathed them, and today, as R. departed to London this morning, the rest of the sauce was to be eaten with pasta, as I live the days once again to my own rhythm, my own patterns, my own desires, for the week to come. I wrote in the studio where the light is clearer, brighter. The rain pounded on the window and Céleste slept soundly on a pile of fabrics kept in an African basket woven from plastic strips, which tend to break off and scatter, and one is never sure at first what they are, these little pink and blue and white scraps. Tomorrow, I thought, I would put away the drawings that have been on the wall for too long and resume my reading of La Fontaine and animals who speak and transform. Back to Barthes, I thought, back to a *vita nova*, back to *marcottage* – the composition by enjambments, insignificant details, but it must be my own way, *to want to*. But of course, part of me longs only for a life of unconstrained and eternal leisure. While I was away, an enormous mushroom was found in a meadow in Bobital, a *vesse de loup*, a giant puffball, *lycoperdon*, wolf's flatulence. It was so big its finder could not get it into his basket. It weighed nearly four kilos. Sliced finely, it is good fried in butter and olive oil with garlic, but the finder doubted he and his family would be able to eat it all.

Nonidi brumaire: *herse* or harrow, a chassis with a grill formed by two series of perpendicular bars fixed at the points they cross. Its pointed teeth flatten the soil, breaking up the muddy clumps, preparing the ground for sowing. It appears late in the year in the calendar. And it is an obsolete word for a hearse in English, the carriage of the dead. Barthes wrote that he writes, he finishes (in quotation marks, and I imagined his hands, which I also imagine as elegant hands, long-fingered, but slightly (perhaps unpleasantly) moist, in the air, his fingers flicking as he spoke the word, perhaps holding a cigarette, no, probably holding a cigarette – once I was told by a man who knew him that Barthes smoked Marlborough, and when I told Jane, she found that hard to believe – and he dies. He wrote that Proust struggled against death, to finish writing before dying. He wrote of reprieve, what Proust would have written, could have written, if he had not died, but a reprieve could be no more than an excess of time, and thus of boredom, and Proust could have only kept on adding to the work, more oil to the mayonnaise (such a fragile emulsion, and one that cannot be made in a thunderstorm; the oil must always be added slowly, but if it breaks, may be repaired by starting again with a new yolk and gently, slowly, whisking in, spoonful by spoonful, the separated disappointing broken mass, then a few drops of lemon juice will improve it, a little spoonful of Dijon mustard helps), paperole after paperole (paperwork or manuscript, but Kate does not translate it, choosing to leave the word in French unitalicised as I do here, but anyway, it is bits of old paper), and his last word, on a sheet of paper, a bit of old paper, the manuscript of *Albertine disparue*, stained with Veronal – a barbiturate with hypnotic effect, dispensed for insomnia

induced by nervous excitability and often the means of suicide for those who sought to escape deportation to the con-
centration camps, was *Forcheville*. The word appears
throughout *In Search of Lost Time*: the Count of Forcheville, a brutal snob and Swann's rival for Odette, Madame
Swann who became Madame Forcheville, who said *faire de
catleyas* for *faire l'amour* (Catleya is a South American
orchid, the queen of orchids, 'mature charm' in the language of flowers, and 'testicles' in its Greek origin 'orchis'),
Gilberte Swann, daughter of Odette and Swann, who
became Mademoiselle de Forcheville, taking the name of
her stepfather after the death of her father, for in the anti-
Dreyfus, antisemitic climate it was better that it should be
forgotten that she was the daughter of a Jew. Proust wrote
that by wasting his time (that of his narrator, of course, who
may be Proust, and/or a literary device, and once at least he
is Marcel, 'my Marcel', 'my dearest Marcel', were the author
to give him his own name), by giving him grief, Albertine
(who might have been Alfred, his occasional chauffeur,
Albert, his occasional secretary, another Albert, his great
pal, Henri, another occasional secretary, Marie, a young
admirer, or another Marie, the daughter of another chum),
with her little pink nose like a cat's, had perhaps been more
useful to him, even from the literary point of view, than a
secretary who would have tidied up his paperwork or manuscripts, his paperole.

Who has died? Odette, Albertine, Berthe, Michèle, Roberte,
Anne-Marie, Marie-Thérèse, Annick, Denyse, Marie-
Yvonne, Yvette, Emma, Paulette, Nicole, Danielle, Eléo-
nore, Rachel, Jeanne, Monique, Marie-Ange, Alice, Colette,
Claudine, Andrée, Yvonne, Françoise, Liliane, Armande,
Fernande, Anne, Janine, Marie, Marie-Louise... *messieurs*
Marcel Boulanger and Marcel Rouillard died as well. So
many deaths in my absence and that was not the half of
them. By now I had narrowed my list to those dying in their

nineties, which as I write would give me another twenty-three years before I am included in the roll call, to meet that final curtain. Barthes wrote that dying could be drawn out; the grandmother (the narrator's) in the garden at Combray, the fact of her body in the garden is the same body as the body that falls ill and dies. That's enough of that for today, I thought, there are too many bodies, even when death takes one by surprise, hallucinating or short of breath.

As I cut in half a pomegranate this morning, I heard a man describing how his small son slipped away from him in the fire that swept Grenfell Tower in 2017. The inquiry has been long-running, the closing statements are issued this week. The police investigation, its decision on criminal charges, will not be made until next autumn. The pomegranate bled its juice onto the wooden board. Tony wrote to me from Beirut, telling me how to extract its seeds without crushing them: you cut the upper part. You remove the crown. You cut the lower part. Then you make incisions with a knife along the white lines. Then you just crack it open. I am accustomed to holding a half over a bowl and giving it a hearty whack with a wooden spoon, but I have found this is not a satisfactory method despite what people say. Ghazal told me that she started growing pomegranate trees by her tiny bedroom window; she said they really need a lot of water. She said in Persian fables each pomegranate has forty women inside it, and when they come out of the fruit, they are very thirsty, so thirsty that they will die of thirst if they are not given water immediately. It is best, she said, to open a pomegranate by a river so the women can survive. The fables, she thought, came originally from Afghanistan. Hajar's poems in *Disbound* take an inventory: exile, yes, and family and language and nation, what is left behind, in Kabul, and what will never return or be returned to; she realigns and is out of line, under excessive stress. There were pauses and gaps as I listened to her reading, a reading about pauses and gaps. She asked me to imagine an apostrophe, cutting it in half. The juice from my pomegranate was bitter. A disappointment.

Today was the day of bacchante, which filled me with excitement. It is *baccharis halimilfolia*, not a raging one but a groundsel tree or sea myrtle or consumption weed. It is a plant of fragrant roots, from which its name derives, *bacchus*, flowering in the late summer. It makes a horrible tea, which may be used to treat inflamed kidneys, fever, and flu. My day was disturbed: I almost forgot two meetings online, discombobulated by events of the morning, and could not concentrate, even when Julia was discussing her use of the apostrophe. I hated the way my face looked on screen, ugly, ugly, and for that there is no cure, no nasty tea or bitter pill (or rather, that *is* the bitter pill).

The saints have been a rather dull bunch recently, so I have not bothered with them, and chose to follow Maréchal, for whom to believe in God was to submit to hierarchy, to masters, to solemnity and memorial, reason should prevail. He gave a hundred and thirteen reasons why women should not learn to read, fortifying eighty-two clauses, to prove that the woman who knows the alphabet has already lost a portion of her innocence. He cited many, including Molière, quoting him on the contagion of reading, that once a woman opened a book, she would think herself capable of writing one, and a woman who 'composed' knew more than she needed to. The night was falling; I spoke to Bernard, with whom I will have lunch in Paris next week to talk about his and Marie-Laure's exhibition about Jacques Lacan and art/artists. How lovely it must be to live at Pyramides, I thought. I miss the city today, any city, with the luxury and ease of leaving the house, but perhaps especially Paris, where I know now that I will never live, whatever my desire. But really, in truth, today, this evening as night falls, all I wanted was to lie on the sofa with a glass of wine, watching a Finnish thriller set in Lapland, which brought together a serial killer and a sexually-transmitted virus, a new pandemic come from Yemen, to watch the strangely beautiful patterns of the virus revolving slowly, inexorably, on the screen of the German expert who is bound to fall in love with the investigating policewoman, who last night looked at herself wrapped only in a towel in a mirror and as she turned, caught sight of who – what – was behind her...

I had to look up *azérole* this morning, uncertain what it was. I found that it is the fruit of the Cretan hawthorn, a mediterranean medlar, orange or yellow or red; Zoë's last line in her poem in her revolutionary calendar reads *vermilion orpiment chrome yellow gold*. The fruit is edible, sweet and sour at the same time, though one seldom sees it sold. It was common on Italian tables in the sixteenth century, called *lazzaroni*, described as good and tasty and healthy for indisposed bodies, beautiful and pleasing to the eye. It has healing properties, relieving the thirst of burning fevers. An infusion of the flowers is a remedy for hypertension, the force of blood circulating through the arteries too great. It was Armistice Day, the day the hostilities on the Western Front ceased, at the eleventh hour of the eleventh day of the eleventh month. A public holiday, it was marked only for me by the fact that no post was delivered, the parcel I had expected. The village *fanfare*, the brass band led by Noël, usually marches around the church on Sunday to commemorate the day. No poppies in France, but *bleuet*, cornflowers. The festival of Reason of the second décadi of *brumaire* in Year II was described as a farcical image by Jacques-René Hébert, the great exaggerator, in his newspaper *Le Père Duchesne*: 'a delightful woman, as beautiful as the goddess she represented, was seated at the top of a mountain, a revolutionary cap on her head, holding a pike in her hand, surrounded by all the pretty excommunicated Opera girls who, in their turn, damned the cloth with their more than angelic singing of patriotic hymns.'

Jean Starobinski wrote that the farce corresponded to a profound contradiction, that instead of creating real presence, replacing dead Christian images by living beings, the festival fell into the old trap of representation, for Reason was no more than a pretty girl from the Opera, no more than a spectacle, simply another cumbersome image, superfluous (he said, *de trop*), ridiculous and obscene. Iconoclasm was accompanied by the appearance of a new idol, a new form; *an image dies; an image is born*. The law of *brumaire*, in Year IV, introduced seven festivals, five of them moral: Youth, Old Age, Spouses, Thanksgiving, Agriculture, and festival followed festival, without (critics said) order or reason, although throughout the Directory, attempts were made to show that they were an inspiring and philosophical series, and Nicholas François de Neufchâteau assembled a handbook of the festivals from the mass of accounts kept at the Ministery of the Interior, selecting what he thought to be the best examples for an exquisite volume to be proposed for emulation by every commune in the Republic. Mona Ozouf called it a dream of unanimity, a dream in which every citizen would recognise the same rites, the same songs, the same plan. From Ukraine came the news that the Russians were withdrawing from Kherson to the opposite banks of the river, and that Ukrainian flags were flying over the city. Russian officials claimed it was a redeployment.

Madder and orange, before entering the final *décadi*, before my last month yet to come. Instead of writing, I spent most of the day yesterday editing the doctoral thesis of a friend, no, one who is not quite a friend, not yet anyway, and oddly, one who writes about a book I wrote over twenty years ago. We share first names, which makes our correspondence oddly amusing, S to S, S from S, signifier and signified. I was painstaking, every comma, every semi-colon, every little flaw of grammar addressed. She had made a most amusing parapraxis, one that would have delighted Freud. When finally, I sent it to her, I apologised for being a pedant, and later, I thought I had written pendant, and yes, I was certainly something hanging around her neck. I was a bit snippy, remarking on the way she disclaimed that her work was therapy; unkindly, I reminded her of Freud's ideas on denegation, the patient who says you know that woman in my dream, well, she's definitely not my mother, and so, of course, it is immediately clear that the woman is precisely, exactly, no doubt about it, you know, the mother.

In 1770 Oberkampf began using copperplate printing at Jouy. While parts of the production process were increasingly mechanised, some aspects, especially at the beginning of the enterprise, could only be completed by laborious handwork. A third of the workforce was comprised of women, earning half the wage paid to male workers. Workers worked in groups, each with its own hierarchy. The *pinceauteuses*, who added colours to the printed toiles, worked in formations called tables. One stage of the printing process of a toile is the *garançage*: the printed cloth is passed through a bath of dye made from the madder root, which reveals the colours printed by the use of mordants, obtaining a range of colours from dark red to pale pink, black to lilac. The background is pink; it is left to bleach in sunlight. Yellow and blue were printed directly on the cloth by the *pinceauteuses*; until 1808 green could only be obtained by superimposing blue on yellow. In my studio I found the remaining packet of madder. I had sent two others to Thomas, which he used to dye his silk thread before making the lace jabot I commissioned from him. The jabot was worn by a cadaver, a Stockman mannequin dating from 1871. It appeared bloodstained, but the blood, one might say, was there from the beginning, that the blood is always there. On 28 July 1794 Robespierre went to the *guillotine* in Place de la Révolution, without trial. When clearing Robespierre's neck, the executioner tore off the cloth holding his shattered jaw in place, causing Robespierre to produce an agonised scream until he was silenced by the fall of the blade. I think of this moment often. I repeat the story.

I bought oranges, a very small mango, six little pears, and a persimmon from Arnaud in the village. My car still did not start, and Denis had not come as he had promised. I thought about what it would be like when R. died, and I was alone here, stranded. I assumed he would die before me. Sometimes I look at houses for sale in small towns, wondering what I would need when I am on my own, and where it would be possible to live as I wished to live. I assumed I would wish to live. I walked with the dogs to the village, the path behind the château, but a longer route as the path that descends from Annick's field, by her walnut tree, is still blocked where it joins the crossroad. Consulting the cadastral plans, Yves found that while the path does not belong to the château as the owners claimed, neither is it a public right of way, belonging instead to whichever farmers own the parallel fields; the track should run across a field higher up, after the cross-paths, through the land where the Bonniers park their many cars and pile up a great deal of broken matter, including rusty machinery. Their yard is overgrown, full of dog shit. We have not seen Christiane for two years, we do not know even if she is still living. We were told she had a liver transplant, that was all, and while Alain and Jerôme wave, and I speak with Geoffroy, none of the sons mention their mother, and when I asked Geoffroy directly, he simply shrugged and changed the subject. I know they were estranged, even though he continues to live next door to his family, with his own family, in the house that was Cécile's, his grandmother's, until her death, where she lingered with a gangrenous leg, and I promised to visit her but never did. On the path I crossed, the man I see often with his two dogs was with a woman and another dog, and I had seen them together before, buying oysters in the village. They lived rough, I thought, they are red-faced, with hard wind scarred faces, too many layers of clothes for the season, a sense of self-containment. But a week later I saw them enter a house in the village after buying oysters. The dogs are lovely. When stroked, their coats are greasy and leave one's hand a little grubby. If I were to touch the man or the woman, there would be the same traces left on my hand. They asked me if there was a hunt today – I thought not.

Arnaud told me he had managed to give away most of the medlars I left with him, and agreed that they were an acquired taste, but Virginie, who sells the oysters and looks like the shrimp girl in the painting by Hogarth that's in the National Gallery in London, loves them, he said, even eating them before they blet, preferring them to figs any day. The shrimp girls were the daughters or wives of the fishmongers in Billingsgate Market, the travelling sellers of shellfish. I bought cheese I did not need, a goat *tomme* with herbs, and one of Erica's that she calls *Nain*, for no clear reason, though one of her children may have named it as dwarfish cheese. I bought good flour, milled across the river by the farm where Erica buys her milk, and a jar of too-expensive crab pâté, made in La Vieille Vicomté, where we almost bought a house by auction, by *vente à la bougie* or *chandelle*, an old custom in which at the time of the last bid, a small wick is lit. After it is extinguished, a second candle is lit, and then a third. Once the last candle goes out, if no other bid is made during this time, the auction is declared in favour of the last bidder. I asked Sylvie to deliver a sack of dog kibble and one for the cats on her way home. The dogs ran cheerfully through the forest, and we crossed once again the man and woman with their dogs. The dogs clustered, sniffing bums, not unfriendly to each other, neutral engagement. Today I would clear leaves at the back of the house and clear the polytunnel of the tomato plants. That was my task. I set to on the leaves.

The polytunnel was not cleared, a job reserved for the afternoon, but the rain resumed its relentless downpour. However, part of the gravel court at the back of the house that leads to the road was cleared of moss and weeds, and a hydrangea that was blocking light from the downstairs bathroom was cut back, even though it is not the right time of year. It is better to leave the dead flowerheads to protect the new buds below them. Yet it was good to have more light in a dark room. On one side, I trimmed the lavenders into satisfying round shapes. On the other side I started to pull up the self-sown verbena *bonariensis*. To my delight, the couple with the donkey walked down the road. With them was a charming Malinois puppy, though the woman was stupid about rushing away with him, flapping her arms, as my dogs approached. It was true that Hera was barking in a fierce manner, but she would not have hurt the puppy, and dogs must learn, as I said to her (the woman) in a stern voice. I patted the donkey, who was completely uninterested in my sentimental attentions, my unsolicited affection.

This morning a pheasant took flight over the path to the Metairie in a flurry of flapping awkward wings, and I saw it was the day of the pheasant in the calendar. This was satisfying. Next, a roe deer bounded across, and I was relieved that the hunters had not culled them all. I dragged home another thick long branch from the forest floor, still determined not to buy wood this year. My electric chainsaw was broken, and R.'s petrol-fired chainsaw was too heavy for me. Yves who works still for the commune used to chainsaw my wood when it arrived. I supposed I could ask my neighbour, another Yves, but really, it could wait. I was as dull as the weather. I am dull. I was, however, rather enjoying the dullness, the sense of one thing after another, the completion of tiny tasks that had been outstanding: the clearing of my desk, the unpacking of boxes stacked on the mezzanine of my study for months, the cleaning of the kitchen cupboards and shelves. I read a fable of the wolf and the lamb, which shows that it is always the best argument (*raison*) that triumphs. I read a poem by Alice Notley in which she writes that she is angry today, trying to think how she wasn't yesterday. I read Jean La Bruyère on the morals of his century, on brutality, chagrin, superstition, and on women, whom he recommends should be judged completely from their shoes to their hairstyle, in the same way one measures a fish from tail to head. I listened to the news on the wireless, as a reporter described the dead bodies lying scattered on the ground in Kherson. A woman market-stall holder, cooking shashlik on a grill, said there was no water, no electricity, no Internet; she had no mobile phone, she said; she laughed, and it was a bitter laugh. I read the letter Rosa Luxemburg wrote from prison in November 1917: she was deep in the study of geology and if one thought this to be a dry subject, one would be mistaken. In another letter she felt her interest in organic nature to be almost morbid in its intensity. Her body was buried, then disinterred, or even never buried at all. In 2007 the director of the Institute of Legal Medicine in Berlin announced that an unidentified mummified torso at Charité Hospital was that of Luxemburg and the body dredged from the canal was that of another. Though he produced scientific evidence, his case came to nothing. He posed with the body for a newspaper photograph; later, the body was turned over to the police and buried anonymously. Rosa Luxemburg wrote of her black wrappings of darkness, tedium, unfreedom.

25 *brumaire* and pistachios or 15 November and Saint Albert. The pistachio is simple enough, green and sweet, growing on its tree like little bunches of grapes, grown by Adam in the garden of Eden and in the hanging gardens of Babylon, travelling on the Silk Road and on the routes of the Venetian sea trade. There is a cake from Sicily made with

pistachio flour, with ginger and lemon peel; the use of Bronte nuts cultivated on the good volcanic soil of Mount Etna is recommended in the recipes. The cracking of its nut brings good fortune, especially to lovers. Saint Albert, on the other hand, is more complicated than a small green nut. A philosopher, a theologian, Albert fought for the right of those in religious orders to teach in the universities, and brought Aristotle to his world, rediscovered through the Arab tradition of Cordoba. He was poorly shod, nicknamed 'Sandals' as well as called master, Master Albert from Padua, Albertus Magus. He was the teacher of Thomas Aquinas, that dumb ox, the doctor of angels.

From Egypt, the news came that Alaa Abd El-Fattah was still alive. On partial hunger strike in prison for seven months, he was now taking water again, he wrote in a letter, held back by the authorities for two days, to his mother; his sister said she could sleep again without nightmares, that she could breathe for the first time in eight days. He asked his mother to bring him an MP3 player, effervescent salts, and vitamins. His British citizenship was denied, and his sister said he was made to disappear by the Egyptian government, even with so much attention on him. From Kherson, the retaliations against those believed to be collaborators began, such as women market stallholders, who were too nice to the Russians. Nadine's French mother was accused of 'horizontal collaboration' during the Occupation; she was one of those women, heads shaved, sometimes stripped and tarred, and paraded in the *épuration sauvage*. Throughout the day once again the rain was intermittent but heavy, and the field where the poultry live looked like a lake. I wanted to plant new trees there, plum, mirabelle, cherry, three or four. I doubted that I would, but if I did, it should be before Saint Catherine's day, when trees put down their roots, *à la Sainte-Catherine, tout bois prend racine*. It was also the day of the *Catherinettes*, young women over twenty-five not yet married, poor spinsters, who would don extravagant hats in shades of green and yellow and decorate a statute of the patron saint of hat-makers with flowers and ribbons in the hope of finding a husband. In a rare moment of sunshine, Julien and Céline arrived to start installing the metal staircase on R.'s studio. I felt I had achieved little, but I re-read Suzanna's book and wept, which I had not done on my first reading. It weighed on me; I wanted to have written it and was glad I had not. It is the kind of writing I have refused for myself while envying it in the writing of others.

On my glass worktable there was a picture that had remained there until today when I moved it, for now it appeared, appears, a card showing a painting of a striped cat, entitled 'Erskine Returning at Dawn'. It is by Tirzah Ravilious, née Garwood, who gave up her art to support her husband Eric in his career and raise their three children. When he died, she painted again. She wrote an autobiography, intended only for her family. Suzanna asked why it was necessary to make art about lived experience, why such a thing should be described as autobiographical, and while that question was explained to her, she would be elsewhere, somewhere phantomic, she said, where that question did not need to be explained. And meanwhile, in a painting, under a crescent moon a cat returned from hunting, and my cats, deterred by the downpours, lay around like discarded old fur jackets, black, calico, white with grey spots, fat black and white, that one with stomach towards the stove, and I thought of Isobel and her mother, Lamé, bringing down the furs from the attic for their cats in the winter. A black dog lay on the kilim in the hallway in the attic and a curly-haired dog lay in a basket under the table in my studio while I was remaking the little painting of a woman with horns sprouting from her forehead, sent to Isabella in return for her book last year and arriving to her creased, damaged, despite the care I had taken in packing it.

26 *brumaire* and the woman with horns, from the series of twenty entitled *Les Maîtresses de la chasse*, is finished, more vibrant, less downcast than the damaged original. The fur on her throat and chest is more finely worked. I noticed that I needed new watercolours, and it would be such pleasurable shopping, for venetian red, brown ochre, magnesium brown, burnt sienna, brown madder, raw umber, burnt umber, sepia, *caput mortum* violet, oxide of chromium, terre verte, winsor deep red. On Friday, I would resume and complete my set of wolves, then start on the bleeding seed pods at last, or rather the roots, the bloody radicals, instead. The rain poured down all day, yet again, but I cleared the paths of the last of the medlars, swept up the fig leaves, and made *focaccia* and soup and hummus with a lot of lemon, parsley, and sumac. I picked radicchio for a risotto for Francis and me this evening and arranged that Régine would collect him from the bus stop in Pleslin, for I was still without a car though I expected Denis to call by at 6.30, when no doubt it would start immediately and he would look both puzzled and patronising. Other travel arrangements failed, as R.'s train from London was cancelled. He might not get back this evening and what was planned, seemed simple, suddenly loomed beset with complications if Francis and I were to depart the next morning as planned.

The entry in the revolutionary calendar was the tuberose pea, *lathyrus*, *macjonc*, which sounds like a character invented by Edward Lear, and should be in a rhyming song, strummed on a ukulele (a word that is surprisingly difficult to spell). I did not hear the news, but I did receive a letter from Eleni in Athens giving me her news, reminding me of our project to reprint the first book in my *Freud on Holiday* series. Its origin was a conference paper, given in 'Dream-Writing' in the School of English, University of Kent, in

2005, convened by Sarah Wood, *int. al.* The paper was accompanied by the projection of a series of photographs, showing a Rome never seen before, or one never consciously recognised. These were views of a city any tourist might see – but captured empty of human activity, as if they were night scenes in broad daylight, and empty arches and cryptic doorways indicated a concealed life. The photographs were taken from guidebooks contemporaneous with Freud's visits to Rome. They were presented as though they were Freud's photographs. Freud, however, did not take photographs while travelling – he bought engravings, prints, cards. After my paper, several people asked me where I had discovered this hitherto unknown archive of Freud's photographs. I think it was this question that set the project in motion. To undertake my holiday work efficiently I read many rail and ferry timetables of Europe. I know a great deal about rolling stock. I am careful to follow city maps and I try (in vain) to stay on described routes and rights of way, to stick to the itinerary. I consulted many travel guides, including the famous Baedeker. I read and re-read the works of Freud, including his letters. I have referred to my impossible reconstructions as an act of ventriloquism, and indeed, as far as speech is concerned, this is true. It was a year ago since my ankle fractured: I have started the same meticulous planning for my return to Trieste and Rome in 2025, when I will be seventy, stepping lightly, with a foot arched.

In Paris, 27 *brumaire*, I found the quartier around Pyramides profoundly changed from when I last walked it, following the Passage Choiseul, now entirely Asian fast-food joints (and one Greek), and I could look out on its glass roof from the long high windows of Marie-Laure and Bernard's apartment, where the other wall is almost entirely bookshelves, floor to ceiling. We spoke about Lacan and art, there was a little gossip (guarded), a delicious lunch though I felt the

Japanese éclairs from Aki with yuzu and matcha were an abomination. They were most hospitable, and I greatly admired the delicate way they ushered me out when time was up, a time I had already signalled that I must be off, yet Bernard gathered my coat, my cane, my bag, in the same seamless flowing gesture that Bruno used in his surgery, taking my hand to say hello or goodbye, while gently moving, almost gliding, pulling me along smoothly to enter or exit his consulting room, as though he feared I might change my mind. I was dismissed in such an elegant fashion, and later wondered if I had overstayed, that I had talked too much about my work even though that was the reason for our meeting. Isabella and Joanna were late to meet me, or I was late to meet them, and there was in the end only time for a glass of *crémant* and not for Alice Neel's exhibition. The bus was stuck in a jam, and even though it was only two metres away from the bus stop, the driver refused to open the door. Some works of mine were chosen by Marie-Laure and Bernard, I thought (though later there seemed to be a difference in recall): a new set of love letters to me from Lacan – as a performance or reading – and a little artist's book. The discussion of erotomania led us to Clérambault, Lacan's only master, and to my text drawings with sanguine crayon on flesh-pink tissue paper. They all were sold in Cologne at the art fair a long time ago, so they asked me to make them again as a third work to include, and I would do so, on Japanese Kizuki Somegani, a thin *kozo* paper, with the same sanguine crayons, frequently used to draw the body, but which body, eh? The story is one of theft, the kleptomania that is the crime of capital. Of desire invented and institutionalised. Of dizzying circulation. Of *'apéritifs du crime'*. Of hysterical causality. The speech of kleptomaniac women interviewed by Clérambault in 1902 is entangled with a medical analysis; the resulting text is an insistent and extended cry of fetishism for silk – an erotic passion, tactile and jouissant. One said that the contact with silk is superior to its sight and that while she would like to sleep in silk, it is not her style; that's for women who are seen in bed. And *la soie a un frou frou, un cri cri*, rustling, squeaking. And I also think the broadsheet *Lalangue* will be included in their Lacan show. It is a report of language without words, where words are replaced by images, and mouths are blocked. It should have been titled *La la langue*, but it is too late now to change it. Women with babies or small children, no matter, all were made mute by me, stoppered up. To be a body is to be woven from language, and the body of the speaking being is determined (imprisoned, as if held between the jaws of the crocodile, snap snap) by the signifiers of maternal speech, so says the master, in whose eighteenth seminar I hear him speaking amorously to me again, a discourse that might not be a semblance. He said that everyone knew that he had to tell in a little gallop, but what matter, everyone has his own rhythm and that was how he made love. There were formulations on the lessons that hysteria continues to teach psychoanalysts, if they have ears to hear, and he made mention of donkey's ears, those he acquired when re-reading like a simpleton, but he was not talking of animal nature, but the relationships between men and women. It is a sign that work has started again for me. A surprise. There will also be my postcards, no, *Jacques's* post-cards to *me*, from Munich in 1958, and I avowed that I found meaning in everything. I am carried away by excitement as my work resurfaces after a time of great quietude – I remembered how this happened when I started analysis so long ago.

So the days passed, of quince (sadly lacking, the tree in the garden survived, revived after its severe pruning, but was still carrying its fungal disease and bore no fruit, which in the past was plentiful, so much so that Kirsten and Dounia and Rosie came to fill their baskets) and the service tree, *cormier*, sometimes called 'chequers', which is a hermaph-rodite. Its fruit must also be bletted, like the medlar, eaten raw when soft or made into preserves or liqueurs. I read somewhere that its use in the treatment of Alzheimer's disease is being explored. In Paris, on the bus, Francis pointed out to me a little park where he said he had first read Foucault. I thought of Foucault's book, *Herculine Barbin*, a girl reclassified as a man, committing suicide in a Parisian attic aged thirty, asphyxiated by the fumes of a charcoal fire. The book is hers/his, not Foucault's, who discovered the memoir in the archives of the department of Public Hygiene while writing his history of sexuality. There are descriptions of her/his body before and after her/his death. One could not have two sexes, no, there could only be one, even with *labia majora* ('very prominent, especially on the right'), a 'feminine urethra, a vagina (with a shallow ending; leading to no cervix or womb). Doctors observed 'a sort of imperforate penis, which might be a monstrously developed clitoris'. Actually, the memoir, while torrid ('I soar above all your innumerable miseries, partaking of the nature of the angels; for, as you have said, my place is not in your narrow sphere. You have the earth, I have boundless space'.) is also rather dull, sad, wretched, and s/he had only four pieces of furniture in her/his garret. The last day of the month was marked by a *rouleau*, a garden roller for flattening, smoothing, but it could also be a scroll, a volute, a manuscript, an embellishment. The month ended and I passed into my last month of the year. At its end, I will have a manuscript, and its embellishment, *enjolivement*, will begin as well as its smoothing and flattening.

FRIMAIRE

I entered *frimaire* with a curious optimism. I was walking without a cane most of the time and though there was still pain at times, it was tolerable. I felt less like a wounded beast. I felt my *almanach* was almost done, as my year, this year of small accounts, drew to its close. It was my final month though it is the third month in the revolutionary calendar. It is a month of cold weather, sometimes dry, sometimes humid, reported Fabre d'Églantine to the Convention nationale on *tridi brumaire* Year II. I made a calendar with Zoë – what, three years ago? – copying an allegory of *frimaire* after Louis Lafitte or Salvatore Tresca or an unknown artist. A woman holds a quiver, from which with her right hand she pulls an arrow, holding her bow in her left hand; at her hip is a hunting horn, in front of her the heads of two dogs are raised, poised for the chase. She is Artemis, of course, and her concession to the cold of winter is just a little fur shawl around her neck and shoulders. In the background there is a snowy landscape, skeletal trees. From her neatly braided and coiled hair, some tendrils escape. I think I sent the drawing to Zoë. I hope I did so. The first day was that of the rampion, the second of turnips (*turneps*), then chicory (variety unspecified) yesterday, and today, the medlar. The shallots, of the variety 'Longor', robust and storing well, with copper-coloured skin and pink flesh, sweetly flavoured, were planted, pushed into the wet soil with their tips protruding. The saints were Cécile and Clément. *Duodi*, no, Monday, was the presentation of the Virgin. Mary's parents, Joachim and Anne, brought their daughter to the temple to consecrate her to God, where she stayed until she was twelve, when Joseph became her guardian. It is told in the apocrypha, the *Protoevangelium of James*. The girl became a temple: *she was planted in the House of God, nourished by the Holy Spirit and kept her body and soul spotless to receive God in her bosom*. On the steps in Titian's painting the child pauses, haloed. James said that when the priest put her on the third step of the altar, God looked down on her and the child danced lightly on her feet. In the foreground, to the right, there is an old woman seated with a basket of eggs and an antique figure.

I woke at four, as I have done for many years, and was unable to sleep again. Sometimes the remains of a dream stay – there was one in which my mother was dying and refused to die, others that I would be reluctant to tell. Saint Flora and the *cochon*, a nice combination. Yesterday evening the post-woman called by, offering the *almanach* for next year. She extracted a pile from her blue bag, and we spread them on the kitchen table. I chose one with scenes of playful kittens yet again, though hesitated over one with black and white photo-graphs of vintage cars. I left for Paris, then for London, with little time to traverse Paris. I had forgotten to note that Bern-ard had told me that Roland Barthes had three sessions of psychoanalysis with Jacques Lacan, and that he felt they had been of no use to him – it was after his lover left him, though one feels, reading Barthes, his lovers were never really with him, and in the end he paid for love. I thought about this only when I was on the *métro*, at Odéon, and I did not know if the stop and the thought were connected. In a *boulangerie* near Gare du Nord I bought two expensive *tartes au citron*, little oblong pastry boats with four perfect piped hills of lemon cream. Packed in a small cardboard box, they bumped rather unsteadily in my suitcase, and I hoped they would survive the journey intact (they did – and were delicious). I read Hilary's script, and decided, yes: yes to her account of futile love, a lover she pursues – she describes the pursuit of an unobtain-able love object as the entry into a black hole – and holes that are felt so strongly they are a presence. I fell asleep, no, half asleep, I think, aware of my open mouth and how at a certain age, when sleeping, one appears to be a corpse. A horrid sight. Animals, like small children, sleep sweetly, beautifully. I read the fourth volume in Anthony Powell's *A Dance to the Music of Time*, whose volumes I re-read every decade with a new pleasure. The two weeks ahead of me in London were full, replete with enjoyment as much as work: dinners with friends, exhibitions.

I read in the newspaper that the Russian soldiers in Ukraine tell women to hang a white sheet in their window, and then the men return later to rape the women. I read this on the bus on the day of lamb's lettuce. In the space of an exhibition, Tai's, there were candelabra with the heads of screaming hags, orbs and pyramids and glass eyes, a bust of a woman made from eyes. Wondrous, yes, but curiously sedate, even polite, so far from the violence of white cloth in a window. Joe cooked a magnificent supper of spiced aubergines, wood ear mushrooms, smashed cucumber with coriander and sesame, phoenix's tails, sticky rice, green beans with ginger. The dog, a dear little anxious Schnauzer, barked fiercely. There was gossip, of course, with Joe and Fiona and Oisín, but in the middle of the evening I felt a malaise descend on me. I fear that I did not hide it well. The next day I was fatigued, but rallied myself, scolded myself for inertia and deferral. The day was that of the cauliflower, the curded *choufleur*, but in London vegetables tend to carry less significance. The day that followed, today, was one of honey, which evoked such sadness, for our hives are dead. I was far from home while still at home, what was once our home and continues for me to bear all the traces of my dwelling, the walls of books, the objects, even the garden, which I intended to revive. Our bill for electricity had more than tripled. How will we survive the winter, all of us? The next winter, and all those still to come?

Louis and I worked on his book, arguing amicably over commas and who or whom. He said he hated the art world. I met Wiebke to look at print samples and we went quickly, too quickly, around the exhibition of Cézanne's works, which was too crowded, and Wiebke was very talkative and sweet. There were many works I did not know, and the small paintings of naked women framed by curtains, drapes, on display (cloth hanging from windows) were strange and compelling. It was not true that he did not use outlines. I was reminded of the paintings of Poussin, and in the first book of Powell's *roman fleuve* he writes of the painting (in the Wallace Collection) from which he draws his title, a scene in which *the Seasons, hand in hand and facing outward, tread in rhythm to the notes of the lyre that the winged and naked greybeard plays.* It inspires in the narrator thoughts of mortality as people *move hand in hand in intricate measure* [...] *in evolutions that take recognisable shape: or breaking into seemingly meaningless gyrations, while partners disappear only to reappear again, once more giving pattern to the spectacle: unable to control the melody, unable, perhaps, to control the steps of the dance.* I prepared my reading for tomorrow in Sheffield, cut it down ruthlessly, lit the fire – David made soup and I felt the day had been long enough. Soup, bread, a glass of wine. A friend.

Juniper and a train journey, one I had made so often over the last thirty years and was relieved, more than relieved, when I knew it could cease. Julie drove us out to the Peak district, magnificent views, glorious light (I know this to be a conventional response to the landscape). I returned to read with Ghazal and Scott in a horrible university building, one that appeared to be constructed only from vanity, which Scott transformed as he moved his body through a desolate atrium, refusing to be constrained by the lecture theatre (where nonetheless some people chose to remain, somewhat sullenly, I thought), speaking at times, breaking through the space the people the words. Ghazal's voice captivated me. She read about love and fables, but really, could have read anything and I would have been enchanted. I met Emma and Rachel, and Andrew for the first time, then Helen and Nia and Mau. Bryan came, ebullient as always, and gave me a drawing. Andrew was speaking to me about my reading while I admired his blue worker's jacket, and a woman said good-bye, interrupting us, not impolitely, yet also without a com-ment on my book or my reading, though later she used my quotation of Brecht without context, calling me 'a friend', and I was jolted into the memory of why I was so glad no longer to have to come here to work among such indifference. It was a silencing, one made again by two more people the same evening, and another the following day. It is so easy to cease to exist, voiceless suddenly, ah, such *amour propre*, and I was pitiful, so self-pitying. One should not allow oneself to be damaged. Nor so pathetic. After the supper, Geraldine spoke with me as we all separated, her eyes filled with pain, but very pleased that she and Agi and Adam and Ghazal had identified the poets who appeared in my reading, all except one.

The next day, Mau arrived at Lisa's reading in London, and took my hands gently in his over the glass case that divided the room. When I left, a little early, tired, and feeling ill, no more than a cold but I could not sustain, Ed rushed around to hug me silently and it felt kind, his gentle bulk. Lisa talked of rime and rhyme, how what appears infantile now was once avant-garde and ain't that always the way; she became an eleventh-century troubadour chanting and at times shaking a rattle with a knowing half-smile, read from *Boat*, stuttering across the gutter where the sentences broke but she called this a parting, like the parting in the hair of the young woman she once saw leaning over a book in a park. Words broke and fell to each side. Rime is snow and ice settling on trees and plants. Rime is the onset. Rime is the word part. Rimes will rhyme. Rhyme is a pattern. In the discussion the young, eager, and intelligent man with a mullet hairstyle and no parting, moaned quietly, nodding, in acquiescent agreement as Lisa spoke, *hmmm, hmmm, hmmm*.

And that was a *décadi* ago, as I succumbed to a cold, ill for the first time in more than two years, a cold that quickly moved to my lungs, a respiratory infection, and it was in a cold snap, a spell of freezing. I coughed through *frimaire*. Today, *roseau*, a reed, and I work backwards through the days I have neglected to count, to mark, to note: heather, a grubhoe, the juniper tree, a hare, the cypress, gorse, the roe deer, a fir tree, a cedar, horseradish, and wax arriving at *pioche*, a pick, where I started again, picking at what I had missed, clumsily. The pick is old, old, old, for mining for earthwork for gardening and its form follows its use. In the garden, it is sometimes called a *serfouette tête et langue*, a hoe with a head and tongue. And I am a head, and then a tongue, sharp, too sharp at times, on my return. The house was cold. The flat in London was also cold. I lit fires of wood and coal. My clothes and laptop smelled smoky. When I ran my finger along the mantlepiece, there was a dark trace of soot; the soot lay on two marbled wooden pyramids from Venice, a glass snow globe with a blue base and containing a scene of a cottage and its garden, two painted tin figures – the Virgin Mary and a Black Madonna, a plastic Madonna from Brazil, two seated ballerinas in porcelain, their heads replaced with the heads of cats, a present years ago from Linda, whom I miss. David told me he liked dusting, rearranging my objects. Unkindly, I thought he did not dust very well all the same. My mother's house was warm, too warm, but still I shivered. Céleste sat on me now as I tried to remember what has happened, at home, abroad, and who has died. I must move her soon. There was a dead fox cub on the road to the sea yesterday. In London, my foxes always come as night falls, hungry. They chatter and scuffle as they emerge from the shrubs, cascading down the brick steps and walls. I saw one in the morning light once, search-ing for food in the compost heap, then a flash, a shape, and it was gone, running along the wall at the top of the gardens, the steep ascent, where mine is the only garden that is gardened. I wanted to return to the saints, I thought, but then no, to the honest people, those I met in the *décadi* of England.

Yet saints returned, in order, the order of those names I liked: Cécile, Flora, Catherine of Alexandria, Delphine, Florence, Viviane, Barbara (little saint of the Eucharist, the tabernacle), Lucie, Odile, and Alice. The Advent came and went, as did the Immaculate Conception, the divinely held Marian truth, the denial of which is heresy, and one knows where that leads: executions, burnings, and so on, the worst. The Virgin Mary had neither original nor personal sin. Régine told me how she had cried like a Madeleine yesterday – I did not know why I thought of this, because, perhaps, in thinking of the two Marys, I suppose, one pure, blessed, the other, not so much... it is only the former who appears like a vision to maidservants and children, or nurses monks at her breast (or so they dreamt), who gives birth to new flesh, sweet fruit, liquid flowing from her heart, and hers and other saintly women's bodies became food, gave forth saliva, milk, oil with the power to cure the sick. Her breast, her son's wound. Christ was formed from her body, was the flesh of his mother. Hildegard of Bingen said it was the weak flesh of a woman that restored the world.

Who has died? Four people in a capsized boat heading from France to England, in the freezing water, and forty-three were rescued. The message came too late or was responded to too late, that there were children aboard the boat in distress. Our Lady, Star of the Sea, *stella maris*. Catherine of Alexandria bled milk, not blood, when she was beheaded, such a miraculous emission from her severed veins. She was the perfect model of wisdom, of ecstatic union, while the Magdalen was stuck with an image of penitence, as well as fasting, for it was said she fasted for thirty-three years. She was present at the crucifixion and Christ's blood covered her, his body hung in the air, as a cloth is hung to dry; she was there at his tomb, where she wept and mistook him for a gardener until he spoke to her, calling for her recognition. He had cured her, expelled seven demons from her (they said). She wept, washed his feet with her tears and wiped them away with her hair (such erotic allure). She kissed his feet and anointed them with ointment from an alabaster jar and he told her to go in peace. In Iran the security forces fired at the face, breasts, and genitals of the women protestors. They were arriving to be treated in secret for their wounds, tiny shotgun pellets embedded in their flesh.

I had almost caught up, but then the necessity of collecting wood, chopping it, keeping fires going in the cold spell, took over – so much energy to expend to keep warm, or warm enough. R. left for London on the day of sorrel, which is abundant though frozen in the garden, the new sowing in a new place. Its sharpness is good in omelettes and lentil soup. The water of the deep basins for the geese and ducks was frozen every morning. It took ten watering cans to fill them, to ensure the poultry had clean water to drink and to wash in. The geese and ducks must be able to clean their eyes and faces. Oddly, there followed the days of the cricket, the *grillon*, which is dormant from October, the male singing throughout May to July when the night falls. A *grillon* is also a kind of crisply fried morsel of pork or a rough textured paté from the Charentes, made with pork or duck or goose, flavoured with nutmeg, the pieces of meat browned before cooking the dish slowly. I sent back to London three bottles of Pineau de Charentes as Christmas presents, two white, made from ugni blanc, colombard, sémillon, sauvignon, montils, merlot noir, merlot blanc, cabernet sauvignon, cabernet franc, jurançon blanc, and folle blanche, one red, from merlot noir, cabernet sauvignon, cabernet franc, and malbec. It is supposed to have been discovered by accident when a winemaker added a quantity of grape must to a barrel containing cognac, and

it fermented to produce a liqueur, a *mistelle*. Francis left for
Paris, and I missed him for a few hours. Last night we had
roasted a chicken from the farm at La Paumerais, as R. was
not there to admonish us for the eating of meat, with the last
of the garden potatoes and buttered cabbage with carrots
and caraway. I read online, with Adrian and Mira, Jess and
Jen, Francesco and Paul, Susan. It was in honour of
Francesco's new book, entitled *Battles*, scripts, scenes, and
Adrian later reminded Francesco of the map of Lepanto,
made at the point of going west to the 'new' world, for him,
a grim and bleak document. On the second expedition they
took a Jew with them; they were expecting to get to China,
he was their only speaker of a Chinese language.

Yesterday: *pignon*, pine kernel, of which those produced in
China are too bitter, and can give you 'pine mouth' when
everything tastes of vinegar for some days or even weeks. I
made three rich fruitcakes, adding this year apricots and
cranberries, using up the remains of port from several old
bottles at the back of the cupboard to marinate the dried
fruits. I collected a syringe with a needle from the pharmacy
to inject each fruitcake with Armagnac every day, curing
them until they will be eaten. The pharmacist was pleased
with this idea, a novelty to him. He keeps bees, but this time
I did not discuss that with him. I decided not to cover the
cakes with marzipan and icing, for the French always pick
this off when the cake is sliced and served; I do not know
why I should find this so vexing, but I do. I have enjoyed the
rhythm of my solitary days this week, walking the dogs,
writing, reading, doing my accounts (salutary – how can we
be so poor? And how will we continue to live on so little
money?), enjoying quietude. It is too easy to live the life of
a recluse, but this is not the same as living as an anchorite,
choosing to be walled-in to a cell in the church, within the
sight of the host kept in the eucharistic chest, living as a
body dead to the world, buried with Christ. Two small win-

dows might look out, one to the church, one to the street, but it was advised that windows should not be loved too well and unbridled conversations with passers-by avoided. My world is larger; at least for the moment, that is, though I sense it closing in.

Rosa wrote to Sophie from her cell in Breslau in 1917 (her third year of imprisonment) that she had been brought a shabby little tree, some of its branches broken, and she did not know how she would fix her eight candles to it. She was surprised at her elation, her strange happiness, her incomprehensible joy, that the deep darkness of night should be as soft and beautiful as velvet. She wished she could share with Sophie her sense of bliss, that Sophie could be calm and happy. Today: *liège*, cork, the light bark of cork oak trees, which I hope continues to be used to stopper wine bottles (for how I hate the increasingly ubiquitous screwtop, which does not pop in a satisfying manner, but also the cork trees in Portugal are dying from drought), even if it may produce cork taint in the wine, and I have spoken with Hilary (barking instructions and information at her) about her book and ordered a case of white Saumur wine. There were endives to be wrapped in Parma ham (again, in R.'s absence) and baked in a cheese sauce for supper. There was reading to done. I was now on volume 6, *The Kindly Ones*, as one must politely call the Furies, the Eumenides, fearful of naming them directly, for they are vengeful, these goddesses of retribution. The Magdalen is often shown with a book; there is a painting, a fragment from an altarpiece, by Rogier van der Weyden in the National Gallery in London: a woman with pale skin, wearing a green dress with a delightful pleated bodice reads from a book wrapped in a white cloth, there are gilded page edges and golden clasps; an alabaster ointment jar by her side identifies her. The raking up of leaves from the magnolia had to wait.

The temperature this morning was minus 6. The water in all the basins was frozen, though I could smash through the ice with my boot on the smaller ones. The chickens did not seem to mind the cold, puffing up their feathers. I soaked stale bread in warm water for them and gave them extra crushed corn and sunflower seeds. I scattered some on the icy ground, to amuse them. Julien was meant to come to demolish the stone steps on the old studio, but he is fragile and easily distracted, and of course did not arrive. The woodpile was worrying low; I am unable to use the heavy chainsaw. Keeping warm demands an enormous effort. The stove in my study refused to light. Blowing on it, I singed my hair and gave myself vertigo. I found the pair of bellows Marcelle gave me many years ago and blasted away with them. My car did not start; it was covered with frost, inside and out. When finally the delicate play with the choke succeeded, I lurched out unsteadily, determined that I must regain confidence in driving. The dogs' breath misted all the windows. The heater rattled alarmingly and loud. In the junk shop I bought a Sarreguemines flat bowl with a blue geometric pattern on a white ground. The Manufacture there no longer exists; it was in the Moselle, annexed to Germany in 1871, then returned to France's possession in 1919, I think. I thought I would give the bowl to my sister, then decided I liked it too much myself and would keep it, then later felt bad about that, and wrapped it in tissue paper for her. I bought a *compotier* in *terre de fer*, with a design of leaves and flowers on one side, then above this, a tiny insect is flying. It is so charming that I kept opening the cupboard to look at it throughout the day. I bought a large linen cloth with a monogram in red, the initials P. B. I bought two linen napkin holders rather crudely embroidered with baskets of flowers and floral borders. I bought two small glasses engraved with flowers, their bases ridged circles, and thought I would give them to Florentine for Christmas, and later I did.

On the road to Saint-Samson the entrances to fields and the forest were blocked by the cars and vans of hunters – I had heard their horns earlier. There is a stupid poem by Alfred de Vigny, with the last line: *God, how sad is the sound of the horn deep in the woods,* and it goes on and on with the ghosts of Roland and Charlemagne, Obéron, dead knights. In the past the hunters would come right into the villages. In the revolutionary calendar it was the day of the truffle. Once I intended to plant truffle oak trees in R.'s field, but it is perhaps now too late, for it is unlikely there will be a yield of truffles before ten years at least. When we lived in Rome, there was always great excitement about the truffle and *funghi* season. That was good hunting. Patrice gave me black summer truffles once (he did not say where he got them), which I kept in a jar of rice until they were gone, eaten with pasta, in omelettes, shaved over potatoes. I placed one in a bowl of eggs. Colette gives a recipe – to steep the truffle in white wine, seasoned with salt and pepper, no other spices, a handful of lardons, twenty or so, she says, 'like Tritons playing around a black Amphitrite, cooked covered then brought to the table, 'and to hell,' she says, 'with your pressed napkin', and if she could not have enough truffles, she would do without them. God, how I love Colette.

Today, 28 *frimaire* or *octidi* of the second *décadi*, and soon I would be back where I started, but this time starting again, from the beginning and from the end, in the circular fashion of all my enterprises. I woke cheerfully (I was not sad), unusually, no longer haunted by the terrible anxiety of what I have not done or will never do or in what I have failed, again and again, which I want to replace with repeatedly, as my ridiculous screen editor advised, as well as cautioning me about certain vulgar turns of phrase, though oddly, not fuck Deleuze, Guattari, *et cetera*, perhaps because it was deserved on their part and the software agreed. I remembered Francis listening in his bath when he was seventeen to Deleuze speaking, his *Abécédaire*, his alphabet, in a series of conversations, interviews, with Claire Parnet: *e* for *enfance* and *d* for *desire*. Deleuze was surprised to be told he was an entry in the Larousse as the philosopher of desire. From *a* for *animal* to *z* for *zig zag*, and Deleuze was ill, terminally ill, a respiratory condition that left him with one lung and unable to read and write. He said it was not complicated; one does not desire something or someone, one desires an assemblage. He would be ashamed to desire a woman, he said, no, he would be ashamed to say something like that, that he desired a woman, since Proust had already said it, beautifully: that an unfamiliar landscape is enveloped in the woman he desires and as long as he has yet to unfold the landscape that envelops her, his desire will remain unsatisfied. Deleuze killed himself, jumping from a window of his apartment on Avenue Niel, on 4 November 1995. He was seventy. He had agreed the year before to the airing of the conversations, and he said it was as if he were already a little bit gone, considering his state, and once he said it was as if any death were double (unless it was Maurice Blanchot who said that), and that death comes from the outside (I am certain it was Deleuze who said that).

Today was the day of the olive, though I thought I might have missed a day or added a day; five or six wizened black fruits are still on one of the little olive trees in pots by the front door. I would love to live where olives grow, and remember the green oil from first pressing, given to me at various times by Greek friends, and that Kostas could not come to my opening in Athens as he had to go to his mother's house to prune two hundred olive trees. I ordered four kinds of dahlia tubers – after the disaster of this year's planting I was cautious – 'Café au lait', 'Honka Black', 'Bohemian Spartacus', and 'Great Silence', and a bare root of thalictrum 'Splendid', rose violet, such airy grace it will have if it comes through. I leafed through my seed catalogues. I made two cushion covers for chairs we never use (but of course, someone might, sitting down to leaf through the stack of books on the table at the top of the stone stairs in the library on the first floor) from scraps of blue and yellow toile de Jouy, fastening them with old yellow buttons shaped like flowers, caught closed in little loops of purple and violet ribbon. I continued my drawings of texts in sanguine conte pencil on the expensive fine pink Japanese paper, the surface of which is a little furry and rubs away under the light pressure of the pencil, and I thought this was good. I was not sad, not at all.

29 *frimaire* and the frost had passed; the temperature rose to 10 degrees by midday and the sun came out in the afternoon. The ground was muddy after the morning's rain. The poultry had nice clean houses now, with a thick bed of old newspaper under their litter of straw and miscanthus. The large basins were filled with clean water and the geese were happy, or so I supposed them to be as they flapped and washed their wings and sunk their heads deep. The house was warm, and the endless recuperation of wood felt less urgent. My car did not start again, and I flooded the engine, but I sought advice online, the Automobile Association recommending the accelerator pedal is pushed to the floor and the motor cranked and revved, and if that did not work, then call for assistance. You may find this rather dull reading, tedious advice, but then again, you may be grateful for this useful tip one day. More tips follow: the *almanach du facteur* proposes mushrooms stuffed with *fromage frais*, onions, parsley, a pinch of *piment d'espelette* sprinkled lightly at the end of cooking. It offers three suggestions on using honey: to heal burns, cleaning the wound then covering with a thick layer; to make hair shine, a good coating left on for several minutes then rinsed; and for sore throats, an efficient remedy when mixed with a few drops of lemon juice.

The High Court ruled that the Rwanda asylum plan is legal, that it does not breach the UN's Refugee Convention nor human rights. There will be an appeal, or rather, the decision whether to allow an appeal will be given on 16 January. The UK Home Secretary had said it was her dream to have a Rwanda flight depart before Christmas. I cannot imagine how one could possibly dream this. What a terrible dream to have. What an odious desire, unimaginable, without honour. A cruel theatre. A bad dream, no, a wicked one. I read a line from Rousseau's *Discours sur l'inégalité*, that he would have liked to have lived and to have died free, that is, so subjected to the laws that neither he nor anyone would be able to shake off its honourable yoke.

The last day of *frimaire*. Day thirty or the tenth day of three decades. A year ago, I came back to France, right leg in plaster (red). A year ago, I entered a depression that endured for three months, unlike the mild depression to which I am subject from time to time. There followed three months of anguish, sleeplessness, dry mouth, vomiting, fear. This continues to return. One can be sure of one thing, that what is repressed always makes its way back. A shovel, *pelle*. Dig my way out. Not half. I thought about some artists who dig, Ronny, Daniel, Keith, Micha: excavations, emptying or hollowing, what does not hold or pass from one thing to another. From tomorrow I have a month remaining, to come back to the beginning – note to self. Then I will re-read, and this time, this book that exists as yet only as a script, re-write. I have thought about what and who is not here. Throughout, still, there is the absence of Louis-Georges, who nonetheless is most present. 'You were always on my mind,' I told him that. But it is the version sung by Willie Nelson, not by Elvis Presley. Maybe I have not loved anyone quite as often as I could. A knife to the heart. In my study, the ashes sent to me a few years ago, in a jar labelled 'I am toxic'; in the glass cupboard, the remains of the homemade absinthe, labelled 'Drink me'. I promised the ashes to Sophie in 2020, in my response to her text, writing this: 'FIRE. "I am toxic", black ash sent to SK from Louis-George Schwartz at a time of suffering, along with a small bottle of home-made absinthe labelled "Drink me".' I sent Louis-Georges a jar of quince jelly, and later some black poppy seeds. The ash is for spells. *Sorts*. It will be a gift to S S-J when we may once again *sortir*.' But it is still with me. I wrote also, and this was my final point for her, point number ten: 'SOPHIE. She tells us about the cigarette packet, a burnt hole. Soiled paper. Red nails. Doughnut. Slapstick (who? Chaplin, Keaton, a clown?). Absinthe – *Verlaine Drinks*: "Ah! How the tangled spindles of the streets/Turn and spin the fabric of men and women, / As if a spider were weaving her web. / With the filaments of uncovered souls." Ashes (phosphorus ashes of the ink? Derrida – again: "The spirit which keeps watch in returning [*en revenant*, as a ghost] will always do the rest. Through flame or ash, but as the entirely other, inevitably"). The evening draws in. Night is falling.' I thought that this gave me the form of what I would write on fire for the *Los Angeles Review of Books* at Chloë's kind invitation, the start of the tenth month.

On the wall of the studio the ten drawings on the stupidly fragile paper are finished. Several edges are ripped, and I must consider if I will retain these or remake. I photographed them *in situ*. Amy wrote to me when she saw the photograph: 'What is this magical space with the cubby holes in the [white stone?] walls? Is it your home? The work is imprinting itself directly onto my subconscious. I anticipate it resurfacing for me in dreams or conflated memory. I hereby promise to remember it is your work under such conditions.' I have not put the drawings in order yet. I do not know what their order is. Now they are in two rows, and reading left to right in translation here from the French, one above the other: strangulations, tears, vomitings, ecstasies; consistence, glow, odour, noise; the coarse silks that rustle, the shimmer and the noise of silk; the evocative value of the fragment of cloth, the voluptuousness responding to frictions; an enduring, dominating, crystallised perversion, an appearance of dilettantism caused by silk; the silk caresses with uniform smoothness, the silk has a rustle, a squealing (or it could be calling, whooping, screeching, crying, and the word *cricri* is also the noise made by a cricket, by the *grillon*). The order of the words, the French syntax is better. I cannot find the ivory moiré silk bookpaper I need to mount the drawings. Are they drawings? I call them this in any case and it is my right to name them. The rain persisted, all day. In the garden I noticed that a few of the Brussel sprouts plants had been ravaged by black caterpillars. The sprouts were no bigger than my little fingernail. The sprouts tops and leaves were gone, leaving only the stalk. It was a great disappointment. There was digging to be done and a letter to write to a dead woman. R. returned from London with a terrible headache, but he could not describe the pain, which to him seemed to be just under the surface of his scalp, acutely fizzing.

NIVÔSE

Today: the ending begins. It is a winding up, to bring to a conclusion, and it is a winding down, to draw gradually to a close. It was remarked of my last book that it was untethered, and of a book before that, that it did not lead anywhere. Well, yes. And no. In the revolutionary calendar it is a day of *tourbe*, peat. Tomorrow is coke, *houille*, and then there follows bitumen and sulphur. On Sunday, Christmas day, there is a dog day. It is a month of fire and grit and stone. *Nivôse* comes from *nivosus*, abundant in snow, and sometimes I hear it as *névrose*, a psychic trouble characterised by conflict, hysterical or obsessional, according to the psychic structure of the subject. I was thinking, am thinking, of what has been omitted in the account of my year and what I will remember when I edit, rewrite, or invent in my return to the account. Scott's poem, the one he wrote to and for me, said he would always tell me the truth. I do not think I always do – tell the truth, that is. I am too often a *fabulactrice*. I started to read, re-read, in both French and English, Lacan's eighteenth seminar, on a discourse that might not be a semblance, from which I would extract all the words, the sentences, that he might have addressed to me as his lover. There is a moment when he said (for the seminars were spoken) that it is very clear he is not talking about everything; the truth, he said, is only a half-saying. But I do not read him for the truth, only for love.

I fed Monique's cats, as I will do until she returns from Paris on Friday with her daughter and my son (and his girlfriend and her dog). The female cat, Yule, was unusually friendly. The male, Peppé, let me stroke him – he came here from Vincent, who is dying or who may have died – there was no news from him, and I was afraid to ask in case there was no answer. I remembered the poem by Jacques Roubaud, waiting for the telephone not to ring for while it does not ring there is a chance it might and Clio, his wife, would be alive. Yule is the solstice, today, the shortest day, associated with

Apollo, Dionysus, Mithra, and in the *almanach de facteur*, with Saint Pierre Canisius, who led the Catholic Reformation of the sixteenth century in Germany and Austria, advising charity and moderation, and if his eyes slept, then let his heart always keep watch for his Lord. The holly and the ivy, the mistletoe... the young sun was born, the fire of the earth, the sun king, son of the goddess, and he brought with him all the promises of the year to come. In the studio I worked on my harpies, six drawings: mine do not have the pale faces of hunger, no, they are rosy-cheeked and lipsticked; their talons are varnished; their feathers are soft, made downy by my tiny brushstrokes until I am bored with these meticulous gestures and throw in the towel, or rather, drop the brush, brushing it off. My harpies do not have breasts; their bodies are entirely avian: only a human face and neck. They have nothing abominable about them, nothing vicious or violent or cruel. Yet, one might imagine their lamentations in the eerie trees. They are seraphim. Holding in hand or claw, a burning coal, touching the mouth, taking away guilt, atoning for sin. I might replace the saints with harpies in my own calendar. Maréchal replaced the sun-king with solar time to organise time anew. All day R. complained of his head pain, until I sent him to the hospital emergency where he waited for six hours and had blood tests and a brain scan. The foolish doctor told him to take paracetamol. After my sister's good advice on the telephone, I sent him a text telling him to suggest it might be shingles, and ah yes, said the foolish doctor, she thought it probably was *zona*, and wrote on her notes *barrière de langage*, which I felt was a considerable cheek under the circumstances.

Coal or coke, *houille*, between lignite and anthracite, sometimes poisonous. The silicone death of miners. In Afghanistan the Taliban prohibit women from going to university. Yesterday women were turned away from the campus entrances. A letter told the universities that women studying were suspended until further notice. Women went to the gates but could not get in, and everyone was crying. There were small demonstrations, women and men, their gathering quickly shut down by the Taliban forces. One woman told BBC reporters that she had lost everything. The Taliban said no one should worry, that they would restore attendance once a more suitable environment was provided. Already women cannot go to public parks, swimming pools, and gyms. One woman wrote that being a girl was a heavy crime. Another wrote that she was very sad and full of hatred. And still they will rise. In the garden there was cavolo nero and there was Savoy cabbage; the leeks had taken a battering, the chard, too; the radicchio now a sorry disappointment after its first splendour. Through the wet earth, however, the shoots of broad beans and peas were emerging, and there were fragile little leaves of spinach and rocket.

The yeast dough for the panettone, rich with eggs and butter, was wrapped and put to prove overnight in the fridge, the golden and dark raisins, the candied orange peel, soaking in a bowl in the dark rum imported by Louis. The cake of cocoa, chocolate, almonds, butter, sugar, and crushed petit beurre biscuits also rested in the fridge – for a moment I thought about adding pistachios but changed my mind. R.'s pain eased during the day but returned at night. I found some codeine and some liquid morphine, and sprayed his head with lidocaine, to which he objected vociferously. There is a rupture in France of the stock of Campari, a catastrophe. My son deferred his arrival to next week, due to family problems for his girlfriend, and decided also to take up the offer of a month's cat-sitting in a house in the countryside an hour from Berlin in January. The Christmas menu would be simplified for only two of us. We were sad.

The day was bitumen, *bitumen*, or asphalt, black and viscous. Bitumen binds the asphalt. Exposure to its fumes is linked to respiratory effects, asthma, bronchitis, to cancer. Inhaling its vapour produces drowsiness, vertigo. I gave R. more codeine and told him not to handle heavy machinery, but as wood needed to be cut, I did not include the chainsaw in this prohibition. The panettone dough rose spectacularly. Taken from the fridge it was rolled into a rectangle on which the rum-soaked fruit and peel were pressed, then an envelope fold made from the long side up, then a half-fold. Formed then into a smooth ball, it was placed in a cake tin for which I had made a high-standing collar of paper and then baked. I feared it was too well-done, the top too brown, but it was still a thing of beauty. Paul said I had created a monster.

I found it difficult to write two things at once and had to reconsider the structure for my essay on fire that is barely about fire at all. I was slow, am slow, and am afraid that I am the victim of my self-imposed constraints. I knew I wanted to include the rockrose, cistus, which is the rescue remedy against fear. It should be made in a crystal bowl in spring water when it flowers. When fire sweeps through the maquis it consumes the rockrose: the plant in peril is the specific against terror, the terror of the rampaging blaze that takes everything. There is a splendid cistus next to the terrace behind R.'s study. It was my delight this summer, velvety and aromatic, with pale-pink papery flowers blotched with dark purple that last only a day. It resents pruning and I am anxious that I cut it back too much. I bought cod from Bertrand, to salt overnight for the Christmas Eve supper before or after mass, to poach lightly in the broth of vegetables, fennel, carrot, broccoli, celery, courgette, the vegetables returned to the broth to warm through, then eaten with a saffron aioli, the saffron sent from Greece. Mélodie and Monique returned from Paris and called round with a bouquet of white lilies, white chrysanthemums, white carnations, and I found my largest Sussex jug for it. It is made of buff-red stoneware with a cream glazed ring around its neck. I found a lump on Nana's belly, under a teat, then another and another, a chain, and feared the worst as I know malignant mammary tumours are common in female cats. She purred very gently as I examined her, then bit me, swatting away my interfering hand. I was again overcome by sorrow. There is too much loss still to come.

This morning, more sad rain, drizzling then a downpour in Dol, and there were very few people in the market, stall-holders and shoppers alike. I bought an orange wine from an estate just outside Aix, *vif*, said the wine merchant, who was nudging me towards one from the Alsace, which I knew would be too sweet. Scallops! Yes! The vegetable man gave me a bunch – a bouquet – of celery, *cadeau de Noël*, he said, and such a very nice present it was. Bistrot Boris also was quiet, and only Boris was behind the bar. On the menu was guinea fowl with grapes and tripes *à la mode de Caen*. We collected four bales of straw on the way home, from a *monsieur* wearing shorts and a tee-shirt; he had red swollen legs with scratches, purple veins. He was very pleasant. There were bits of straw sticking out of the boot, and at home, R. having let the car open, I was too late to stop Aristide pissing over the seatbelts in the back. The cat did not seem at all sorry, simply irritated that I shouted at him. We came back through the village of Miniac-Morvan, where there is a street called Rue Bienheureuse Thérèse Fantou, which delighted me.

In the afternoon I met the man who walks his donkey when I took the dogs up to the forest and learnt that the donkey is seven years old and his name is Gatsby – the man paused, then added *le magnifique* before I could do the same. Today is sulphur: the beast and the false prophet were thrown into a lake of fire and sulphur in Revelations, along with the cowardly, the faithless, the detestable, all the liars, the immoral, the murderers, the sorcerers, and so on and so on, and fire and sulphur and smoke came out of the mouths of horses of the Apocalypse. As for the wicked, well, fire and sulphur and a scorching wind shall be the portion of their cup. It was the day of Saint Adèle, who had a devout life filled with good works and communion with God. It is doubtful that will be said about me, but I would like to be the *bienheureuse*, even when I am not. The elect among the Manicheans were the *bienheureux*, those who entered divine knowledge and followed rigorous rules, including mortification and abjection of the body. They did not kill or torture beasts, not break even a stem of a plant. One garment sufficed them for a year. Susan wrote to ask me what I would be wearing for our reading in Brussels next month; she had seen a dress in the sales but was hesitating: buy the frock, I said, and continued making saffron aioli, pale orange-yellow. I had only one egg from the hens, from the young Araucana with the ear tufts, peduncles, abnormal flaps produced by a gene that can be lethal, and it was a delicate task to keep the emulsion from separating. The Romans burnt sulphur to protect the home against witchcraft, sulphurous flames with the odour of rotten eggs, brimstone. I did not feel quite up to removing myself from the material world, however, nor to advising anyone else to do so.

Dog day, dog days... a period of stagnation and inactivity, but usually in the late summer. I supposed that description of lassitude might apply to Christmas day. One says, *un temps de chien*, and that has certainly been the case, rotten weather, execrable, one would not put a dog outside in it, or dogs were kept outside, miserable and wretched. It is an expression designated by an excess, the contemptible dog, dirty and impure, like the bitch of a life, or the life of a libertine, debauched, living like a dog. Or what it is like to be treated as a dog. I counted the dogs we have had: Laila, Rosie, Ruby, Florence, Harry, Lucy, Millie, Molène, Gustave – and R. had Olive and Francis had Falcon. Now we have only Ida and Hera, who have become unaccountably jealous of each other, which appeared to start around Julien and their vying for his attention. I would like another, a third, dog, and look wistfully at photographs of Border Collies who need homes. Perhaps, however, I thought, it would be easier to live without animals altogether, as both dogs hurtle down three flights of stairs barking ferociously and stupidly as the postwoman arrives with a small package or someone has the temerity to walk past on the road, or even drive by the houses. Largely, apart from a walk by the sea, the day was disastrous, and I have nothing to say about it. My anxiety returned. It took a long time to fall asleep and then my dreams were troubled. I woke early, restless, and took the dogs out into the dark of the morning. I do not know if I have a human or animal relation with them. I do not know if I am a fool, sentimentally forcing them into my way of life, or if I live as they live, if we have chosen our servitude or if we build our worlds together, entangled and in alliance; familiarly, one might say, kin, one might say. One must say, I think.

Sextidi, lava and Saint Etienne, the first Christian martyr, stoned to death for pronouncing the name of God, a miraculous child of a barren couple, a thaumaturge, once a principal saint of Paris who has ceded to other saints, though some of his story remains depicted in the south portal of Notre-Dame. I think he is also known as Saint Stephen, the patron saint of stonemasons. His body was left unburied for the dogs to take but the animals did not come for it. The disciple Paul moved the body to a secret cave near Jerusalem, and the location of the tomb appeared in dream to Lucian four centuries later. When the entrance was opened, the earth trembled, and a gloriously sweet fragrance filled the air. Lava will not turn a body to stone – no, it burns it to ash and the ash becomes a statue through ingenious means, a negative corpse, flesh and organs decomposed, a shell of hard material around absent form. In Pompeii a dog straining at its tether to escape left its void. The animal is twisted, its forelegs raised, in the position assumed when the pyroclastic flow overwhelmed it. Its mouth is open, its teeth visible, barking or whining or trying to breathe, inhaling the poisonous gases. Poor old guard dog, tied to a post in the atrium of the house of Marcus Vesonius Primus. The atrium filled with ash and debris and the dog struggled to get free, but its chain, fixed to its collar with two bronze studs, kept it there. *Cave canum*. Poor old Deleuze could not breathe towards the end he decided for himself, tied like a dog to his oxygen tank, reaching the limit of his chain, and desiring an unleashing in the hard winter of his long suffocations. He felt he was treated like a dog by his doctors. It was, he said, not men but animals who know how to die.

Yannick the magnetiser came, as R.'s head was still very painful. She works with horses and with elderly people in care homes. Her car was yellow, painted with flowers, and had a small vase on the dashboard holding a small bunch of artificial flowers, daffodils and something bright and unidentifiable. She was less flowery than her car and appeared to be a sensible woman. When R. lay on the sofa for his treatment, eyes closed, he thought she was tickling him with the fur collar of her jacket, which surprised him, but not as much as when a moment later he felt his ear being licked. It was, in fact, one of the cats. Yannick said only one session should be necessary, but he would feel very tired for several days. R. told Yannick he felt a difference but when she had gone, he said he felt exactly the same and had lied so she would not be disappointed, and I felt a surge of resentment of the unnecessary expenditure of fifty-five euros.

At the vet Anne felt the chain of little tumours on Nana's belly and said they had to be removed, that perhaps there were two chains, two operations for which I must find the money; my mother's money goes out on her care, and I try not to resent this either. Francis arrived at Dol, and R. failed to identify white miso in the shop even from a photograph I had taken as a reference for him. I was unable to suppress the resentment of his return with a jar of expensive dark miso that I am unlikely to use. It was the day of topsoil, and I crumbled some wet earth from the spinach bed between my fingers, pulling out green weeds that I used to think were Fat Hen but are not, for the poultry. We ate blinis with taramasalata and a glass of prosecco, then a Savoy cabbage stuffed with chestnuts, mushrooms, porcini, coriander, with sour cream with smoked paprika, a Ukrainian recipe, accompanied by a joking Ukrainian conversation in which our accents ended up as Italian. I thought about who might read this with annoyance. I thought about remembering, that as I re-read, edit, rewrite, it is a poor sort of memory that only works backwards. At first, when I remembered this sentence, I could not remember from where this came – the White Queen says this to Alice? Yes. The White Queen spoke of living backwards, too, and Alice had never heard of such a thing. The White Queen said it had many advantages. And then there was all that running one had to do, just to stay in the same place, so oh lord, twice as fast. I forgot that Simon and Valérie called by for breakfast, that Monique and Mélodie came for tea and fruitcake, which they did not like at all, struggling to get through their really quite small slices and declining a second slice with barely concealed expressions of horror or disgust. The modification or construction of the past re-describes it, performs it; it is not simply bearing it, after Richard Terdiman – or after Édouard Glissant, 'remembering is not the opposite of forgetting', and 'memory has to be a selection; only some features of an event are preserved, and others are dropped and forgotten, either straightaway or little by little'. Remember-ing – an action – produces memory, but it is not always full, complete, it may be even without affect. What is the memory, then, a narrative with which to act, re-enact, to repeat, to work through? A scrap here, a scrap there. Little bits. It is like the grit from the cat's paws on a clean linen bedsheet.

On the day of manure, we drove to the centre of Brittany for lunch with John and Julia, sitting in their glass house to eat, facing out onto their wild and extravagant garden through the rain, and it was like being on a boat. Francis drove and we listened to a programme about haiku on France Culture. In my reading group with my doctoral students, I was relieved when Barthes's haiku seminars ended and we could move on to some nineteenth-century novels, though I liked it when Barthes said he could find something in a story that jumps out at him, like a film jumping, a sliver flying off, something that has all the spirit of haiku but is in fact no way related to the story: something that *sets a bell ringing*, that brings with it all the particular features of haiku he tried to articulate. His voice on the radio was rather lovely. In re-reading *The Preparation of the Novel*, I was surprised by how much I had forgotten: the seminar on the labyrinth, of course, the edifice of many rooms from which one cannot escape, the combination of bifurcations and dead-ends, obstacles produced by choice, and for Barthes, a beloved at the centre.

In the car I read to Francis a selection of articles from that day's edition of *Ouest-France*: Paul Ricœur's joyfulness, his cascading laughter, even after the suicide of his son Olivier, the death of his wife Simone; the armed revolt of young Palestinians in Naplouse; the production in Scotland of a whisky called 'Cosa Nostra', its bottle in the shape of a machine-gun; the suicide of an Iranian man in Lyon, throwing himself into the Rhône, recording himself first on video: 'by the time you see this, I will be dead'; in the Orne, the body of a woman found stabbed many times, then her husband found hanging from a beam in the garage adjoining their house; the forthcoming evening race through Dinan in fancy dress (*déguisements*). By the time we returned, R. complained of pain and fatigue and had to sleep. His outbursts of rage have increased; sometimes he holds his head between his hands, shaking it from side to side; he understands less and less, and it is unclear if it is because he cannot hear (he will not wear his hearing aids) or if he is not listening or if he cannot process the information the words the events the memory. It was the day of the Holy Innocents: Childermas, the slain children, the first martyrs, the boys. It was also the Feast of Fools when parents abdicated their authority to the rule of their children.

Today: saltpetre, incendiary, yes, but also for preserving, *salaison*s, salted, hams, sausages, retaining the rosiness, the salt of Peter. R. was feeling very rough, so we called the doctor. But it all seemed normal under the circumstances, Marion and Benoît wanted to come to tea, but I felt it was not possible, that I did not have the force to lurch from the preparation of breakfast to coffee to lunch to tea to supper, without end. On my own, I can live to my own pattern. I clipped Ida and bathed both dogs; they were silky and fluffy, but still smelt a little. From Holland, I ordered nine bare-rooted plants of cranesbill, 'Samobar', royal purple flowers almost black held high above maple-leaf-shaped foliage, which may be planted in full sun and in deep shade and will go under the medlar tree in the garden, and 'Album', showy white flowers and fragrant leaves, full sun to partial shade, and who knows where I will plant these. Who has died? The artist Dorothy Ioannone, three days ago, whom Robert Filliou called a freedom fighter, and the artist Milly Thompson, sharp-edged, two women who thought about bodies and aging and pleasure; Marie-Annick, Maria, Marie-Thérèse, Maria, Paulette, Jeannine, Monique, Victoire, Marie, Marguerite, and Sœur Marie-Louise, and yes, we have the sadness, even without the offering of flowers and cards, and are touched by the number of signs of sympathy and friendship. Others died, famous people, and the wireless transmitted their eulogies without cease.

The tenth day, flail, *fléau*, a tool to beat the wheat, to separate grain from husk; but it is also a scourge and a curse, a calamity and a plague, a catastrophe and a disaster. The day passed quickly, with little achieved; the passing-by of Céline and Julien to take down more granite steps and Julien admitted he had been obliged to cut two of the thick vines of wisteria. When I looked later, I found it was three thick twines and my heart broke. Marion and Benôit, Laure and Samuel came for tisane (raspberry leaf and lemon balm) and coffee (the Arabic blend from the Algerian Coffee Stores in Soho, with cardamon, cloves, nutmeg, and cinnamon), and Christmas cake that they called pudding and claimed to enjoy. I darned two holes in a dark blue Guernsey jumper for Francis, red wool weaving at his request, one done well, the other less so. The weather had changed, cold, a sharp wind was blowing, the kind that pierces like a spear. I felt the end of writing nearing, the winding down, my own dullness, the grind of working-through. Chateaubriand noted there was in the Middle Ages an adequacy between life and work (or *the* life and *the* work). I knew what I was doing was not literature. Sometimes any words might do, like the thrushes warbling Greek words from the balustrades of Roman palaces (whose words? A prize might be offered to anyone reading this. The words of birds).

Today I could not grieve as others appeared to, for the loss of a fashion designer, no. Shelling continued in Ukraine; three strikes hit Semenivka, and one dead person was known, it was reported, but no name was given. Xi Jinping called Vladimir Putin his dear friend. Ukraine air defences shot down sixteen Russian kamikaze drones. The exiled chief rabbi of Moscow advised Jews to leave Russia while they still could before they were made scapegoats for the hardships of the war. The Italian government imposed anti-immigration measures that require migrant rescue boats to request a port and sail to it after undertaking a single rescue, rather than remaining at sea to rescue more people from other boats in difficulty. There will be longer journeys and less time at sea saving lives. It was the day of the Holy Family, the model of family; its members extended to include Anne and Joachim, others. Elizabeth, John the Baptist, holy kinship, a few more cousins. I set out a celeriac and a big fennel to roast in brown butter with clementines, to serve with the remains of the aioli, and a grain as yet undecided, a salad of apple and chicory, toasted walnuts and *bleu d'auvergne*, walnut oil in the dressing. I counted my words as they amounted. I thought of Mallarmé's distinction of a double state of speech: *here*, brute and immediate, *there*, essential. I could not remember what Barthes said about that – will I return to it, I wondered. What is the language of birds? It is mystical, or perhaps it is merely ordinary conversation. They will speak or sing the last human words. In any case. Ukrainians call their language *nightingale speech*.

The eve of an old year in the Gregorian calendar and the day of the new... in the Jacobin calendar, 11 and 12, *primidi* and *duodi* of the second decade, and on the eve of the old, Saint Sylvestre, who killed a dragon and built some basilicas, and evil spirits are chased away. There was no saint for the first day, when I was cooking lunch for guests, including a tart with ricotta pastry, filled with roasted pumpkin, mushrooms, chestnuts, parmesan), but there followed days of granite and clay, *argile* – the green-grey clay of my poultice last year. I noted that two years ago I had written an essay entitled 'The Years', each entry starting with a narrow image of the gutter of Annie Ernaux's eponymous book. It is published online in various places, and in one, the final day is missing, replaced by a repetition of the preceding day. I was attentive to reading what was now a public exchange founded on an intimate engagement between people whom I had met only once or twice, and those were on occasions in the past. I would, I said, write in instalments, a discipli-ned activity, but my attention wandered and I felt unkind, impatient with ambiguity and opacity, missing the points on which the conversation turned, a poor listener, one who interrupted with her own stories, an impolite guest who did not know her place, a ghost on the stairs. I did not write every day. As I wrote, a storm raged for several days. I fell into the gutter, into the blur produced by scanning a book, which would not lie flat, unless of course I were to break its spine, for books are no longer bound in such a way that they fall open softly, with a gentle curve, so one may weigh each side in each hand, like the scales of Justice, who closes her eyes and does not speak. The snow did not settle. I was unable to place myself, no longer certain if I was an eaves-dropper, a note-taker, a commentator (on the text or on events), a respondent (one who is called upon to supply information; and then I remembered that in French a respondent is a *défendeur*, a *personne interrogée*, and it was perhaps true that unconsciously I felt that I had a posi-tion to prove or an appeal to make). In my last note, my final margin moved to centre (because ending is so difficult, as hard as beginning, tongue-tied, no, word-tied), I returned to the book I had been re-reading since I assumed my task as commentator, a task that I did not know if I had per-formed adequately, elegantly, generously, clearly, attent-ively, carefully, or if I had written in wilful obscurity. The book had provided a page marker, a curvature, a shadow (or a haunting, if that were not fanciful), a gutter. It gave me stuttered words, fractured words. I was seeking a fine turn of phrase or thought or echo. Its author wrote that there was only 'one' and 'we', as if it were now her turn to tell the story of the time before, and I knew that was not my place: *it will remitting present* (this is not a typographic error, I assure you).

Passing to the second day of the old, *tridi* of the new. Slate, a new slate, wiping the slate clean. *Tabula rasa*. Turning over a new leaf. Letting bygones be bygones. Burying the hatchet (never. I will bear certain grudges to the end of days). In French, to pass the sponge, absorbing, mopping, soaking up, blotting; to turn the page, put the counter back to zero. My son worked in the room that is not his room, snarling at anyone who approached him. R. cut wood. I did my accounts, pretending I understood what I was doing. I broke my resolutions immediately, the first of which had been to let tiny matters go and internalise my snappy replies – Doliprane *is* paracetamol, burnt toast does *not* give you cancer, the knife handle *was* broken, the porcelain spoon had *not* been put away carefully. The failure was mine. The great cookery writer and broadcaster (also a doctor, and scientific researcher at Institute Pasteur), Édouard de Pomiane, describes in *Cooking with Pomiane* how the emigré Polish children were given a crust of bread with which to wipe clean their school slates; they became very good at spelling for, as they were so hungry, they preferred to eat their crust. He writes in the same book that to invite relations, friends or business contacts to a meal is a most complicated business, for one must be responsible for their entire happiness while they are under your roof, and one must put all one's affection and goodwill into the cooking pot, all one's gaiety and zest, so a waft of happiness escapes when the lid is lifted. The pumpkins were declining rapidly; cut into slices, trimmed of the bad parts, they must be cut up, frozen in pieces or purées, and made into soups, stews, curries (tonight) all week. There *can* be too much pumpkin, to be honest. I thought about the actions, the gestures of Janine Antoni washing a floor with her hair, her ponytail dipped in dye, crouching, not cleaning, not at all, in the figure-of-eight swooshing movement, and Mierle Laderman Ukeles scrubbing the steps of a museum, moving to the marble floors inside, on her knees with a rag (a diaper, I think) or mopping for nine hours. Endless labour: start, end, begin again. Infinite cycle. Year in, year out. Repeat. Perhaps one would prefer to clear away everything, for once and for all.

Sandstone: and following the theme of cleaning, I started to clear some shelves in my study. I found R.'s collection of books on boats, tides, sailing, weather, and placed them on the shelves Gareth built in the summer, I found a small painting that had disappeared, a twenty-fourth or -fifth birthday present to my son, who claimed he did not remember it. It is a baroque gold mirror frame painted loosely on a dully reflective metal plate, like the tain of the mirror, the lustreless back, a surface without which no reflection is possible. Mirrors once had a tain of mercury and tin, the point of touch separate from its reflection, sparkling and crystalline. Once I showed Tyler the scene from Cocteau's film, *Orphée*, in which the Underworld is entered through a mirror, the molten effect produced by a bath of mercury, which unlike water, made no ripple, no concentric circles, and in a rather accusing tone he asked me why I had never shown him this before. Sandstone, composed of feldspar or quartz, silicates, is used in the production of television screens, but a play on screens eluded me. Francis took back some books, severely Marxist tomes, but fiercely rejected taking other books, those that appeared frivolous, such as novels. Some of the bookcases gape, like mouths with missing teeth. I must reorganise the alphabetical distribution – and would be pleased as Punch to acquire two empty shelves, if I were to do so. Many friends and acquaintances were making lists of what they had read in 2022, some in order of merit, the best book – what a stupid idea, sometimes, it seemed to me (perhaps unkindly), to curry favour with the author, though of course I was flattered in the most absurd way to find myself on two lists. Goodness, how unattractive bragging is, especially to oneself. My reading was as indiscriminate in 2022 as in any other year and there was no best of... no, certainly not.

I finished reading Lacan's eighteenth seminar yesterday, a book on the letter of sexual enjoyment, writing, and castration. He chided his audience, his mind seemed to wander, he was aging, becoming gaga, *làlà*, but nonetheless it was a move from the clinic of Oedipus to a clinic of writing. It did not, despite this, lend itself easily to my intention, that of the erotomaniac transference, a transference into letters, that then would have to be translated back into French for my reading in the autumn. I needed to find a different approach, to fold in the hysteric's false connections, somehow to make a commentary that excuses or justifies why her (my) beloved was not speaking to her (me) directly but about her (me) – the woman who is not one. Yes, *faire semblant*, for there is no discourse that is not a semblance, and it is only stated from the truth. (I thought again of the poem Scott wrote to and for me, that he would always tell me the truth.) The (mad) woman (I) would try to explain that it is she (me), the woman at stake, Lacan's truth. Easier said than done, of course. I could probably write anything if I gave it less thought. I returned to the bodies of birds, the heads of women, the language of the harpy, her harsh shrieks and her gentle coos. I understood more about the depiction of feathers today, but the reproduction of the fine plumage of a blackbird eluded me.

Though today's date is marked by a rabbit, here we seldom

see them now. In Dol market there is a stall selling rabbit, from fresh meat to terrines and rillettes, which I used to buy. Once I made a first course of these, with a salty radish butter, chilled radishes and good bread, but such delights are now prohibited – the rabbit parts anyway. The rescued rabbit who no one liked went to Emmanuelle, in whose loving care became a reformed character. The day she went into hospital to give birth to Kate, Neal found him dead under the apple tree, and had to lie to her, telling her he had brought the rabbit to his cage from the garden. It is a long time since we have seen them, Emmanuelle, Kate, and Neal, as it is with so many old friends.

I explained to Régine this morning about coercive control; carefully, she wrote down the term in her notebook, along with the telephone number for the women's shelter and advice centre in Dinan. It was unlikely she would call them on her daughter's behalf. Strikes and disputes continued in England, and I felt great relief that I would not have to be the one chasing colleagues to join the picket nor observing colleagues slipping past the line, aggressive or sheepish or apologetic or simply (and perhaps this was worse) ignoring us entirely. I read with incomprehension about exchanging my UK driving license for a French one, getting a new UK passport quickly, and did not win anything on the Premium Bonds, when even a thousand pounds would have come in very handy. Nearing the end of Powell's long novel in twelve volumes, I was struck by his references to Proust (which I did not remember), with whom he has been compared. Perry Anderson felt them to be significantly different: that Proust handled time erratically and history had no meaning for him in the present, his characters were caricatures ('garish dummies') or without complexity: Powell's work was historical, events orchestrating the narrative, his characters delivered with detail and precision, speaking expressively. But I do not want to write an inept essay on either author, though as usual I digressed: a rabbit hole: a journey that unfolds chaotically or strangely. I noted that I had adopted Powell's use of the serial colon. Bridget was disconcerted, even shocked, when she noticed this sudden introduction. It separates time, of course, and ratios and biblical verses but also joins sentences, the following sentence sharpening or explaining the former. In French, the expression of the rabbit hole does not exist, save in *Alice au pays des merveilles* the *terrier du lapin*, and is heard instead in such terms as 'the invocation of a fallacious pretext' or 'adventuring on an unknown way' or 'undertaking research that leads nowhere'. Alice did not stop to think how she would get out when she followed the White Rabbit into the hole that was a long straight tunnel until it dipped, and she found herself falling into a very deep well: she fell slowly and observed the walls were filled with cupboards and bookshelves: there were maps and pictures hung upon pegs: from a shelf she took down a jar labelled 'orange marmalade', but it was empty and she was disappointed. Who would not be? There is disappointment even in dreams.

In 1966 Lacan paid homage to Lewis Carroll in a broadcast on France Culture, later published in *Ornicar?* He said that only psychoanalysis sheds light on the scope of the absolute object that the little girl may assume. It is because she incarnates a negative entity. Carroll has made himself the servant of the little girl, she is the object he draws, she is the ear he wants to reach, she is the one, out of us all, whom he truly addresses. I think I failed to translate this correctly, that something is lost. With Lacan, it is difficult to tell. I have a work by Jeannie, a print, a drawing of a child falling: her daughter is called Alice and I have known her, that other Alice, since she was ten, when my son said she was the most beautiful girl he had ever seen.

A wandering sort of day, grey. An hour in the forest, gathering wood, nearly a cord. To Saint-Servan for three new paintbrushes, very fine, o, 1, 2. I will improve my plumage, fine, finer feathers. *Silex*, flint, flintstone. Firestone. A kind of quartz. Tools, fires. Chips and breaks, sharp-edged pieces. Sparks struck. Smashed against iron. Flintlock. Tinder, a fungus that grows on trees, a dating app: *coup de foudre*: to get the sparks flying. I was not so interested, at least, not as much as I thought I might be, struggling instead to light the stove in my study, which resisted paper, firelighters, small kindling, sticks and small logs and three attempts. I thought about how much time I spend in winter trying to light and keep the fires burning, collecting wood, chopping and chain-sawing. Fourth attempt, a spark, and I gave up. The departmental magazine arrived. There was an article about the small museum in Saint-Nicholas-du-Pélem, the musée-école de Bothoa. There, a school from the 1930s has been recreated, the classroom with a stove, a playground, the house of the teacher, *la maîtresse*. Children used to walk to school, wearing their wooden shoes, often walking as many as ten kilometres, following the deep tracks, like trenches – there were no tarmacked roads until the 1960s and then you could go on your bicycle, if you were lucky enough to have one. Sometimes there would be six or seven of you *en route,* you and your sisters and brothers. The stove in the classroom was lit but still it was cold, for the ceilings were high and the windows large, to let in as much natural light as possible for as yet there was no electricity, and also because of the prevalence of tuberculosis – the air had to circulate, be renewed. On the walls, there were those large posters: geographic maps, human anatomy, steam engines; three blackboards, a new moral passage was chalked, and you had to learn it by heart each day. The desk tops were stained with blotches of violet ink, there were porcelain inkwells on the right because everyone had to be right-handed and if you were not, your left hand was tied behind your back until you learnt better, and if you spoke Breton, like Marcel, you were put in the corner with your wooden clogs hung around your neck until you spoke French. There was dictation, you copied letters and lines. You had a morning break and you played in the courtyard, skipping, hoop and stick, hopscotch, marbles. The girls pissed in the cubicles on the left, the boys in the *pissoirs* on the right. You went back to the classroom for arithmetic. At lunchtime some went home but if you came from a long way you went to the café in the village and had bread soup, made by the baker, with a little bit of bread and butter, and then you went back to school for history and geography or science, and then the day ended with recitation and singing, or manual work for the girls. Often you got a rap on the hand with a ruler, and sometimes a good point, but not often. But you know, when you lived in a dark little house with a beaten earth floor, it wasn't so bad to come to school, with the stove, the wooden floor, the window on a world.

Augustin Meaulnes turned up at the village school where the father of François Seurel (who tells the story) was the director, teaching the older children, and his mother Millie taught the younger children. Meaulnes arrived as night fell, wearing the felt hat of a peasant tipped back on his head in a jaunty way and a black shirt belted round the waist like a schoolchild might wear. He took fireworks from his pocket. François had been ill, he was fearful and unhappy; the arrival of Meaulnes was the start of his new life. And then Meaulnes went missing for a few days, he disappeared into the forest... How I have loved this book all my life, it is intricate, romantic, improbable, and I think it brought me to France, seeking the enchantment of the hidden chateau, the *fête champêtre* where the children ruled, which I imagined as a painting by Watteau, and Meaulnes met a girl and experienced the wonderment which I felt when I read it. In English, the book was entitled *The Lost Domain* or *The Magnificent Meaulnes* or *The Land of Lost Content-*

ment or *The Wanderer*. Sometimes I think I see the château across a field in the winter, when the trees have lost their leaves and the view is clear.

It almost escaped me that today was the Feast of the Epiphany, marking the visit to the Holy Family by the three kings bearing gifts after the birth of Christ. It is not marked in my new *almanach de facteur* as the sixth of January but as the coming Sunday, a moveable feast. The mortal remains of the kings were taken from Constantinople in the year 314 to the church of Sant'Eustorgio in Milan, where a Roman sarcophagus housed their original shrine, a large star incised on the sloping roof. In 1164 their bones were taken to the cathedral in Cologne. A fragment of their remains was returned to Milan in 1904. Giotto painted their arrival, guided by the star, in the Scrovegni chapel in Padua. They moved from Persian mythology to Christian legend – in Ravenna, in the Basilica of Sant'Apollinare Nuovo, a mosaic shows their exotic arrival. I took down the Christmas tree and wrapped each bauble in tissue paper, putting them away until next year. I am the only one here who cares about them, fondly believing the decoration of the tree on Christmas Eve with the carol concert from Kings College on the wireless, opening with a solo child soprano, to be a family tradition despite the many years of wretched evidence to the contrary. The library looked empty without the tree, its lights, but in truth it was much tidier.

It is customary to eat the *galette de roi* on Epiphany, two layers of puff pastry with a layer of frangipane between them, concealing the china *fève*, the little bean that might be anything from the Christ child to a Schtroumpf, and that tradition is nothing to do with the advent of Melchior, Balthazar, and Gaspard, but lies in Roman antiquity, the feast of Saturnalia, when slaves ruled over their masters for a day. I used to take a galette back to England and at the airport, we amused ourselves, the baggage controllers and I, putting the cake through the machine to find the *fève*, to the surprise and in some cases, irritation, of other travellers, The large collection of *fèves* gathers dust in a guestroom: many donkeys (some blue), cows (standing and lying down), camels, elephants, kings, three Josephs, six Marys, two priests, four nuns, a flock of sheep, a woman riding a donkey, three men carrying lanterns, many common folk, and various others, including Gandalf, a Renault 4L, a block of *savon de Marseille*, a blue Schtroumpf, and a yellow crown. The best galettes in Paris this year included those from the Boulangerie MieMie (crumbcrumb!), made with Montaigu butter, whole almonds, and muscovado sugar, and from Nina Métayer – 'The Crown', named for its lace-like pastry crown instead of the usual golden paper one. Akim Bouhadda from the Val-de-Marne bore away the laurels among the hundred and eighteen entrants to the concours of the *Ile-de-France de la meilleure galette des rois aux amandes 2023*, and in second and third place, there were Eric Taboul and Christophe Pryzyaniak, from the eighteenth and third arrondissements. As yet there have been no reports of the best *galette de roi* in Brittany. A little collection of golden crowns hangs from a pair of horns (a gazelle, I think) on the stone stairs. It was once the custom that the youngest child in a family should go under the table while the galette is cut, calling out the names of those gathered for each slice, allocating them in fair neutral distribution – the *fève* brings good luck to one who finds it and the lucky finder is the king of the feast, whose desires must be met for the day. Customs change, of course. Once Francis would do it gladly, until the time arrived when he refused. During the years of the Revolution, there was neither *fève* nor king in the *galette* of liberty or the *galette* of equality, and the day of the kings was the day of the *sans-culottes*, and then the feast of good neighbours, for the *galette* must be shared.

Conrad sent me a photograph of Freud's cabin trunk from Berggasse; he said he saw it and thought of me: the case is stamped S. F. Wien. It had gone unopened for decades; in 2015, preparing its display for 'Freud's Travels', a little jeweller's giftbox from A. Böttager, was found therein, the inside of the lid inscribed with a message in pencil from Freud: *to my dear Martha on her twenty-first birthday, from a poor, happy man.* A winnowing basket, *vanne*: yes, an object used to separate grain from chaff after flailing, and from the woven basket the grain is tossed high in the air to allow the wind to blow away what cannot be eaten. I wrote (at last) my letter to a dead woman, (one with whom I never had much sympathy when she was alive but now, I felt I could share something with her) about the harpies, all these fabulous bird-women, personifying the storm winds, called 'rainstorm' and 'swift-wing' and 'light-foot', and variations that evoke the winds and speed. One of them at least gave birth to horses, four beasts that ran like the wind, taking after their mother, though their father might also have been a wind (paternity was often uncertain in these reports and it could have been a west wind or an east wind or both). Their images showed them to be pale-skinned and attractive (like the sirens, with whom they were also confused), with delicate features, but in the written accounts, they became hideous, these bird-women with the face and upper body of a woman and the lower body of a bird of prey, but neither woman-body nor bird-body was lovely, no. Their pallor was that of hunger. Everything they touched with their claws, their ugly curved talons, gave off the terrible odour of putrefaction, and they left the most disgusting stink behind them, in the currents of the air, the soft breezes that bore them.

I missed the days of limestone and marble. A year ago, the cast was taken off my leg, revealing two large scars, one still partly open and infected, and I sloughed skin, disgustingly.

I cried then and I cried, am crying, now. Nana, the little black cat, was diagnosed with an untreatable cancer that is spreading very quickly to her lungs. There is a large tumour in her thorax, and when she can no longer breathe easily, she will have to be put to sleep, killed, that is, to be blunt, that she will shuffle off this mortal coil, *et cetera*. And I will be responsible for her death. She sits now, patiently and neatly, looking calmly out of the window at the road behind the house, and will each month – and it will be six months at most, Anne tells me – have the injection of a painkiller that will last for four weeks, until the moment of decision comes, inexorably. I had no spirit to write of limestone, the stuff of quicklime, which preserves corpses and eradicates the odour of their putrefaction, lime and marble, the stuff of tombs and monuments.

Today, gypsum, a soft sulphate mineral, alabaster, satin spar, selenite, but I was heavy-hearted, broken-hearted, and in consequence, today I did not write about:

1. Gypsum, pure and translucent, carved and polished.
2. Saint Guillaume, who was not William of Aquitaine, the troubadour, but Guillaume de Bourges, before whose tomb miracles took place.
3. Those who have died: two protestors in Iran, for instance. And Robbie, whom I had not seen for over forty years, but remembered his visits with bread rolls in the shape of animals when he was in London, acting out scenes of violence and lewdness until I cried with laughter, and only some time later understood these to be acts of seduction.
4. The pro-Bolsonaro riots in Brazil.
5. The Bill before UK Parliament to restrict strike action.
6. My vexation with Isabella for her constant failure to reply, and then my feeling of regret about my impatience when she did get back to me, followed by a cross feeling that she was not more apologetic. She may be reading this now and I apologise. She will not.
7. Wasting time looking up on the Internet how to pronounce *gomasio* (go-ma-sio).
8. The enormous unexpected medical bill from the Emergency Department at hospital in Dinan for R.'s

treatment, especially as I made the diagnosis.

9. My great annoyance with R. this morning before he left and my immense relief at being on my own for a week.
10. The disappointing leeks in the garden, despite the mesh against the Leek moth, their caterpillar larvae causing the plants to rot and die.
11. The new growth of radicchio, deep red and white-veined.
12. Three loads of laundry, including three patchwork quilts that had to be repaired.
13. The cat sick on the bed (see item 12 above), perfectly formed, moulded in his œsophagus and extruded as if it were cast.
14. The great kindness of my friends on learning of Nana's diagnosis.
15. A new drawing of a Dunnock harpy, more delicate than those preceding it, and my irritation that Su described them as being done with felt pens, as though I were a child, rather than the walnut ink the expensive pigments the gouache the watercolours the costly paper the fine brushes and so on and so on.
16. That I still had not written the essay on fire for the *Los Angeles Review of Books*, and what I had done so far did not do its work. Slow, slow.
17. My embarrassment, even shame, at re-reading the good review of my book by Louis Lüthi in *Full Stop*, the ridiculous pleasure I took in it, especially his view that I share something with Hélène Cixous, the impulse to write as closely as possible to the unconscious. Again, unappealing bragging.
18. The pleasure I took in reading *Faux Pas*, a collection of essays by Amy Sillman. My surprise at my pleasure.
19. My envy of those who are cleverer and more successful than I (see items 17 and 18 above).
20. The thought that today these were quite enough items not to write about. More than enough, actually.

22 *nivôse*, a day of salt. In the kitchen: a small glass jar of *fleur de sel* from the Guérandes, fine light crystals, cultivated for several centuries, the 'flowers' blossoming from the surface of the salt marsh harvested by the *paludiers* in the evening during the summer months, before the crystals are destroyed by rain, with a tool, a *lousse*, made of chestnut wood; a rectangular white china terrine dish with a lid, small handles of a lion's head on each side, found at the

recycling bins, containing Maldon sea salt, brought back monthly from London, harvested by hand by members of the same family for over a hundred years; smoked sea salt from the fish shop in Hastings, in an old Le Parfait jar; a German Weck preserving jar containing large salt crystals and lavender flowers, a present, I think, from Kristen; above the stove, an old blue enamelled sheet metal salt box with a wooden lid, *sel* in a black ornate script, a raised sunburst design on the back, holding *gros sel*, rough, grey, slightly damp. The salt of my tears. Dolly Parton sang that he never cared about her, hurting and deceiving her, and after all those years she realised he was not worth the salt in her tears. Pure salt has no odour. Tears have no odour. I had no will to work. I was weighed down by sorrow. Sadness has no odour, but it fills the room, and tears, when women weep, it is said, undo desire.

The third day of the third decade of the month, my last week of writing and not-writing daily. A day of iron. On the news, from Ukraine, the report of a field of bodies, Russian infantry, the foot soldiers sent out in wave upon wave as if from the trenches of the First World War. It was the day of Saint Tatiana in Ukraine, the patron saint of students. Her eyes were torn from their sockets with hooks, for she refused to offer sacrifice to an idol, but four angels surrounded her, protecting her and striking her tormentors. Her wounds healed by the following day, such miraculous healing, but that was not enough for her torturers, and then she was stripped and beaten, her body slashed with razors. A sweet fragrance rose from her bleeding wounds and filled the air. Her torturers felt they were being beaten with iron rods wielded by angels, and nine of them fell to the ground, dead as doornails. It went on: by the next day she had healed again, no wounds, no bleeding, and she called down thunder and lightning in the temple, destroying the idol. She was hung up, lashed, her breast cut off, which healed again, so this time she was thrown to a lion, but the creature just licked her feet. She was thrown into a fire, but the flames did not burn her (like the bacchantes). At last, as clearly this could not be allowed to continue, she was beheaded with a sword and that put an end to Saint Tatiana, for heads do not grow back but instead circulate as relics.

Blood smells of iron (Katharina noted: or *vice versa*, yes, iron smells of blood): bleeding cuts, menstrual bleeding, blood rubbed on the skin, metallic, old or fresh blood smell, rich and fragrant or sickening. Awash with the blood of the lamb, a vivifying sacrament, Saint Beatrice had visions of blood, and Christ's blood flowing from his wounds flooded into her heart, *imitatione Christi,* joy and redemption, pain and loss. On 21 January, allegedly, Maximilien Bourdaloue dipped his handkerchief in the blood of Louis XVI after his decapitation. The handkerchief was stored in a calabash. Robespierre asked the legislators, who should be the organs and the interpreters of the eternal laws that the divinity dictated to men, to erase from the code of the French the blood laws that command judicial murders, and that their morals and their new constitution reject. But the king must die so the republic can live, and a people does not judge as does a court of law. It does not hand down sentences, it hurls down thunderbolts; it does not condemn kings, it plunges them into the abyss. Tulips were emerging from the black earth in their pots: the tips of 'Purple Prince' and 'Elegant Lady', the tiny points of 'Red Riding Hood', which will be bright scarlet with a black heart inside, toxic to dogs, cats, and horses. The last two lines of Zoë's poem for today: *air reddens to the taste of blood / on the edge of the lung.*

Copper: twenty-fourth day of the revolutionary calendar and Friday 13 January in the Gregorian calendar. In the Julian calendar it appeared as 23010, which seemed more or less the same – I did not understand the Julian measure of time, and time is always a great complication, as Ele-onora and I found this morning in a confusion about where I was and where she was, and in which time zone (this was one of the reasons my *Capital* reading group in two contin-ents stopped meeting – we were either too early or too late, like revolution itself). There is a timepiece called a Complic-ation. Copper smells like blood, dulled and old, or blood smells like copper. In the kitchen there is a very heavy cop-per pan, found in a junk shop and re-tinned at great expense; I never use it now, for it is too heavy. Somewhere I have my father's copper pans, but they are of poor quality. Copper may be cleaned with a cut lemon rubbed in coarse salt, scrubbing until the tarnish has gone. In Ukraine the Russian forces gained control of the salt-mine town of Soledar. There are few walls that remain standing in the town. A report in *Le Monde* said Russian criminals, 'recruited' from prisons, were being sent to their deaths on the frontline, in a scene of uncontrollable street battles. Blood and tears.

It is the day of Saint Yvette, an anchoress, the healer of lepers, a prophetess denounced by the clergy and canons. The name Yvette derives from Yves, which in turn comes from 'if', the yew tree (*taxus baccata*), and if one is honest, if one is frank, one is said to be as straight as a yew. The yew is the tree of the cemetery, the threshold between life and death; its poison, for which there is no antidote, can kill but it has the power to cure certain cancers. Its branches age and touch the ground, and there, they root and form new trunks. The commissioners of the new revolutionary gov-ernments failed to remove all the calvaries (nor did they succeed in displacing a single village saint); crosses taken down in the day were restored at night, crosses proliferated in the graveyards, like mushrooms after a storm, a commis-sioner noted, that their seeds were in the heads of the people from which they would grow again, but veneration of the dead required tolerance. There may be little distance between the living and the dead, after all, and daily life may entwine with a life still lived after and through its death. Vinciane Despret asks if the dead yearn to be remembered or if it is the living who impute this desire to them. A line from a poem by Denise Riley struck me from memory though I could not find its source: *I swan with the chatty dead – numberless uncalculating familiars*. A blow from a phantom.

I bought a wooden lamp this morning in a junkshop, with the engaging form of a crudely made and painted profile of a cat, the Puss-in-Boots, in fact, *le chat botté*, the master cat. He is wearing a striped flared blue and black frockcoat, high boots, a lavish cravat or jabot around his neck, and his eyes are oval, green, painted as though full face, like an Egyptian. His tail curls erect, up his back, folding to his head. He holds the light fitting for a candle bulb in his hands/paws. His nose is large and painted pink. He looks like one of my drawings, I thought, and sought out a folder with the series of women's head with cat ears and whiskers I made a few years ago. Their ears poke through their stylish hats (I noticed that I had written 'stylish cats' and although now corrected, well, of course they are). They are perhaps unconvincing. In the story of Puss-in-Boots, a miller bequeathed his mill, his donkey, and his cat to his three sons; the youngest son got the cat and was very unhappy about it, for he thought he would starve, well, after he had eaten the cat and made a muff of its fur. But the cat, like all cats, was a remarkable one, not least one who could speak, and he asked the young man for a pair of boots and a bag, and from thereon, the cat performed many amazing things, catching rabbits and partridges which he took to the king, and it is quite a long story, including an ogre, which ends up with an introduction of the young man to the princess, of course, and their marriage, and the cat became a great lord and no longer had to run after mice. When rewired and with a new shade, the cat-lamp will light my writing table, standing next to the Belgian figure of a smiling sitting cat and two small Staffordshire spotted dogs, *couchant*. Next to these is a blue leather-bound edition of Rousseau's *Émile, Education-Morale, Botanique*, against which leans the little faded bear sewn from blue and white toile de Jouy, which Nicole gave to Francis when he was three, and he called her Lully and loved her, until a few years ago he said he thought that he had grown out of Lully, whom he used to take everywhere at one time. It was the day of the cat in the calendar. Trying to get the stove to light in the dark of the early morning, I thought of all the cats who have passed through here: Alexandre from Rome, Cosima from the Czech Republic, those who simply turned up or were left with me or were found abandoned: Bella, Zéphir, Bevis, Fidèle, Jean-Balthazar, Pilou, Aristide, Céleste, Nana, the three cats from the farm: Limpet, Smudgelina, Minouche, Orphée whom Martina and Cécilie gave me when we came back from Lecce, driving miles to St-Val d'André to collect him. Francis made little models of some, not all. Céleste pushes them over, knocks them to the ground with a swat of her cross little paw.

The Jamieson Library of Women's History in Penzance has had a number of library cats, listed since 1986, among them Grace Melbury, Lucette Le Soeur, Arabella Donn, Florence Hardy, Emma Hardy, and Tabitha Lark. In 1936 a cat was reported in the *Herald Tribune* as appearing in the middle of the reading room of the salle de Richlieu in the Bibliothèque nationale. A long, lean, completely white cat, it jumped from table to table, but the readers scarcely noticed its passage. In Flaubert's *Bouvard and Pécuchet* Victor, the horrible child (their Émile) the two copyists attempted to adopt and educate, boils a cat, which bursts from the pot, howling terribly, its dilated eyes as white as milk, and it dies as it rolls in agony in the ashes of the fireplace. It took a long time to clean up the kitchen. Bouvard quoted Rousseau that a child has no responsibility and cannot be moral or immoral, as if seeking an excuse for the child's act. Pécuchet thought they might follow Bentham, that the punishment should be in proportion to the offense, a natural consequence, but none of the deprivations they considered would affect horrible Victor, whom they decided to treat as if he were ill, putting him to bed, but he was quite contented with that, lacking intellect and heart. They tried to cram his head with literary fragments, and following the advice of Madame Campan, selected the entire works of Rousseau. I could not remember what happened to Victor, nor to sly Victorine, his nasty sister, who were confined to the kitchen and the role of servants, and Flaubert's manuscript breaks off in any case, leaving no certain ending.

Sunday, a day that is not *décadi* but *sextidi*, and is a day of tin, so the cat, its day, snuggled between copper and tin, elements which when mixed form bronze. The bronze of bells and cymbals! The sounds of celebration! The commissioners serving the *Directoire* were instructed to note if the bells were still rung, in their observation of communal life. If the churches and chapels were shut, well, people could kneel in the village square, but sometimes the clappers were removed from the bells in the church towers, or the bell towers were demolished. The days were no longer broken up by the bells. One can see how difficult it must have been, in the villages and small towns, in the provinces, to adhere to the new measure of time, now there was no longer any religious authority over its distribution. If the only day of rest was a *décadi*, a day that had to prevail over the Sunday of the past, that would make for a long working week and a rather exhausting rhythm of time, despite Rousseau's ideas about a natural religion in which every day was a shared collective holiday and nice work if you could get it, in that neat circle of equality.

Sunday and *décadi* had to meet on equal terms, or rather the first be subsumed into the latter, despite the arithmetic and the disruption of seven into ten, ten into seven, and an hour being twice as long, a minute a little longer and second a little shorter. Robespierre commissioned Maréchal to write thirty-six hymns of the *décadis*; they addressed such diverse subjects as hatred of tyrants, the liberty of the world, maternal tenderness and paternal love and filial piety and so on, from the plurality of the universal to the singularity of the domestic – that was certainly one way.

The village market was quiet, almost deserted, but then I was there early, before the church bells started to ring, drowning out any conversation. A bitter wind blew, and two stalls had moved into Claude's courtyard on the corner. I met Marie-Laure at the cheese stall, and she spoke about her son's depression and her inability to help him. He was a friend of my son at primary school and for a year or two at *collège*, and was often at our house, a stoic sort of child without many flights of fancy. I thought of him now, living on his own in a dark basement, lost, another lost child. There was a blue egg in the straw, and later, a brown one. The hens were starting to lay again after a winter's break, but the serious business of egg production, including the goose and the duck, would begin after Saint Valentine's day – and look, how easy it is to slip back into the old church measure of time. Victorine became honey-tongued and shy and knelt before the Madonna; she stole violets (she denied this) to decorate the altar and stole twenty sous from Bouvard for the collection plate; she was sent away from catechism when she was caught kissing the notary's son. Later the two men discovered her entwined naked in the straw with a hunchbacked tailor. There were natures bereft of moral sense, Bouvard and Pécuchet concluded, and in those cases, education could do nothing. Their experiments in agriculture fared no better.

The day of lead, and indeed, the day was leaden, sleet and rain and wind, very strong winds from the Point de Raz. I fell asleep for an hour or two in the early afternoon, both dogs at the foot of the bed and one cat on my chest, waking to a very dreary feeling. Who has died? On Friday, Gerald, our old solicitor, taken to hospital where he died unaware of his death; he had been unable to breathe without oxygen for a long time. He had sold his model trains, and his remaining pleasure was music. In Kabul the former Afghan MP, Mursal Nabizada, was shot in her house, with her bodyguard, killed in darkness. She chose to stay in the country when the Taliban returned to power. Lena sent me her book, *Memento Mori i Ni una mas !* In 2003 she made her first *plomb,* her first lead tube, in an old factory for the production of ochre in the Bourgogne, returning there every summer to make and leave her leads. Each folded lead was in memory of a murdered woman in Ciudad Juarez and Chichuachu. The site *Casa Amiga*, established by friends and families of the victims, published a list of the murders, the disappeared. The leads were sent or given to people to carry, to hold, and where Lena knew or could find the person, the keeper of the lead, the memory, she photographed them. On each page of her book there is a photograph, the lead held in a hand or hands or lap, the keeper anonymous. The image is preceded by a short account in each case, the name of the dead woman commemorated, and with whom, where, and how the photograph was taken. In 2004 I carried the lead in memory of Miriam de Los Angeles, holding it like a baton in my right hand, resting the right wrist on my left hand on my knee. It was taken in my garden in June, and Lena writes that I carried it from friendship and from my political and militant conviction. The lead is in my study, on a narrow shelf that runs under the eaves. From time to time, I pick it up, weighing it in my hand. I do this with some of my books, too, those whose binding allows the weight of the pages to open, no broken back, lying flat between my two palms: a measure, a scale.

Alone in my house, my rooms, I get up, walk about, sit down again quite differently from when there is another present – I felt I was quoting someone here, Simone Weil, perhaps, an early essay, and did not know why I had retained this. I have always struggled with Weil, yet no more than she struggled with herself, I imagine. In the studio, my harpies finished, flown off (hah!), I started new drawings planned over a year ago, but then I could not stand or move without pain and effort. I follow the Jacobin calendar still, even as – because – this book draws to its close, and I know I must end it, even if there is no happy end and the work is in a sense unfinished. When the plant of the day has a root, it is copied (I am a copy-ist, too, after all), and the tangled roots bleed (recalling the mandrake, perhaps). The first was coltsfoot, *tussilago*, derived from *tussis*, cough, and *ago*, to act upon or to cast, a plant of wastelands and paths, spreading by rhizomes and seeds; sometimes it is called ass's foot or horse-hoof. Today, a viola, but I did not copy its heart-shaped leaves nor its stamens or other flower parts, concentrating on its fine fibrous root system. The drawings are not well done but they are made to the best of my ability. I have the title, and it is the title that makes sense of the work: *The Bloody Radicals*. I must not overdo the blood. Note to self.

In two days, this almanach of Year I ends, and today is the day of zinc, burnt by alchemists to form philosophers' wool, white snow, and it is the day of Saint Roseline. I signed an agreement for a crown of porcelain at the dentist this morn-ing, fifty euros more than the composite. I should have called upon Saint Apollonia, saying the novena prayer: *O Glorious Apollonia, Patron Saint of dentistry and refuge to all those suffering from diseases of the teeth, I consecrate myself to thee, beseeching thee to number me among thy clients.* After my appointment, the dogs ran on the beach for a while, but mostly stood looking out to sea or snapping at each other – they have been ill at ease together lately. I too am ill at ease, with myself, with R., with the dogs who bark too much at anything at all without reason. There would be a general strike called in France on Thursday, *décadi*, my final day (odd that I thought of it as this, the end, the end, grant me patience and endurance, grant me a last word), and my train journeys were cancelled. I spent a great deal of time cancelling and booking new tickets, then at night, had to do the same for R. in London, as his train from Paris tomorrow was cancelled suddenly and he was unable to understand how to book a new ticket and be reimbursed. I shouted at him too much, I fear, with no calm at all, and was relieved when David took over at the other end. I thought about the pleasure of sleeping, lying in bed doing nothing, not even reading, and of course that recalled the years of depression as a young woman that went unrecognised, undiagnosed by anyone but especially not by myself. I lived at times under violence, but no one came to save me. I thought that was how things were, that I had to simply *faire avec*. Saint Rosaline had unusual power over demons (such a gift); she had many visions; this 'radical' nun was much given to the infliction of harsh self-mortification and favoured by exceptional mystical graces (more gifts). Five years after her death in 1359, her body was exhumed, found to be intact, and her eyes were as lively and brilliant as they had been in life. She was conserved in a glass casket like the Sleeping Beauty until she was embalmed at the end of the nineteenth century. The miracle of the preservation of her eyes was witnessed by Louis XIV's physician on the king's orders in 1660. The weather report predicted snow, but instead a layer of hail fell with great force, settling on the pots of tulip bulbs, icily concealing their green tips.

Today, *octidi*, has passed too quickly, as indeed it should, being the day of mercury or quicksilver, used in measurements of temperature and weather, and speed and mobility are the characteristics of the messenger to the gods. As Hermes, winged time, he also is the god of travellers and boundaries, of fertility, of sheep, of all flocks and all their shepherds. When mercury is found as cinnabar, it is ground to make vermilion pigment, the red of my discretely bloody roots, of the light droplets that fall from their tips. Once it was used for tooth fillings, quicksilver crowns, an amalgam of mercury, silver, tin, and copper, but fear of mercury poisoning made people anxious. In the local news: the tempest deprived over ten thousand households of electricity, a street in Lannion will be named for Mona Ozouf, the cycling fair returns to Dinan in April, a man was condemned to a year in prison for years of violence – intimidation, control, and humiliation – against his wife and children, another man sentenced to seven months for violence towards his partner and he said he would change, a course in wild basket-weaving was offered in Évran, *Ouest-France* sought a local correspondent for Pleslin-Trigavou, the schoolchildren of Saint-Charles received two footballs from the football club of Les Dahus du Mont Bel-Air, the choirmaster of the parish church in Saint-Briac gave up his baton for good, nine children were confirmed in the church of Saint-Pierre-de Plestan, and the poet Fañch Péru died, who wrote in Breton, which came from his mother who ran the station café in Kerauzern and spoke in rhyme (rime) all the time. Who else has died? Marie, ninety-two, Jeannine, ninety-one, Thérèse, ninety-six, Anne, ninety-four, Janine, ninety-four, Jacqueline, ninety-two, Madeleine, ninety-five, Marie, ninety-six.

Rosa wrote to Sophie in October; it was her final letter, fuming, full of complaints: *things can't go on like this for much longer*, she said, and they did not. John Berger offered her a posthumous gift in an essay of 2015, in the form of a letter: *Dear Rosa*, he began, *I've known you since I was a kid.* He wanted to send her something his Polish friend Janine had bought for sixty kopeks when she took the train to Moscow to buy gold (three rings, which she hid about her person on the train home). It was a thin cardboard box with a picture of a Flycatcher on its lid, and printed in Cyrillic Russian below the picture: SONG BIRDS. It contained eighteen matchboxes, three rows of six boxes, with pictures of songbirds on their covers, the names in Russian. The boxes were *full of matches with green striking heads. Sixty in each box. The same as seconds in a minute and minutes in an hour. Each one a potential flame.* His friend Janine kept the box among the plants on her windowsill; it gave her great pleasure, and in winter it reminded her of the birds singing. Berger recognised only five birds, one of which was the linnet, two white streaks on his tail and pink-breasted. Dark times, he wrote, then and now. The sky was dark grey and luminous for much of the day.

So this was it, the last day of *nivôse* and the ending of my almanach. Of course, it ended and did not end, for now was the time to return to the day it began and work through the year that had passed. Hah! To edit the past. How I wish that were really possible. The real problem with repression is that it never works fully; something always escapes over the border, often returning in those dark hours of the morning. It was the day of the *crible*, the sieve, and that is what remained for me to do, the sieving of the words, the sifting and riddling, examining what passes through as much as what remains, or perhaps it is the other way round in respect to worth. In the studio, that little pair of patent cream and red boots still stood, now on a wooden *sellette* (I don't know what it is called in English, something like a turntable, but it does not turn. It is a table with a small top and a shelf near the bottom, holding the long quite spindly legs together, probably made to support a vase of flowers or a potted plant). The child's shoes were joined by another pair, little soft black leather slippers with ankle straps fastening in front where they crossed with a leather and metal button, in a small cardboard box. The box was labelled in black ink, now faded, in a cursive script: *Premières petites chaussures de Raymonde*, then below this, to the right, in brackets *(1930)*.

Last night I finished the final volume in *A Dance to the Music of Time*. The narrator ends *Hearing Secret Harmonies* as snow falls, quoting from Robert Burton's *An Anatomy of Melancholy*: 'I hear new news every day, and those ordinary rumours of war, plagues, fires, inundations, thefts, murders, massacres, meteors, comets, spectrums, prodigies, apparitions. Of towns taken, cities besieged [...]'. The novel's last line is *even the formal measure of the Seasons seemed suspended in the wintry silence*. In Poussin's painting the four dancers circle endlessly, the Seasons, or Poverty, Labour, Riches, and Pleasure, while Father Time plays on his lyre. One of the dancers is Bacchus, a young man with a crown of flowers and vines. When next in London, I will visit the painting in its home in the Wallace Collection.

For some reason, Watteau's painting, *L'Indifferent*, came to mind: look, that mysterious figure, arms outstretched, is stepping forward to meet me from an obscure landscape, so abstract it is almost a void. He is in the Louvre, but I have not seen him for a long time, though I made a poor copy of him for a book cover in 2021. Him, too, I will stop by to greet when next passing, meeting his gesture, extending my arms as though to embrace him and raising my hands, palms cupped outwards, in the opening that Vladimir Jankélévitch calls 'the elusive and controversial I-don't-know-what (which) is the most important thing in the world, and the only thing worthwhile'. Above all, I wanted to stop writing and I wanted above all to keep writing.

FIN.

POSTSCRIPT

It is the 1st of May and it is 12 *floréal*. It is the day of sainfoin and of Saint Joseph. It is the *fête de travail* and labour day. This Saint Joseph is the worker saint, the carpenter, patron of artisans. I have worked today to make sure my writing is ended, so that I may send it to its first readers, those who stepped forward, and then later others, all the honest people, in any case: Allie, Bridget, Brian, Bryan, Cécile, Chloë, Danielle, Florian, Isabella, Jess, Jo Aurelio, John, Katharina, Ken, Laura, Louis-Georges, Lucy, two Marks, Marita, Martina, Sarah, and especially, Zoë for allowing me to include her poems. I asked some to look for infelicities and repetitions, for blunders. Several would not start or complete their self-assigned task, while others did not reply in the end or felt it was not for them – no matter. From the months of editing, the sieving and riddling, I decided to keep, yes, to retain the debris, all the lumpy matter, the nasty things, closely examining them in my *crible*. Though I might have honed, embellished, and all that, shined them up to present a more glorious picture, I think, in the end, *à la fin*, I have not really done so.

And then suddenly (it seemed) it was the 14th of July 2023, in the second *decade* of *messidor*, CCXXXI (the years may be disputed). It was the day of Saint Camille and it was the day of sage. What was written had to stand, for it was written as it happened and as it will continue to happen, time after time. *You may say to go slow but I fall behind, but if you're lost you can look and you will find me, and if you fall, I will catch you. Time after time,* I sing tunelessly to myself.

Also available from grand**IOTA**

Production of this book has been made possible with the help of the following individuals and organisations who subscribed in advance:

Rosa Ainley
Aris Anagnostopoulos
Tony Baker
Christopher Beckett
Paul Bream
Andrew Brewerton
Ian Brinton
Jasper Brinton
Hamish Buchanan
Thomas Carroll
Rosie Dastgir
Sam Dolbear
Susan Finlay
Allen Fisher/Spanner
Benjamin Friedlander
Paul Green
Penelope Grossi
Leopold Haas
Michael Hampton
Randolph Healy
Lindsay Hill
Jeremy Hilton
Gad Hollander
Fanny Howe
Elizabeth James
Lauren Kalita
Alexandra Keramidas
Ian Land
Sophie Lee
Katharina Ludwig

Julia Luebbecke
Murdo Macdonald
Michael Mann
Michael Maranda
Eleanor Margolies
Timothy Mathews
Rod Mengham
Paul Nightingale
Joseph Noonan-Ganley
John Olson
Irene Payne
Sean Pemberton
Bridget Penney & Paul Holman
Frances Pinnock
Samuel Regan-Edwards
Adrian Rifkin
Elaine Rose
Lou Rowan
Assunta Ruocco
James Russell
Valerie Soar
Zoe Skoulding
Gavin Traeger
Keith Tuma
Roxy Walsh
Keith Washington
Tony White
Isobel Wohl
Shamoon Zamir

www.grandiota.co.uk

www.ingramcontent.com/pod-product-compliance
Lightning Source LLC
Chambersburg PA
CBHW032148080426
42735CB00008B/629